DEMOCRACY IN THE THIRD WORLD

ISSUES IN THIRD WORLD POLITICS

Series Editor: Vicky Randall, Department of Government, University of Essex.

Current titles:
Heather Deegan: The Middle East and problems of democracy
Jeff Haynes: Religion in Third World politics
Robert Pinkney: Democracy in the Third World

DEMOCRACY IN THE THIRD WORLD

Robert Pinkney

LYNNE RIENNER PUBLISHERS
Boulder, Colorado

Published in the United States of America in 1994 by
Lynne Rienner Publishers, Inc.
1800 30th Street, Boulder, Colorado

Library of Congress Cataloging-in-Publication Data
Pinkney, Robert.
    Democracy in the Third World / Robert Pinkney.
      p.   cm. – (Issues in Third World politics)
    Includes bibliographical references and index.
    ISBN 1–55587–454–1 (alk. paper)
    1. Developing countries – Politics and government. 2. Democracy –
– Developing countries. I. Title. II. Series.
D883.P56 1993
  320.9172′2—dc20   93–16049
                                                               CIP

Printed and bound in Great Britain

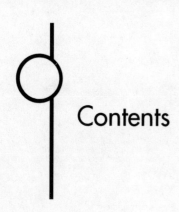

Contents

Series editor's introduction

When I was invited to edit this series, I thought long and hard about what it should be called. I ended up going back to the well-worn phrase 'Third World' but recognizing that this very term raises problems that both this Introduction and the books in the series would need to address. Its advantage is that to most people it signals something fairly clearcut and recognizable. The expression 'Third World' has come to connote the regions and individual countries of Africa, Asia, the Caribbean, Latin America and the Middle East. It is the politics, in the broadest sense, of this part of the world, and of its relationship with the rest of the world, that constitutes the subject matter of this series.

Yet the notion of a single 'Third World' has always been problematic. When it became clear that the nations so designated were not going to follow a third, 'nonaligned', economic and political route between the capitalist West and the communist world, it was argued that they none the less shared a common predicament. Directly or indirectly they suffered the after-effects of colonization and they came late and on disadvantageous terms into the competitive world economy. Even then there was tremendous variety – in culture, experience of colonial rule, forms and levels of economic activity – between and within Third World regions.

Over time this internal differentiation seems to have grown. On the one hand we have the oil-rich states and the Newly Industrializing Countries (NICs), on the other the World Bank has identified a 'Fourth World' of lower income countries like Bangladesh or Tanzania, distinguished from the lower-middle income countries like Mexico and Malaysia. Then from the later 1980s we have witnessed the disintegration of most of the 'Second World' of state socialist societies – where does that leave the First and the Third?

These developments certainly threaten the coherence of the concept of a Third World. They must make us wonder whether the concept is any longer plausible or useful in categorizing what are by now well over 100 countries, containing three-quarters of the world's population. Recently writers both on the Right and on the Left have suggested that the notion of a Third World functions primarily as a myth: for the former it is a projection of the guilt of First World liberals while for the latter it evokes for the West a reassuring image of its own opposite, all that it has succeeded in not becoming.

The arguments are not all one way, however. When Nigel Harris writes about the 'end of the Third World' and its dissolution into one world economic system, he is referring to objective economic trends which still have a long way to go and which are by no means automatically accompanied by a decline in Western economic nationalism or cultural chauvinism. Third World countries do still at least some of the time recognize their common status *vis-à-vis* the developed world and the need to stick together, as was apparent at the Rio Earth Summit in June 1992. The fact that some Third World nations may have 'made it' into the developed world, does not negate the existence of the Third World they have left behind. It does, however, undermine the more deterministic arguments of dependency theorists, who have maintained that it is impossible to break out of economic dependence and underdevelopment. The dissolution of the Second World, it could be argued, leaves the confrontation and contrast between First and Third World starker than ever (this might of course indicate the use of a different nomenclature, such as North and South). On the other hand the countries of the old Second World will not be transformed overnight into members of the First and there is a case for retaining a Second World category to refer to countries only recently emerged from a prolonged period of communist rule.

But my purpose here is not to insist on the continuing usefulness of the notion of a Third World so much as to signal the question as part of the agenda I hope that authors in this series will address. It seems to me that there *are* respects in which most of the countries conventionally included in the Third World do continue to share a common predicament and about which it is up to a point legitimate to generalize. But unless we also explore the differences between them, our powers of political explanation will be limited and it may be that it is these differences which now hold answers to the most important and interesting questions we want to ask.

Recently 'democratization' has become perhaps the key political issue in Third World studies. First in Latin America, then, more tentatively, in Africa and the Middle East, the trend has been apparent. A rapidly burgeoning literature has begun to examine the origins of democratization, or redemocratization, the process of transition, the process of consolidation, future prospects and so forth. In this masterly review, Robert Pinkney not only brings together the insights of this diverse literature but locates them firmly in the context of a consideration of the meaning and place of democracy since independence in the politics of Third World nations.

Vicky Randall

Acknowledgements

Many people have made the completion of this book possible. Dr Austin McCarthy, the Faculty Librarian at the University of Northumbria at Newcastle, was always helpful in guiding me through the maze of literature, and students at the university provided many helpful comments when I tested my ideas on them. My wife Mary eliminated many of the typing errors and much of the inelegant prose from the first draft. Dr Vicky Randall, the Series Editor, made sure that I kept to the publisher's deadlines and offered constructive criticism at every stage. Dr David Brading of Cambridge University kindly answered my queries about race relations in colonial Latin America. I am grateful to everyone who helped, but take sole responsibility for the opinions expressed and for any errors that remain.

Introduction

A book on democracy in the Third World would have been a very short book if it had been written 20 years ago. Competitive elections and civil liberties had survived since the achievement of independence in India, the Gambia, Botswana, Mauritius and some of the West Indian islands and, since the ending of civil war, in Costa Rica, but these were oases in a desert dominated by military governments, one-party regimes and personal dictatorships. Today virtually all the governments of Latin America have been chosen by means of competitive election. In Asia, South Korea, Pakistan, Bangladesh, Thailand and Nepal have all emerged from military or personal rule, and in Africa 25 of the 41 nations have held contested elections within the past five years, or expect to do so in the near future (see *The Economist* 22 February 1992: 21–3; 6 June 1992: 21–3). This leaves Burma, Indonesia and much of North Africa and the Middle East under authoritarian rule, with question marks over whether the dominant one-party systems of Singapore and Taiwan can yet be regarded as democratic. The transformation over so much of the world in so short a time is re-markable by any standards. Why should democracy have emerged, or re-emerged, what is its significance and what are its future prospects?

To use the terms 'democracy' and 'Third World' in the same sentence is to provoke immediate arguments about definitions and the utility of par-ticular concepts. The term 'Third World' is probably no more illuminating than the terms which preceded it, such as 'developing countries', 'under-developed countries' or 'emergent countries', but it has come into common usage for want of anything better. We can argue about where the Third World ends, and where the First and Second Worlds begin, but I shall accept the common usage and take it to include the countries that are characterized by greater poverty, compared with Western Europe, North America and the Antipodes, yet have not had their political systems trans-formed by membership of the communist bloc. The poverty can be measured not only by narrow material indicators such as per capita income, but also by such indicators as illiteracy, low life expectancy, high infant mortality and unsafe drinking water. It is these social and economic circumstances, together with an unequal relationship with the 'developed' world outside and, in many cases, a recent experience of colonial rule, which help to give Third World politics its distinctive flavour, even though there is much diversity between the individual countries. In particular, it has frequently been argued that these countries are the ones least likely to be able to sustain democracy, since politics is more of a life and death struggle, in which those who possess a disproportionate amount of the meagre resources available are not likely to risk electoral defeat if it means losing these resources.

How, then, can we explain the emergence of democracy in such a hostile climate? The literature on the subject has ranged from individual case studies, especially in Latin America, to ambitious comparative studies, but all too often the reader is left wondering about the extent to which the different authors' ideological preferences have stood in the way of objective analysis. Assertions that free-market economics is an indispensable complement to democracy, that Nicaragua could not be a democracy while it was governed by Marxists, that moderate and consensual moves away from authoritarianism are the only means of achieving democracy, or that the restoration of nominal political competition is a device for securing the privileges of indigenous elites and their foreign backers, are all plausible in their own way, but they are not always tested, or compared with other hypotheses, with the rigour one would expect in other areas of political analysis. There is, inevitably, controversy about the nature and objectives of democracy. To some it means giving citizens equal political rights while defending large areas of society and the economy from 'political interference'. To others, democracy has only been achieved when the aspirations of the masses are no longer thwarted by powerful elites. But one might expect academics to clarify the type of democracy they are discussing, to acknowledge that it is only one of several types, and that it may sometimes be established or maintained by political actors whose motives and beliefs are less than pure. Despite the rich variety of literature available, we find all too often that authors are talking past each other instead of comparing their own positions with those of others who start with different assumptions.

While I can lay no greater claim to objectivity than anyone else, I have tried to distinguish between the different types of democracy for which different groups are striving, and to look critically at arguments that take too many ideological assumptions for granted. In this way, I hope that I have brought together some of the different strands of the debate on how and why democracy, in its various forms, is emerging. I begin by looking at the question of what we mean by 'democracy', and its various definitions and forms are discussed in Chapter 1. While we are no nearer than the Ancient Greeks to arriving at a universally agreed definition, or to deciding

which form of democracy is 'best', there has been some process of elim-
ination. 'People's democracy', as practised until recently in Eastern Europe,
is out of favour, and the practicability of 'socialist democracy', at least in
the old-fashioned sense of the common ownership of the means of production, has come increasingly into question as the limitations of the capacity of the state have come to be recognized. The focus has thus narrowed,
at least for the present and the immediate future, to variations on 'liberal
democracy', with free competition for elective office complemented by a
'free economy'. Many advocates of democracy might want to go beyond
this stage to a more participant, egalitarian system, but most would still
accept liberal democracy as a necessary stage along the road, and it is therefore this form of democracy which occupies much of our attention.

Whether it is a staging post or an ideal in itself, or even the final destination marking the 'end of history', liberal democracy offers Third World
countries something that is in stark contrast to the alternatives most of
them have experienced. At the very least, it implies an absence of arbitrary
arrests, tortures and executions, of costly decisions taken by arrogant rulers
whose fallibility no one could question, and of demeaning personality cults
which encouraged sycophancy in place of informed debate. Even the
achievement of such practical objectives as stability, order and development has generally eluded authoritarian rulers and, while democracy has
seldom been canvassed primarily as a means of achieving these objectives,
it can help to check the worst excesses of corruption, prestige spending or
individual short-sightedness, through the checks and balances it provides.
What, then, are the opportunities available for, and obstacles in the way of,
achieving the democratic goal?

After discussing the meaning of democracy, I go on in Chapter 2 to
examine the debate on the conditions conducive to its emergence. Much of
the debate is centred on developments in the West, but I consider the extent
to which the theories can be adapted to the Third World, and the extent
to which new explanations of democratic development need to be added.
Most of the Third World countries were colonies of European powers
before they attempted to develop democratic institutions, and the varied
effects of colonial rule are considered in Chapter 3. The majority established
some form of pluralism after achieving independence, although this involved a long time-interval in Latin America, but these eras generally
proved to be false dawns, with incipient democracies superseded by authoritarianism. The explanations of this eclipse of democracy are discussed in
Chapter 4, while Chapter 5 looks at the exceptional cases where democracy
has survived continuously since independence.

For the majority of countries where democracy was eclipsed, or has
so far failed to materialize, the debate on the feasibility of establishing or
restoring democracy has centred not only on what sort of social, economic
and political conditions are most conducive, but also on how to achieve the
necessary transition from a variety of different starting points. Weaknesses
in authoritarian systems need to be pinpointed and exploited, support has

to be built up to embrace not only the committed opposition but previously neutral groups, and even individuals within the ruling regime, and varied demands and interests have to be reconciled. Chapters 6, 7 and 8 look at the dynamics of transition from three different, but overlapping, perspectives.

Finally, I look at the prospects of democracy being sustained, bearing in mind the earlier false dawns. The unattractiveness of the authoritarian alternative and the consequently greater will to make democracy work are important factors, but the new democracies are emerging in circumstances very different from those which sustained democracy in its early years in the West. There is the obvious difference of Third World democracy emerging in a period of economic recession, whereas democratic development in the West was generally accompanied by industrialization and social transformation, but there is also the difference that there are fewer long-standing political institutions that might be adapted for democratic purposes, and that the relatively homogeneous social groups on which mass political parties were built in the West are generally lacking. While democracy in Europe often acquired a 'social democratic' element as universal suffrage appeared on the horizon, and the masses were thus given tangible benefits in terms of social welfare and income redistribution in return for their votes, democracy in the Third World is emerging at a time when the ideology of the New Right is in the ascendancy, and extensive state economic intervention is deemed to be impracticable or ideologically unsound.

If democracy does enjoy a longer life in Third World countries this time than it has done after previous attempts, it will be operating in a very different context from democracies we have known in the past. For the moment, participants in the political process may embrace democracy out of a sense of relief that authoritarianism has been toppled, but if governments fail to tackle the persistent problems of poverty, inequality or a sense of social injustice, political systems are likely to face new pressures. The real challenge will then be to resolve, within a democratic framework, the new conflicts that emerge. Three-quarters of a century of experiments with various forms of Marxism have generally failed to meet people's aspirations, as have less deeply rooted forms of authoritarianism. Democrats promise much less than authoritarians in terms of material salvation, yet the key test for the survival of democracy may lie in its ability to produce adequate sustenance as well as liberty and political choice.

The nature of democracy

There is a growing belief that authoritarianism in the Third World has served people ill, in terms of providing material prosperity, stability, order, the protection of human life or the pursuit of goals that in any way reflect the wishes of the majority. Occasional exceptions may be found, such as the rapid rate of economic growth in Brazil and South Korea, or the relatively benign nature of one-party rule in Tanzania, but the vast majority of Third World citizens, whatever their degree of political influence or perception, have little reason to favour the continuation of military governments, single-party regimes or personal rule.

The obvious alternative to authoritarianism is 'democracy', but democracy is elusive both as a concept and as a feasible objective. I shall consider feasibility later, and concentrate for the moment on the varied conceptions of democracy, the ideologies underlying them, and their implications for the state, society and the citizen. The classification of democracies is as old as political science itself, and we have an embarrassment of typologies to offer the aspiring Third World country. For our purposes the works of Dodd and Sklar help to illustrate some of the more obviously relevant types (Dodd 1979: 176–8; Sklar 1983: 11–24). After eliminating Dodd's 'direct democracy', which is hardly feasible in any but the smallest communities, and Sklar's 'participatory democracy', which seems to overlap with the other categories, Table 1.1 offers a five-fold classification and summarizes the features of each type of democracy in terms of objectives, conceptions of society, the role of the state, the political process, citizens' rights, citizen participation and the practical problems to which each type gives rise. Each category is, of course, an 'ideal type' and most countries claiming to be democracies will contain elements from more than one category, but we shall begin by looking at each category in its abstract form.

Table 1.1 Types of democracy

	Radical democracy	Guided democracy	Liberal democracy	Socialist democracy	Consociational democracy
Objectives	Enabling undifferentiated individuals to exercise their rights and protect their interests	Achievement of the 'general will'	Representation and protection of diverse interests	Equality, social justice	Consensus between diverse groups
Perception of society	Aggregation of individuals	Organic whole with common interests	Aggregation of diverse individuals and groups, autonomous from the state	Potentially organic whole, but requiring transformation through state action	Aggregation of diverse groups, autonomous from the state
Role of the state	Executor of the will of majority	Executor of the general will	Referee	Redistributor of resources and guide action	Referee
Political process	Provision of arena for pursuit of individual interests	Unchecked pursuit of objectives proclaimed by the ruling elite	Checks and balances to prevent tyranny of the majority, or its representatives, or of powerful minorities	All citizens given an equal voice by reducing inequality of wealth and resources	Recognition of the diversity of interests and identities by bringing leaders of all major groups into the governmental process

Citizen participation	Active participation is encouraged; electoral contestation	Mobilization by ruling elite; no elections to key institutions, or only non-contested elections	Permitted but not actively encouraged; electoral contestation	Popular participation to offset elite power; may involve mobilization or coercion; electoral contestation possible, sometimes only intra-party	Participation within constituent groups, and by group leaders in the allocation of resources; electoral contestation
Citizens' rights	Individual interests are subordinate to the interests of the majority, but are protected by equality before the law	Individual interests are seen as synonymous with state interests; rulers decide on the extent of equality	Constitutional safeguards of individual rights; equality before the law	Attitudes to civil rights ambiguous; objective of social equality	Variable; may be safeguarded by state, or within constituent groups
Actual and potential problems	Tyranny of the majority	Tyranny of the elite	Elite domination on account of unequal distribution of resources	Extent of coercion required to achieve objectives	Reinforcement of social divisions; immobilism

Radical democracy

Dodd traces the ancestry of this type from the Ancient Greeks through Tom Paine and Thomas Jefferson to the utilitarians (Dodd 1979: 176–8). Society is seen as an aggregation of individuals, without the allowance made in subsequent literature for the existence of people as members of groups with common interests and resources, which mark them off from other groups. The democratic ideal is to enable these undifferentiated individuals to exercise their rights and protect their interests as active participants in the political arena. Citizens' rights are protected to the extent that all are equal before the law, but there is not the same emphasis as in liberal democracy on protecting the individual against the power of the state, since the will of the majority is paramount and the state exists to execute that will. Even if the method of establishing the will of the majority is impeccably democratic, problems remain with regard to the position of minorities, whether they be permanent minorities such as a particular ethnic or religious group, or more transient groups such as residents living close to a proposed hydroelectric dam that is purported to be in the public interest.

The complexity of group interests and the need for governments to retain the support of these interests in order to survive make this form of democracy unusual in the modern world. Elements of it may survive in the United States, where political decisions in many states are taken by referenda, and governments at all levels are regarded as executors of the popular will rather than means of striking corporate bargains between groups enmeshed in the political process, but in practice the sanctions that various groups can wield (including votes), and the checks and balances written into the constitution, prevent a crude majoritarianism. In the Third World the network of influential groups is generally less extensive, and the assertiveness of citizens wanting to safeguard their rights against the 'tyranny of the majority' is lower. Some governments have thus been able to claim a mandate from the majority to pursue radical reforms, even if this meant riding roughshod over the wishes of minorities or imprisoning 'subversives' who stood in the way. Ghana under Nkrumah, Guinea under Sékou Touré or Sri Lanka under successive leaders might be cited as examples. Yet experience suggests that a country will not approximate to the radical democratic category for long. The democratic element is suspect, not only because first-past-the-post elections can give extensive power to rulers who have not received a majority vote, but also because the absence of checks and balances may tempt them to retain power through elections and referenda which are increasingly unfree, with opposition groups harassed or banned altogether. If democracy is not to degenerate into authoritarianism in this way, or if people want to restore democracy after authoritarianism has already been imposed, they may demand more checks and balances to restrict the power of those claiming to represent the majority.

Guided democracy

This type of democracy also borders on authoritarianism, and on the 'people's democracies' recently in power in Eastern Europe. Society is perceived as an organic whole with common interests, unlike the aggregation of undifferentiated individuals in radical democracy. Leaders claim to know what these interests are (the 'general will') and the state exists to execute the general will without being inhibited by constitutional checks to protect minorities or even, unlike with radical democracy, by majorities who have a false perception of their real interests. There are thus no individual 'rights' that might obstruct the execution of the general will, and citizens only enjoy equality, whether politically or economically, to the extent that their rulers deem this desirable.

One could ask whether the term 'democracy' should be used at all to describe such a system but, unlike in totalitarian systems, contested elections are permitted as long as they do not threaten the power of the executive. Kenya and Tanzania thus allow a choice between parliamentary candidates of the same party, and military governments in Brazil and Indonesia have permitted rival parties to compete for seats in the legislature. General Ayub Khan openly proclaimed his system in Pakistan to be one of 'basic democracies', in which competitive elections were held at a local level and provided the base of a pyramid for the election of higher authorities. (Colonial rule might be regarded as a form of guided democracy, in which people were not given rights for which they were not yet considered 'ready'.) Such arrangements may be regarded as long-term political solutions which avoid the 'divisive' effects of inter-party competition or threats to the presidency. Why should Africa follow the 'Western model' when it did not have the class divisions of the West and did not want a more rigid polarization along ethnic lines? Why should Pakistan tolerate competition between corrupt party politicians whose dishonesty and incompetence had been clear for all to see?

Supporters of guided democracies have been more on the defensive in recent years. Like radical democracies, they can easily degenerate into crude dictatorships, but if some opportunities for dissent and participation survive, people may question the legitimacy of those who claim to rule in the public interest without allowing the public to pass judgement on them through the ballot box. Brazil, Pakistan and Zambia have already moved from guided democracy to a form of democracy in which the top political offices depend on popular election, and similar pressures from within individual countries and from external powers may push more countries in the same direction.

Both radical and guided democracy thus exist as ideal types which have a philosophical claim to be regarded as forms of democracy, but they are not forms to which politicians or reformers outside a small privileged elite are likely to aspire. Even in their pure form they leave the governed with only limited control over the government, and in their corrupted form they may be little more than a cover for crude dictatorship. To understand the aspirations of those who seek an alternative to authoritarianism, we need to turn to the remaining three forms of democracy cited in Table 1.1.

Liberal democracy

Liberal democracy is more willing to recognize society as an aggregation of diverse citizens acting as both individuals and members of groups. It aims both to secure the representation of these individuals and groups, and to protect them from other groups and the state. There is thus a notion of a clearer separation of the state from society than in radical and guided democracies. The state does not exist to execute the 'general will', whose existence is denied on the grounds that people's interests conflict rather than conform to an organic whole, or the will of the majority, which may be incompatible with the rights of minorities. The state thus exists as a referee to ensure the representation and protection of diverse interests. Citizens enjoy equality before the law, but not necessarily 'social equality', and their rights are protected by constitutional safeguards, whether enshrined in writing or by convention. Citizen participation is permitted, but not actively encouraged, and the main democratic emphasis is on 'representative government' chosen through competitive elections, rather than on direct participatory democracy.

A frequent criticism of liberal democracy is that it merely allows political competition between nominally equal citizens without taking into account the unequal resources that citizens possess. An elite enjoying superior wealth, contacts, education or political skill in general may thus be able to perpetuate its privileges at the expense of the majority by manipulating the key political institutions and the media, and influencing public opinion so as to minimize public debate on issues which bring its privileges into question. This can be seen clearly in many Western countries, where the wealthier sections of the population are numerically over-represented in executive and legislative bodies, and sources of inequality, such as inherited wealth, private profit from land and profits from capital which owe more to imperfect markets than entrepreneurial skill, are seldom subjects of debate between contenders for power. Nationalist politicians in the Third World who have experienced foreign exploitation may seek not merely a set of rules to govern political competition, but also a means of achieving greater social and economic equality. To them, liberal democracy may offer an inadequate solution to their perceived injustices.

Socialist democracy

Socialist democracy is concerned more explicitly with equality and social justice. Like the advocates of guided democracy, its supporters see society as a potentially organic whole with common interests, but only after society has been transformed. This is to be done through the actions of the state, which exists to redistribute resources, generally through greatly increased public or cooperative ownership and extensive welfare provision, and provide a moral guide to political action. The greater equality of wealth and resources enables the political process to operate without the built-in advantages that are enjoyed by privileged groups in liberal democracy, and the threat of elite power is largely offset by the 'popular participation' of the masses, though it is not always clear whether this activity is purely voluntary, a process of 'mobilization' in which social pressure is put on people or even compulsory in some instances. Democratic socialists generally insist that they have no objection to electoral competition, even if they do not treat it with the same enthusiasm as liberal democrats, but they face a dilemma in deciding how much electoral freedom to give to those who want to restore capitalism. Nicaragua conceded that freedom, with the result that its membership of the socialist democratic camp is now in doubt, while Tanzania has so far restricted competition to within the confines of a single socialist party.

Socialist democracy's attitude to citizens' rights, like its attitude to electoral competition, is ambiguous. Its supporters may insist that they are as keen as any liberal to protect the citizen but, if the pursuit of equality and social justice take precedence, this may heighten conflicts between the state and the individual, often to the detriment of the latter. This leads us on to one of the central dilemmas of socialist democracy. How far can the ideals it enshrines be achieved without considerable coercion? This is not merely a matter of progressive taxation or the appropriation of private property (possibly with compensation), but also of policing a variety of activities that might detract from the egalitarian, socially just ideal. How does one respond to private education or medical care, varied forms of entrepreneurship or the importation of goods which upset the government's economic plans? If the material progress necessary for the well-being of society is not to be achieved through the profit motive, what part will state compulsion play in securing an efficient use of resources? At the extreme, there is even the danger of censorship to prevent indigenous minorities or foreign publishers from spreading bourgeois values.

Much of this has to be in the conditional tense since the countries that can be regarded as socialist democracies, unlike guided and liberal democracies, are few in number. Democratic socialists would disown the former 'people's democracies' as undemocratic, and would have doubts about many of the African and Asian leaders who claim to be socialists but rule over countries in which widespread inequality and capitalist ownership continue to predominate, and in which electoral competition continues to be restricted. Nicaragua in the 1980s, or Tanzania, might qualify as members of the democratic socialist camp, but for the most part socialist democracy remains an ideal which has yet to be tested in the real world. The age-old question of how far the pursuit of equality requires a sacrifice of liberty, or even economic efficiency, has yet to be resolved.

Consociational democracy

The term 'consociational democracy' was first used in relation to the Third World by Apter, to describe the way in which a culturally diverse country such as Nigeria ensured that all significant groups were incorporated in government without any being frozen out by crude majoritarianism (Apter 1961: 20–8). The system recognizes society as consisting of these distinctive groups, based on language, race or religion, autonomous of one another and the state. The state exists not to promote any utopian ideal such as socialism, the will of the majority or the general will, but to act as a referee in the process of inter-group conflict. While groups based on social class may blur into each other and there is normally some mobility between groups, people cannot change their race and only infrequently change their religion or principal language. The exclusion from power of a social class is thus seldom total, because people with working-class backgrounds may be recruited into the elite, or governments with mass bases may be leavened with intellectuals from higher up the social scale, whereas the exclusion of Catholics in Northern Ireland, Tamils in Sri Lanka or Africans in South Africa represents a much sharper break between 'ins' and 'outs'. The object of consociational democracy is to seek consensus between the different groups through a political process that brings all their leaders into the governmental process, whether through carefully tailored forms of proportional representation or federalism, or by specifically reserving offices of state for members of the different groups. In these ways, each group will have an ultimate veto power over the others, though it will normally be retained only as the 'ultimate deterrent' if the system is to work smoothly.

If the cleavages between the groups are sharp, citizen participation will be mainly within each group, with the respective leaders then negotiating with each other over the allocation of resources. Electoral competition is open to all, as in liberal democracy. Voters may polarize between monolithic groups, but in Europe there are often divisions within the groups, as between working-class and middle-class Calvinists or radical and conservative Flemish-speakers. In culturally diverse African states such as Kenya and Nigeria, the divisions within each group are less marked (at least in terms of voting behaviour). Each group has a geographical area in which it predominates, and is thus likely to gain representation in the legislature proportionate to its size, even without a formal system of proportional representation. Citizens' rights may be safeguarded specifically by the state, or the state may leave the constituent groups to fill in much of the detail. Thus the degree of freedom to deviate from Muslim orthodoxy in Malaysia may depend heavily on social pressures within the Malay community.

One obvious problem created by consociational democracy is that of 'immobilism', with political change moving at the pace of the slowest, and possibly the most privileged, and with the political system reinforcing cultural divisions that might otherwise wither away. In rejecting crude majoritarianism, consociationalism may go to the other extreme of giving

minority groups influence, and enabling them to retain resources, disproportionate to their size. Thus the solution of consociationalism canvassed
as an answer to South Africa's problems might be supported on the grounds
that it is preferable to either violence or a mass exodus of Europeans whose
skills and capital are vital to the economy, but it could still leave the
political system a long way short of 'one vote, one value'.

There are also practical questions of whether the conditions which
have sustained consociationalism in European countries, such as Belgium,
Holland and Switzerland, are so readily available in the Third World. The
normally accepted requirements of the legitimacy of ruling elites – respect
for well-established institutions and procedures, a spirit of compromise and
an overarching sense of national loyalty – may be less strongly developed
in the Third World (Berg-Schlosser 1985: 95–109; Tindigarukayo 1989: 41–
54). Many elites have lost their legitimacy as a result of their performance
in government, institutions are generally new and ill-developed, a 'winner
takes all' attitude often prevails over one of compromise, and national
loyalty, although developed in the struggle for independence, is often less
deeply rooted than in European countries that have spent centuries assert-
ing their identities in the face of hostile neighbours. If the preconditions for
consociationalism remain inadequate, a country may be left with a loose
marriage of convenience rather than a durable form of democracy.

The democratic melting pot

The purpose of the outline given above is not to offer Third World countries a consumers' guide to the forms of democracy available but to present
a range of ideal types in order to show the range of theoretical possibilities
and dangers inherent in taking any one form of democracy to extremes.
The practical problems in achieving any form of democracy are immense,
let alone in achieving one unadulterated form. What is interesting are the
ways in which different blends of the different types are being canvassed or
attempted, not as means of achieving perfection but as alternatives to hith-
erto undemocratic systems which have frequently produced tyranny, social
inequality, the plundering of public resources or plain incompetence. Just
as Aristotle urged the Greeks to develop a synthesis of different types of
political system, so modern political scientists have sought to learn from
the failures of those who have peddled their own exclusive brands.

Sklar sees signs of the emergence of 'developmental democracy', which
accommodates the goals of social reconstruction implicit in socialist democracy, the resistance to authoritarianism implicit in liberal democracy, as in
the struggle for trade union autonomy in Zambia, and the recognition of
cultural diversity implicit in consocialism, as in federal experiments in
Nigeria (Sklar 1983: 19–21).

Glickman sees a convergence not only between different types of democracy, but also between 'left-wing' and 'right-wing' ideologies, which are

both rejecting authoritarianism in Africa (Glickman 1988: 234–54). Table 1.2 attempts to spell out, and perhaps extrapolate, some of Glickman's ideas. A growing body of opinion on both left and right, he argues, rejects authoritarianism, apparently on the grounds that it has proved both harsher and less efficient than was once anticipated. The distinction between 'left-wing' and 'right-wing' authoritarianism in Africa has, perhaps, been rather blurred, with right-wing governments like those in Kenya and Côte d'Ivoire using the mechanism of the one-party state once associated with Leninism, while nominally left-wing governments use international capitalism to bolster their authority, as in Ghana or Zambia. One can none the less make a broad distinction between left-wing authoritarianism based on state control over the economy and political patronage, with political competition and dissent explicitly suppressed, and right-wing authoritarianism based on the power of economic elites, which use the machinery of state to protect their privileges but without necessarily imposing a monolithic political structure. One can see the distinction more sharply in Central America and the Caribbean, where left-wing authoritarianism is preserved in Cuba through one-party exclusiveness and extensive state penetration of the economy and society, while right-wing authoritarianism survives in Guatemala and El Salvador, despite the existence of nominal party competition, because economic elites ensure that no political force challenges their domination.

At one time most of the opponents of left-wing and right-wing authoritarianism had little in common. Opponents of right-wing dictatorships, including colonial regimes, sought an end to economic exploitation and poverty without generally being concerned with democratic rights. Castro, or even Ho Chi Minh, was more likely than politicians who had won contested elections to be a hero. Opponents of left-wing dictatorships, such as the opponents of Nkrumah and Rawlings in Ghana, were more concerned with restoring or establishing pluralist competition and civil liberties than with building an economic base or maintaining a degree of social justice that might sustain democratic government. But Glickman suggests a growing convergence of views, or even a search for similar solutions under different names.

Thus the left speaks of reduced dependence, the right of self-reliance; the left of popular control of government, the right of reduced government control over the economy; the left of government more responsive to the popular will, the right of individual rights. One can still detect elements of socialist democracy and liberal democracy in these different approaches, but the gulf between them is not unbridgeable. Points have been conceded on both sides. Few people on the left still accept the practicability or desirability of an omnipotent state controlling the economy and dispensing patronage to the extent that few groups in society are left with political or economic autonomy. In 1988 Glickman saw prospects for the emergence of 'non-liberal democracy', with the general retreat of the state, inter-party elections in Zambia (subsequently followed by inter-party elections in 1991),

Table 1.2 Left-wing and right-wing democracy and authoritarianism

Left-wing	Right-wing
Democracy based on:	*Democracy based on:*
1 Development to reduce economic dependence	1 Self-reliance
2 Popular control of government	2 Reduced government control of the economy
3 Government more responsive to the popular will	3 Individual rights
Authoritarianism based on:	*Authoritarianism based on:*
State control of patronage, and repression of political competition and dissent	Class exploitation

the development of the ruling party as a watchdog over the government in Tanzania, the search for greater political participation in Ghana, and the growth of such groups as cooperatives, trade unions and professional bodies (Glickman 1988: 241–50).

The collapse of the Soviet Empire, and the limited achievements of Third World governments that attempted to insulate themselves from world capitalism, have hastened support for less centralized, more participatory brands of socialism. And if socialism based on coercion is deemed impracticable or morally undesirable, it is a short step to accepting that socialists must win power through pluralist elections, or even risk losing it through such elections, as in Nicaragua in 1990 and Zambia in 1991. The line between socialist democracy and socialism within liberal democracy becomes blurred.

At first sight the right does not appear to have travelled as far as the left along the road to democratic convergence. The notion that economic liberalization is a precondition of political liberalization, to which we shall return in later chapters, is not a new one, and the demand for individual rights in the face of state encroachment has for centuries been the battle cry of privileged groups that do not want their privileges attenuated, but a more populist strand has come into right-wing thinking, with the emphasis on 'self-reliance'. If it came merely from the well-established elites it might be dismissed as a new version of 'let them eat cake', but if it comes, however inarticulately, from small entrepreneurs who see more future in working out their own social or economic salvation than in relying on a corrupt or inefficient state, then we may be witnessing a strand in pluralist development that complements the left-wing emphasis on reduced economic dependence on the outside world. Chazan suggests that the growth of autonomous economic groups is helping to strengthen conditions for democracy in Ghana (Chazan 1989: 349–50), while much of the literature on 'social movements' in Latin America, covering such groups as shanty-town dwellers, relatives of victims of political persecution or the unemployed, suggests a comparable autonomous base for political participation (see especially Lehmann 1990: 149–86). If the reader questions whether the terms 'left' and 'right' are still appropriate to describe such ideas and developments, then the point about convergence has been made.

Another way in which the right may be yielding ground is in its greater reluctance to shelter behind the military in preserving its privileges. The obvious contrast between past and present is in Chile, where right-wing politicians who were part of a democratic system in 1973 either actively supported the coup to overthrow President Allende or offered little resistance. By the late 1980s most politicians and elites on the right had rejected the military solution on the grounds that it was no longer practicable in the face of public resistance at home and external pressure, or desirable in view of the human suffering and economic devastation which military government had created – an indiscriminate sledgehammer to crack a left-wing nut that might now be cracked more easily through electoral competition. Other right-wing military governments may have been less extreme than that in Chile, and the extent of right-wing conversion from authoritarianism to democracy less remarkable, but a comparable trend could be seen in most of Latin America as well as Pakistan and, somewhat earlier, in Southern Europe. Capitalists, like socialists, were less willing to impose their ideas without democratic consent.

Sceptics might argue that it was the right who got the better of the democratic bargain, and that nominally democratic systems can sustain privileged elites as effectively as military governments, especially if parties demanding radical change are banned or harassed by authority, or if it is made known that votes for them may provoke military re-intervention. Jonas calls for 'real democratic transition', which requires structural changes to reduce inequality, working-class involvement and mass participation (Jonas 1989: 150). The point is reinforced by a study of Central American republics such as Guatemala and El Salvador, where the change from military governments to elected civilian ones has done little to widen political choice or participation, let alone tackle the inequalities in society which many people would regard as inimical to the democratic process.

In contrast to Jonas's search for 'real' democracy, Karl prefers a 'middle range definition' of democracy, which requires a set of institutions permitting the entire adult population to choose leading decision-makers in competitive, fair elections within the context of the rule of law, political freedom and limited military prerogatives (Karl 1990: 2). More rigorous requirements for democracy, such as non-discrimination against any party, equality or active involvement of the subordinate classes would, she argues, restrict unduly the number of countries qualifying as democracies.

Such conflicting views could take us back to the arguments about whether liberal democracy is preferable to socialist democracy, or even whether some of the real-life approximations to 'liberal democracy' are really democratic at all, but there is also the dynamic question of how democracy, in its various manifestations, evolves. Is liberal democracy, or still more the crude form of limited political contestation found in Central America, a blind alley that enables elites to retain effective control of the polity and the economy without the embarrassment of having to be sustained openly by brutal military dictators, or is it something to be valued not only because it is less repressive than military government or personal rule, but also because it provides a relatively peaceful means of responding to changing pressures and ideas in society? Does it, in other words, provide potential openings for those who would pursue their own versions of equality, social justice and mass participation, just as in the West it facilitated a transition from oligarchy to universal suffrage, and responses to the social and economic demands of the newly enfranchised middle and working classes?

In this chapter I have concentrated on the nature of democracy, and have noted the diversity of the groups which now prefer to strive for a pluralist order rather than pursue their more exclusive goals by less democratic means. But is the mere desire for a particular political solution sufficient to guarantee its adoption? We must now look more closely at the forces that shape the evolution of democracy and at its potential for meeting new challenges.

2

The conditions for democracy: its evolution in the West and some lessons for the Third World

The question of whether 'democracy' existed in the pre-colonial Third World is an interesting one, but is of limited relevance to this study. Decision-making in some communities undoubtedly involved widespread participation and a search for consensus, but the link between decision-making in such communities and in the modern state is a tenuous one. The greater size of the modern state, the heterogeneity of groups within its boundaries, the range of functions it attempts to perform and the resources at its disposal make even the poorest modern state a much more complex entity than the political systems of most pre-colonial communities. Different types of political skill are required if the loyalty and compliance of diverse groups are to be achieved and maintained, and delicate decisions have to be taken that can make enormous differences to the wealth and lifestyles of the 'winners' and 'losers'. Does village A obtain a new school at the expense of village B, with the result that children in village A grow up literate and acquire new opportunities for employment, while children in village B are deprived of these? Does the proprietor of firm C obtain a large government contract which can enrich him overnight while the proprietor of firm D goes hungry? Is the currency overvalued to the benefit of urban elites consuming luxury imports, while peasants find it difficult to sell their crops in world markets? And will a devaluation of the currency increase the wrath of the urban elite, who then persuade the military to displace the politicians responsible, so that new groups now gain access to government patronage while former rulers and their clients are thrown back on their own resources? Whatever the nature of pre-colonial politics, the political skills displayed will be of limited value in coping with the intricacies of modern government, even if traditions of tolerance and experience of containing conflict offer some cultural bases for democracy. It is not therefore for reasons of ethnocentricity that we begin our search for democracy in the West, but because one modern nation state, however

poor, may learn more from another modern nation state than from its
distant ancestors, who were generally concerned with the administration of
much smaller areas and with a much less complex range of functions.

Democracy is clearly not part of the 'natural order' of life. For most of
human history rulers have ruled without being chosen by the majority of
their subjects and with, at best, only limited opportunities for subjects to
make their views known on decisions affecting them, let alone participating in these decisions. This remained the situation in virtually all the countries of the world until well into the nineteenth century. Why, then, did the
situation change?

In searching for clues we can note what is different in the countries
where democracy now prevails, compared with the days when it did not.
In most of these countries industrialization has occurred, accompanied by
such developments as migration to urban areas, vast educational expansion,
longer life expectancy and, of course, improvements in material well-being
and increased leisure time, which have enabled people to think more of
requirements and aspirations beyond mere survival. Society is also different
from pre-democratic times in terms of the social groups which exist and
the ways in which they interact with one another. While the earlier relationship between lord and peasant could remain largely static for generations, the relations between different sections of the middle and working
classes today are less bound by tradition and are more likely to be characterized by conflicting demands, which governments will be expected to
resolve. This leads us on from the nature of the groups to their political
attitudes and actual behaviour, which again imply an expectation of governmental responsiveness rather than fatalistic acceptance, especially if the
groups have the means of articulating their demands and of threatening
sanctions if they are not met. Such articulation, and the governmental
responses to it, is possible because of the existence of a complex network
of political institutions both within the formal state structure and in the
'political sub-system' of groups from the wider society interacting with it.
Finally, it follows that if society, the economy and the political structure
are different from those existing in pre-democratic times, a variety of different changes must have occurred at different times to bring about this
transformation. Nowhere was there a 'big bang' which immediately
ushered in industrialization, urbanization, new social structures and new
political institutions simultaneously.

I have not so far attempted to 'prove' that democracy was the result of
a process of cause and effect. I merely note a correlation between democratic developments and the other developments, and even here there are
exceptions. Countries in Eastern Europe achieved many of the other developments without democracy, while countries such as Botswana and the
Gambia, with few of the developments described, have sustained pluralist
systems. And where democracy and other developments have gone
together, the pace of each has been uneven. Consider, for example, the
way in which economic development outstripped democratic development

in Germany before 1945. But in attempting to generalize, we can at least enumerate the ingredients that are commonly found in the democratic cake, even if we are not yet in a position to specify the proportions in which they may be best combined, or to offer a recipe to show how they should be processed.

If we want to move on to search for a causal relationship between other developments and democracy, we can pick out several explanations of democracy, as indicated in Table 2.1. As in Chapter 1, each variable is taken as an entity in itself for the sake of simplicity, without implying that the authors cited necessarily accept one explanation of democracy to the exclusion of all others.

Economic development

One of the pioneering explanations of democracy was made by Lipset (1959). Lipset noted the correlation between the existence of democracy and such variables as per capita wealth, industrialization, urbanization and the level of education, and saw these variables as causes of democracy. With increased wealth, he argued, the question of who ruled became less important, because governments had less power to affect the 'crucial life chances' of the most powerful groups, who now enjoyed sources of wealth independently of the state, while poorer groups could secure some redistribution of wealth relatively painlessly without the rich having to make any great sacrifice. Such redistribution need not, of course, be seen purely in terms of the size of pay packets, but in terms of, for example, sacrificing private sector investment to expand education and social welfare, or permitting trade unions to pursue demands for better working conditions. In such circumstances the 'lower classes' would be less likely to turn to extreme ideologies, and would be more likely to be integrated within the polity (Lipset 1959: 84).

To be fair, Lipset did acknowledge the possibility of a legitimacy crisis if rising social groups were denied political access, or if new class divisions reinforced older divisions based on ethnic or religious affiliations (Lipset 1959: 87, 97), but the general assumption was that economic development was the main driving force for democracy, albeit a rather narrowly conceived democracy in which opportunities for constitutional changes of government were given greater prominence than political participation or social equality. It is certainly difficult to refute the fact that virtually all the countries of Western Europe, North America and the Old Commonwealth have achieved substantial economic development and arrived at the democratic destination, despite their different starting points, different problems along the road and the different beliefs and responses of political actors, but the question of causality is still not resolved.

Did the Industrial Revolution in Britain produce the wealth that enabled elites and the masses to achieve consensus on the right to electoral participation and the benefits which flowed from it, or was the Industrial Revolution only possible because elites which had dissipated their resources in civil war in the seventeenth century were now able to agree on a political settlement that was conducive to both economic growth and the co-option of other social groups into the political process? And even if we concede that industrialization then produced the wealth which lubricated democratic evolution, we can point to countries such as Germany, Japan and Russia where industrialization was fostered by authoritarian governments and, at least in the short term, helped to strengthen these governments by providing them with more resources for repression. Democrats might seize on the phrase 'in the short term' to argue that a wealthier, more educated population will eventually find authoritarianism intolerable. Other things being equal, that might be true, but democracy has been helped by quirks of history which were not economically determined. What if the twentieth century's greatest totalitarian rulers, Hitler and Stalin, had preserved their non-aggression pact instead of turning against each other, or if another authoritarian regime had not provoked the United States, through the bombing of Pearl Harbor, into supporting the Western European democracies in the Second World War? Would we still be boasting about democracy as the end-product of economic development, or would many of George Orwell's forebodings have proved more accurate? A Europe dominated by Hitler or Stalin might have enjoyed substantial economic prosperity (especially if it had been spared the ravages of a costly war), but the achievement of even the limited form of democracy envisaged by Lipset might have had to wait for several generations.

Political attitudes and behaviour

Almond and Verba's *The Civic Culture* shifted the focus from material wealth to the willingness of people to accept government by consent as a means of resolving conflict (Almond and Verba 1963). There is no obvious reason why such a willingness should require a high per capita income. The Ancient Greeks managed to sustain such a culture, whereas relatively wealthy people in modern Cyprus or Northern Ireland have been unable to agree on who should rule over whom or by what means. Greater wealth may help to take the rough edges off political conflict because, as Lipset argues, differences between winning and losing are less a matter of life and death, but whether one is willing to compromise with one's adversaries, and to concede advantages to them as a result of majority decisions or the working of constitutional checks and balances, will depend on a variety of cultural and historical factors. If a rival group is seen to enjoy particular privileges, or to threaten aspects of society or the political system which another group holds dear, consensus will clearly be difficult, but the existence of such attitudes and perceptions may have to be explained in terms of either inflexible elite domination (the preservation of apartheid or of landed elites in

Table 2.1 Conditions conducive to democracy

Conditions	Supporting authors	Arguments	Problems
Economic development	Lipset (1959)	Correlation exists between wealth and democracy; increased national wealth makes competition for resources less desperate	1 Correlation is not the same as cause 2 Greater wealth may strengthen the resources of authoritarian rulers 3 Process and rapidity of economic growth is not specified clearly
Political attitudes and behaviour	Almond and Verba (1963)	Democracy requires a willingness to accept government by consent as a means of resolving conflict	Attitudes may be shaped by social and economic circumstances
Inter-elite relations	Rustow (1973)	Democracy emerges when elites agree to the rules of the political game rather than risk national disintegration; these rules can subsequently be adapted to accommodate non-elites	1 Why is a point reached where national unity is preferred to violent conflict or disintegration? 2 How can elite attitudes be ascertained?
Social structures and interaction between social groups	Moore (1967)	Democracy is most likely to evolve where the monarchy checks the power of the nobility, and the aristocracy goes into commerce	How to explain the existence of democracy in countries with a diversity of social antecedents

Political institutions	Heper (1991), Stephens (1989)	Democracy requires the development of institutions (especially pressure groups and political parties) which can filter public demands and thus facilitate compromise	1 Danger of historical determinism 2 Role of economic changes, external influences, and even society, not clear
Sequences in development	Binder *et al.* (1971), Dahl (1971)	Democracy is easier to establish if political competition precedes mass participation, and if major conflicts over the role of the state are resolved one at a time	1 Danger of historical determinism 2 Problems of recognizing and quantifying the variables
External influences	Seldom offered as a principal explanation	Foreign governments, institutions or individuals may supply ideas, offer inducements or apply sanctions	Influence can only be indirect; democracy cannot be imposed

Central America) or the impact of particular historical events (the partition of Ireland, the colonization of Cyprus). Yet we are still left with the question of why key groups in some societies eventually arrive at a consensus, despite previous intractability, while groups in other societies do not.

Inter-elite relations

Rustow, like Almond and Verba, puts the emphasis on a willingness to compromise by subscribing to democratic rules, but with a greater emphasis on groups as collective bodies or on elites leading the groups, than on a collection of individual attitudes (Rustow 1973). In Rustow's model, a prolonged and inconclusive struggle between groups ends when neither genocide nor expulsion (nor, presumably, secession) are possible. Decisions are thus taken to come tō terms with the situation by agreeing to peaceful competition for power. This requires the adoption of democratic rules, including the appropriate checks and balances, and the protection of rights. Once such a framework is in place, it may be consolidated by subsequent generations of politicians, elites and voters, and may be adapted to bring previously excluded groups, such as the poorer classes, into the political process. One could presumably adapt this model to include the middle and working classes as combatants in the 'long and inconclusive struggle', as well as older elites and ethnic religious groups, in attempting to trace the democratic compromise.

While no one would dispute that democracy is likely to work more smoothly if key groups are willing to compromise rather than fight, we are left with a model which may prove too narrow to offer general explanations of democracy. There may be cases where one group takes control of the political system from another, as in the American Revolution, rather than having to compromise with other groups of comparable strength, and then absorbs other groups into the democratic process, or where incremental concessions are made without the need for prolonged conflict, as in much of Scandinavia. Even where Rustow's model, broadly interpreted, does apply we are still left with questions about cause and effect. If rival groups acknowledge the need to live together within the boundaries of one nation, what brings about this desire? External threat might be a significant factor, as in the Low Countries, or economic factors may increase the inducement to moderate conflict. Thus businessmen, and possibly state bureaucrats, had a strong interest in resisting the fragmentation of Nigeria after 1966, and this required a search for means of accommodating diverse groups. Democracy itself might even be a cause rather than effect of reconciliation between groups. Perhaps democracy is established for reasons other than group reconciliation, such as the insistence of a departing colonial power or military government, and rival groups then work within the democratic framework.

There is also the converse problem of explaining why group conflict is *not* resolved through democratic accommodation in many parts of the world, even when this would seem to be the 'rational' course to follow. I have already cited the cases of Cyprus and Northern Ireland, where external pressures may help to keep conflicts on the boil and where, especially in the latter case, elites have only limited control over the behaviour of their followers. The relatively lowly social position of the followers may be such that they have much less to lose from continued conflict than the elites. For Third World countries seeking elite compromise as a recipe for democracy, the experience of the West may be of limited value. It is more difficult to envisage a democratic settlement in Third World countries based on the masses marching obediently behind rival leaders until the latter have achieved a democratic settlement at elite level, for at least two reasons. First, the masses already have the vote and, even if this asset is frequently devalued by rigged or non-competitive elections, it gives them a degree of autonomy from elites which the masses did not enjoy in most of Europe until well into the nineteenth century. Second, indigenous elites in the Third World are frequently enmeshed in alliances with groups or governments abroad, which may provide them with additional resources and thus enable them to win or retain power without the need for compromise with their adversaries.

A final problem with Rustow's model, like that of Almond and Verba, is that of ascertaining what people's attitudes really are. Whereas Lipset's social and economic variables can be quantified, can we really be sure that particular democratic outcomes occurred because certain groups favoured particular courses of action? Did elites in England after the seventeenth-century civil war, or Spain after the death of Franco, make a conscious effort to resolve their differences in order to enjoy new-found prosperity? Or were they merely abandoning a form of conflict that was no longer appropriate to the new political, economic or ideological order (the abandonment of the doctrine of the divine right of kings, the demise of the republican threat, the defeat of fascism in Europe)? If that was the case, any democratic settlement would depend less on reconciliation between old warhorses and more on the constitutional adjustments made by members of more narrowly 'political' institutions (the constitutional monarch or leaders of parties with effective power bases, rather than royalist absolutists and republicans, or communists and fascists) who had moved to the centre of the stage, if only by default.

Social structures and interactions between social groups

Barrington Moore, like Rustow, focuses on the interaction between groups in society, but with greater emphasis on whole social groups rather than elites (Moore 1967: 413–70). While Rustow sees democracy evolving out of reconciliation, Moore sees it as emerging out of revolution, with the victories of the Puritans in England, the Jacobins in France and the anti-slavery states in the United States paving the way for democratic development. He offers an elaborate model in which democracy is facilitated by the emergence of a strong bourgeoisie, or an aristocracy going into commerce and shorn of feudal tendencies by the counterweight of the monarchy, in contrast to the communist model, where the aristocracy remained indifferent to commerce and a large peasant mass survived, thus facilitating revolution in the absence of the safety valve of bourgeois democracy. This is also in contrast to the fascist model, where the upper class used political and social levers to keep the labour force on the land and make the transition to commercial farming in this (non-market oriented) way. This, together with industrial growth, which was again presumably controlled by the levers of state power rather than market forces, again left limited room for an autonomous bourgeoisie (Moore 1967: 413–22).

Moore's approach, with his emphasis on the interaction between social classes, is perhaps the closest we get to a Marxist explanation of democracy, although Marxists have not, until recently, shown any great interest in pluralist democracy in the West. It is (or was) seen as a necessary staging post on the road to revolution, and as something preferable to bourgeois rule without political competition, but not as something to be remarked upon or admired for its own sake. While liberals celebrated the benefits that political competition and participation brought to the citizen, Marxists dwelt on the limited scope for political choice while the ruling class controlled the means of production (see especially Miliband 1973).

Moore's model obviously ignores the fact that communism and fascism spread to many countries through conquest or contagion, but even if we focus on the countries where these systems were home grown, we are asked to make lengthy teleological links between past and present. Did the social structures of nineteenth-century Germany and Russia make communism and fascism more likely outcomes than democracy, or did the outcomes depend more on responses to such events as the 1918 Versailles settlement, which provoked a nationalist reaction in Germany, or the crippling effect of the First World War on the political order in Russia? Even if one argued that the social histories of these countries made them less able than others to cope with such strains in a democratic way, the experience of West Germany in achieving democratic consent after 1945 might suggest that the pathways to democracy mapped out by Moore are too restrictive. A society with a tradition of order imposed through upper-class manipulation of state structures may find that this order helps to facilitate the moderation of political demands associated with democracy, once an authoritarian regime has been defeated. As Huntington observes,

> Countries that have had relatively stable authoritarian rule (such as Spain and Portugal) are more likely to evolve into relatively stable democracies than countries which have regularly oscillated between despotism and democracy. . . . A broad consensus accepting

authoritarian norms is displaced by a broad consensus on acceptance of democratic ones.

(Huntington 1984: 210)

This is in contrast to the British model of order and democracy emerging out of elite competition within which the rules were gradually institution-alized. Democracy today, like communism and fascism in earlier times, has spread through conquest and contagion to many lands, including those which Moore would regard as fertile ground for authoritarianism, but its survival cannot be attributed to conquest and contagion alone. Each coun-try will have elements in its history and culture which can be exploited as democratic assets, whether they be the tradition of pluralist competition in Britain, egalitarianism and participation in Scandinavia or order in Germany.

Political institutions

The question of the ability of the political system to channel and contain conflict, without being driven to authoritarianism or chaos, leads us logi-cally to consider the role of political institutions. Heper contrasts the success of Spain and Brazil in achieving relatively stable democracy with the more halting progress in the rest of Latin America and Turkey (Heper 1991). Spanish-speaking Latin America, he argues, evolved from nineteenth-century societies in which *caudillos* (personal rulers) ruled over an 'inchoate, inarticulate populace' in which there were few shared norms. Diffuse, vertical hierarchies of patron–client networks continued into the twentieth century with the object of gaining the benefits of distribution through direct access to the executive without the medium of political parties. If parties did not perform their textbook role of aggregating interests, governments could not moderate demands, and attempted instead a strategy of 'co-optive in-corporation', which failed on account of their limited distributive capacity. In the absence of adequate institutionalization, and therefore legitimacy, governments resorted to repression. Spain was different in that the nine-teenth century saw the transformation of an oligarchic structure into one of 'bourgeois hegemony'. This brought the idea of common (as against indi-vidual) interests expressed in the form of ideologies, and the development of coherent policies with legal–rational bureaucracies to implement them. Interest groups and parties linked to different sections of the economy evolved, together with pragmatic political parties. All these institutions made democratic compromises easier after the end of Franco's authoritarian rule.

Brazil was closer to Spain than the rest of Latin America. In the absence of much European settlement, Lisbon had a free hand in transforming a hierarchical and authoritarian polity and the idea of 'organic representation of the community' based on Lockean pre-democratic principles. Political institutions were thus strong and, when authoritarian rulers gave up power, they were able to exercise firm control over the process of transition to democracy. We are again led to the conclusion that democracy is more likely to endure if it stems from strong, rather than weak, authoritarianism, but with the emphasis this time on the underlying strength and adaptability of institutions rather than on the characteristics of political culture. Yet Heper concedes that over-powerful institutions can be as damaging to democracy as weak ones. In Turkey, the state was re-consolidated along bureaucatic lines and remained isolated from society (Heper 1991: 201–2). In functionalist language, the political 'sub-system' remained stunted, and the sort of autonomous political activity accepted as healthy in most Western democracies could easily be interpreted as a threat to the public interest.

Heper (1991: 202) argues that one of the strengths of his approach is that democratic evolution is seen in a broad historical perspective, instead of being explored from the starting point of conflict within the previous authoritarian regime. There is also the advantage of focusing more directly on 'the political'. Material wealth, democratic attitudes and an interdependent relationship between social groups will be of little use in facilitating democracy unless institutions evolve that can translate political choices, demands and decisions into actual 'outputs' via institutions such as parties, pressure groups, legislatures and bureaucracies, whose roles and existence are accepted by most of the population. Some critics may rush in to argue that such institutions as develop will merely be a reflection of social and economic development, and Heper hints at such a link when he describes the transformation of an oligarchic social structure into a bourgeois hegemony, but the precise nature of the link remains unclear. An institution such as the office of prime minister in Britain may come into existence by historical accident, yet have a significant bearing on democratic development by making the head of government dependent on both the majority in the legislature and the wider electorate, while the decision of Latin American countries to adopt a directly elected presidency has left them with relatively weak political parties in systems where capturing the executive prize becomes more important than building a winning coalition in the legislature. In the absence of the checks and balances of the United States system, this can strengthen authoritarianism at the expense of democracy.

Stephens's study of Latin America offers a useful detailed complement to some of the questions raised by Heper (Stephens 1989). While acknowledging that initially the economy and the class structure, and the class alliances it generated, shaped the prospects for democracy, she goes on to argue that the institutions shaped by these forces subsequently acquired a weight of their own, and contributed decisively to regime outcomes (Stephens 1989: 331–3). Thus the willingness of elites in the Southern Cone to accept working-class participation in the political process, in the belief that their own interests were secure, facilitated the development of durable institutions which could survive the rigours of economic depression and military intervention, while elites in Central America were unwilling to make comparable concessions, and the institutional basis for democracy remained fragile.

We are still left with insufficient clues as to how far institutionalization can develop autonomously of social and economic developments, still less of external pressures from foreign governments or international capitalism. And if it is wrong to seek an understanding of democratic development by taking strains within the pre-democratic regime as a starting point, is it not equally dangerous to go to the other extreme of implying that countries which followed the wrong sort of evolution in the nineteenth century are pre-ordained to remain authoritarian or, at best, unstable democracies? No doubt the historical pedigree will help, but what are the prospects for countries which were not born with such silver spoons, but have the will to build democratic institutions and an extensive knowledge of the experience of democracy elsewhere?

Sequences in development

Having considered what are said to be the basic ingredients of the democratic cake, and noted the extent of disagreement as to the proportions in which they should be combined and the distinctive flavour which each contributes, we are left with the question of the sequence in which the ingredients should be added. Dahl explored this question in 1971 and concluded that 'polyarchy' (his real world approximation to the ideal of liberal democracy) fared best if political competition preceded 'inclusiveness' (Dahl 1971: 203). In other words, Western countries enjoyed the advantage of a long period of competition for power based on a narrow franchise, during which the main rules and conventions of political decision-making were able to evolve. When political rights were gradually extended to the rest of the adult population, they could be admitted to the club, to change the metaphor, on the understanding that they abided by the existing rules, or only sought to change the rules in certain accepted ways, thus ensuring stability and continuity. Many Third World countries, in contrast, began their independent existence with universal suffrage, and with an awareness on the part of party and pressure group leaders of the ways in which participation through lobbying and the ballot box had advanced the claims of diverse groups in the West. There were thus high expectations, and pressures on the political system, at a time when the system had barely become institutionalized and when the resources available to meet mass demands were meagre.

The contributors to the volume by Binder et al. look at a wider range of chronological orders of events (Binder et al. 1971). They suggest that a country may be confronted with a variety of 'crises' in the process of 'political development': crises of identity, participation, penetration, legitimacy and distribution. An ideal path on the road to democracy would, perhaps, be one along which the question of identity – which areas and groups belong within the boundaries of the nation state – is resolved at an early stage, as in Rustow's model, with the question of legitimacy – who is entitled to rule and how they should obtain office – also resolved before the demands for increased participation, and a redistribution of resources to less privileged groups, put too much pressure on the system. The 'crisis of penetration' – how adequately the writ of the state can run through society in collecting revenue and enforcing its authority – is also resolved better before the participative and redistributive pressures become too great.

The obvious inference from this model is that Western democracies have had in-built advantages in being confronted with these crises in the best chronological order, and with ample time for consolidation between one crisis and the next. The question of legitimacy in Britain was largely resolved with the 1688 revolution, which settled most of the outstanding questions about the role of the monarchy in a parliamentary system and, disregarding Ireland, the question of identity was largely resolved by the Act of Union with Scotland in 1706. State penetration increased steadily in the nineteenth century with the development of a professional civil service and a growing volume of social legislation, despite the facade of a *laissez-faire* economic policy. Only late in the day were there irresistible pressures for universal suffrage or a significant redistribution of wealth. Such developments can be contrasted with those in many Third World countries where the 'crises' all crowd in on one another. Newly established governments with limited penetrative powers tried to cope with the demands of newly enfranchised citizens, which could not easily be met, for universal education, hospitals, piped water and adequate roads for marketing their crops, or even for sufficient foodstuffs in the shops, at a time when questions of the scope or desirability of one-party rule or the right of Ashantis or Biafrans or the Baganda to autonomy or independence were still in dispute.

As with the Moore and Heper models, the Binder *et al.* approach risks the charge of historical determinism, or of giving advice of the 'If I were going to Dublin I wouldn't start from here' variety to Third World democrats. Are we to argue that prospects for democracy are irredeemably poor because the crises of legitimacy or participation occurred at the wrong time, or can a determination to establish democratic norms, especially after experience of the alternatives, together with the benefit of knowledge of the experiences of long-standing democracies, which the latter did not enjoy when they started along the democratic path, enable countries which went through the 'wrong' sequences to arrive at the 'right' destination in spite of themselves?

For analytical purists the words 'crisis' and 'development' leave the Binder *et al.* approach open to further criticism. It is not clear how one recognizes the beginning or end of a crisis, or even its existence. Did the 'crisis of participation' in Britain begin with the pressures leading to the 1832 Reform Act, or that of 1867, or with the later demands for trade union recognition? Was it resolved with the completion of universal suffrage in 1928, or did it re-surface in the 1960s with the rise of 'direct action' pressure groups which rejected the underlying consensus? Was the crisis of legitimacy resolved with the acceptance of parliamentary democracy by the eighteenth century, or did it re-surface in the 1980s when people questioned the right of a government to pursue extreme policies under an electoral system that gave it 60 per cent of the seats in Parliament in return for 42 per cent of the votes? As for identity, the question of whether Northern Ireland should belong to the United Kingdom or Eire has been in dispute for the past three decades after a long period of apparent calm, and the right of a government whose party holds barely 12 per cent of the seats in Scotland to rule that part of the kingdom may yet be called into question.

The propensity of apparently resolved crises in the West to recur calls into question the concept of 'development', as does the inability of many Third World countries to resolve any of the crises outlined by Binder *et al.* The concept is, perhaps, discredited because of its association with the 'modernization' theorists of the 1950s and 1960s, who envisaged Third World countries treading the same paths that Western countries had trodden in earlier centuries, without making sufficient allowance for indigenous culture and social structure, and economic dependence on the West. What the critics of the modernization school would put in its place in assessing the prospects for democracy is less clear. Some, such as Huntington, argued the case for 'order' and strong institutions as preconditions for democracy, whose imminence now receded beyond the distant horizon (Huntington 1968: 244–5), while others insisted on a more self-sufficient economy to end the undemocratic process of Western exploitation, and/or the development of working class participatory structures to ensure equality of wealth and resources as well as political rights (Amin 1987; Jonas 1990), but the practicability of either course is open to doubt. If rulers are strong enough to impose order in the way advocated by Huntington, and many clearly lack this strength on account of limited resources and dubious legitimacy, why should they subsequently want to share their power with anyone else? The self-sufficiency argument has been abandoned by some of its strongest advocates (see especially Frank 1991) in the face of the reality of international interdependence and the absence of much economic or democratic development in the countries where it has been attempted. The mass participatory argument fails to explain how elites are going to be persuaded to enter a bargain which gives all the benefits to their adversaries, in contrast to the more subtle democratic transitions in the real world where both authoritarians and democrats have been willing to concede on some points if their interests could be guaranteed on others.

At this point, participatory democrats might plead that they are merely setting out an ideal at which to aim, which may be very noble, but tells us little about the route by which they expect to get there; or that they believe that it will all come to pass 'after the revolution' in which the elites are overthrown. Sceptics might then enquire as to how many revolutions have ushered in democracy, given the economic hardship and social polarization frequently necessary to provoke such an event. Nicaragua may be cited as a useful model, but it remains an exceptional one in that neither elites nor their foreign backers normally allow governments to become so inflexible and vulnerable as to provoke such a revolution as the one that overthrew President Somoza.

The advocates of economic autonomy or participatory democracy, like the developmentalists they criticize, are open to the charge of operating from too high a level of generality. Even if we can separate their political analysis from their ideological preferences, we may find that they offer us a useful impressionistic picture of processes that may help or hinder democratic development, but the actual objects in the picture become blurred on closer inspection. Achieving national identity with a legitimate centre of government, building up effective state structures and responding to (or articulating) pressures for participation, distribution and economic autonomy are clearly tests which many political systems and political institutions have to undergo. The ability to achieve sufficient consensus in surmounting them will augur well for democracy, but the actual processes are often difficult to recognize until they have receded into history, and sometimes not even then. Do we know, for example, whether the Nigerian Civil War finally resolved the 'crisis of identity' or merely ushered in a truce, or whether the current attempt to impose a two-party state within a federal structure will go far to resolve the 'crisis of participation', or will merely offer one means of channelling political demands until a change in the balance of power between different civil and military elites makes for further extra-constitutional conflict? Those who are doubtful about the value of such broad concepts as have been examined above may prefer to take refuge in narrower studies of transitions to democracy in individual countries.

External influences

No authors, to my knowledge, have offered external influences as a primary explanation of democracy, but it is obvious from what has been said already that democracy would not have taken root when it did in many countries without the impact of external forces. These may be direct, as with the Allied occupation of the former fascist countries after 1945, or may involve sanctions against non-democratic governments, in the form of trade boycotts and the withholding of aid and investment, actual or threatened, as in Chile and South Africa, or merely the influence of ideas and political practices. Just as many African states succumbed, one after another, to one-party or military government, so many are now contemplating the return of multi-party politics. While their own experience of authoritarian rule may be a major reason for this, the success of neighbouring countries is also likely to have an influence. Authoritarians who had previously been able to praise the achievements of authoritarian rulers in more developed countries ('Mussolini made the trains run on time', 'the Russians were the first to put a man in space', 'Franco resisted decadence and social permissiveness in Spain'), were left with fewer models to emulate as these regimes collapsed, with their achievements appearing more modest and the levels of both repression and incompetence laid bare. In the West, friends of Third World authoritarian rulers became fewer and less reliable. President Carter had more scruples in his dealings with these rulers than had his predecessors, and even the more conservative American Presidents have had to face a more critical lobby opposed to 'aiding the dictators', while the ending of the Cold War has raised questions as to whether there are any good practical reasons for supporting foreign despots who were once seen as a bulwark against communism.

This is not to argue that Western pressure has been entirely on the side of the democrats. United States support for the Contra terrorists who opposed the elected government in Nicaragua had much to do with the electorate's eventual decision to remove the Sandinista Government, in the hope of ending terrorism and the economic deprivation that went with fighting the terrorists, and one could argue that American support for the ruling elites in Guatemala and El Salvador has provided them with a lifeline and enabled them to use repression rather than reconciliation in dealing with the opposition, which in turn has continued to resort to violence in the belief that it would not be allowed to compete in free and fair elections. Similarly in Africa, European powers have sustained General Mobutu in power in the hope of maintaining stability and protecting foreign investments. International businesses may have no specific ideological preferences between democracy and authoritarianism, and may even prefer a sustainable democratic regime to an authoritarian one which is losing its capacity to rule in the face of popular resistance or internal intrigue, but businesses want a return on their investment, low prices for their raw materials and a minimum of competition from countries building up competing industries. This may lead them, and the Western governments over which they have influence, to support the suppression of democracy if there is a prospect of people electing a government that threatens their interests.

External pressures can quite easily topple a democracy, through means such as economic sanctions, support for subversion or even invasion, but their ability to create a democracy is more limited. By its nature it cannot be imposed in the way that authoritarianism can, and external influence can only add a helping hand if some of the preconditions I have mentioned are already there. Foreign influence has fluctuated over the years but, with modern communications and a realization of the impact of pressure group politics, there must be few countries under authoritarian rule today in which opposition groups do not have allies in the West to speak for them who can, at the very least, embarrass Western governments that are on friendly terms with the authoritarians.

Lessons for the Third World

Many of the lessons for the Third World arising out of the literature reviewed appear to be negative. Most Third World countries have not enjoyed the economic development cited by Lipset, or the civic cultural attitudes cited by Almond and Verba. The sequences in development conducive to democracy in the West have not generally occurred in the Third World, and the 'developmental crises' have frequently crowded in on one another over a short period of time. Institutional developments have generally been limited. We have seen that most Latin American states, despite their long period of independence, have built only rudimentary links between government and governed, while the more recently independent states of Africa and Asia have had little time to develop institutions. The structures bequeathed by the colonial powers were more concerned with sound administration than democracy, and most political parties only appeared in the decade or two before independence. The long history of the Congress Party in building a base of support in India is very much an exception to the general rule. The pressures on, and willingness of, elites and social groups to achieve reconciliation are limited, if only because the benefits derived from membership of the nation state are limited if the nation is poor and the state's administrative capacity limited, though many Third World countries may begin with the advantage that the initial animosity between rival groups is less than that between groups such as the Protestants and Catholics in much of Europe, or even between the working and middle classes in some instances. Informal coalitions do clearly emerge between different ethnic and religious groups, as in our earlier example of consociational democracy in Kenya, and the government of larger countries such as India and Nigeria would be impossible without such coalitions.

We thus need to remind ourselves that Third World countries are not just poorer versions of those in the First World, or imitations of those countries as they existed a century ago. Countries in Europe did not have their economic systems transformed to meet the requirements of wealthier nations on another continent, since none existed, and although their frontiers were sometimes drawn arbitrarily, a sense of nationhood based on language, culture and history was probably more easily recognizable in nineteenth-century France, Germany or Spain than in twentieth-century Sudan or Nigeria. Whether these differences are differences of quality or quantity is a matter of debate. The dependency school, as exemplified by Wallerstein, argues that the advancement of Western countries necessitates the continued impoverishment of the Third World (Wallerstein 1974), though critics have argued that this view is over-deterministic and that governments and their citizens can, within limits, make their own political choices, which may either stimulate development or preserve dependence (Chazan et al. 1988: 21–5). Similarly, with regard to the question of 'artificial' frontiers, one could argue that ethnic conflicts in Nigeria and the

Sudan are different only in quantity from disputes about the positions of Northern Ireland or Quebec in relation to Britain or Canada. Yet in the case of both dependency and national identity there is surely a difference between countries where such problems exist alongside a range of others, and are not necessarily the most serious, and countries where survival depends on fluctuations in the price of a single primary product, or on preventing a major ethnic group from seceding or massacring its adversaries, without having much conception of the well-being of the 'nation'. This is not to argue that all Third World countries are equally at the mercy of international capitalism or that all are artificial shells with no focal points of national unity, but merely to note that the closer they are to such conditions, the greater will be the difficulty in establishing democracy.

While the national frontiers drawn by the colonial powers make little sense in terms of ethnic homogeneity, the fact that the international community guarantees these frontiers, in a way that it did not when the nation states of Europe were emerging, imposes a certain discipline on rival groups. Irrespective of the economic damage that national disintegration might cause, this option is seldom available, except in the case of secession from loose federations by countries such as Bangladesh, Singapore and the West Indian islands, where the facts of geography made for little national unity in the first place. Secessionist struggles continue to be waged by minority groups within countries such as India, Indonesia, Morocco and Sri Lanka, but most rival groups have accepted the need for some form of accommodation in the absence of any realistic alternative. One question mark over the preservation of existing frontiers is, of course, the impact of the breakup of the Soviet Empire and Yugoslavia. The emergence of an independent Croatia or Ukraine might create a precedent for Tamils, Ibos or Sudanese Christians to demand their own territories, but the viability of such territories might depend heavily on the willingness of the West to provide sufficient aid.

Whether the need to live within most of the existing frontiers will provide a basis for democratic competition in the way described by Rustow is another matter. The group leaders might merely share the spoils of office, and allow some trickle-down of wealth and patronage to their followers, without necessarily permitting free elections. A major challenge might emerge if some of the followers were dissatisfied with their share of the spoils, and thus demanded greater control over their leaders, but whether this would lead to democratic concessions or greater repression would presumably depend on the relative resources of leaders and followers.

As for Moore's thesis about democracy depending on the evolution of an autonomous bourgeoisie, the prospects again appear unpromising. Many Third World countries have achieved little of the industrialization which is concomitant with the emergence of a large middle class, and where industrialization has taken place, it has often been dependent on the good will of the state rather than the efforts of an autonomous middle class. Whereas entrepreneurs in nineteenth-century Britain could build factories, seek their own raw materials and markets, and promote legislation to provide an infrastructure of railways, ports and urban developments to house their employees, and ultimately use their independently earned wealth to enter politics and shape society more to their own requirements, their Third World counterparts are more dependent on the state for the provision of import licences, contracts, foreign currency and means of transport. The entrepreneur who falls foul of the government will find it difficult to survive if these favours are withdrawn. It is significant that those who have done most to sustain opposition to authoritarian governments in Africa have come from professions such as the law and academia (and in Latin America the church), which enjoy the greatest insulation from government. If they have contacts with popular opposition leaders in exile or power bases in local communities led by sympathetic chiefs, they may be able to offer a 'government in waiting', but the length of the wait may then depend on the willingness of the military, whether out of sympathy for opposition groups or for their own reasons, to overthrow the authoritarian regime and then permit free elections.

The extent to which the state does actually constrain autonomous behaviour has been questioned by writers using the concept of 'civil society' to indicate the presence of increasingly autonomous groups, whether they be the grass roots 'social movements' which have arisen in response to repression in Latin America or the more staid 'autonomous groups' which have grown in stature in much of Africa as the state has become increasingly incapable of performing its basic functions. I shall look at these developments in more detail in subsequent chapters. Here I merely caution against exaggerating the importance of these developments. The state may have lost much of its effectiveness, but it would be stretching Moore's model unduly to argue that the conditions that he pronounced as conducive to democracy exist in much of the Third World today.

It may in the end be the external factors that will do most to provide a democratic opening, though this is not because all the external powers are anxious to promote democracy or because indigenous populations are hostile to it. At first sight, the external forces seem to be on the side of repression, both directly and indirectly. Where democratic elections have produced governments which were hostile to Western interests, as in Guatemala and Iran in the 1950s and Chile in the 1970s, Western powers were quick to subvert them and sustain their authoritarian successors, while the nature of economic dependence on the West is said to maintain societies where ruling elites collaborate with international capitalism while the majority of the population remains in poverty – a situation not conducive to democratic consensus. Yet one can find examples to illustrate a less one-sided set of relationships. Entrepreneurs in Kenya and Zambia have pursued interests which have reflected their needs much more than those of international capitalism, and Western powers have failed to subvert many rulers hostile to their interests. These have often been dictators, such as Ayatollah Khomeini, General Amin and Colonel Gadaffi, rather than democrats but their longevity might also give hope to democrats standing on platforms that are not entirely subservient to Western interests.

At least as important as the policies of foreign democratic governments is the experience they can offer. Democracy emerged only slowly in the West, and was not generally an outcome for which political actors actually strove. If we go back to the developments which were said to have helped the evolution of democracy, there is no reason to believe that this was the outcome sought by entrepreneurs promoting economic development, rival groups seeking to bargain with their adversaries, or political actors building institutions to strengthen their own positions or attempting to resolve developmental crises. Even the cultural conditions cited by Almond and Verba as conducive to democracy are as likely to be a response to a democratic environment as a precondition for its emergence. Yet when democracy did emerge, it became valued in its own right as a more equitable and efficient means of resolving competing demands.

When the colonies of the Western democracies began to demand independence, it did not occur to them or their colonial masters to demand anything other than a constitution which embodied democratic values. (The case of the Latin American colonies, which gained independence from non-democratic Spain and Portugal in the nineteenth century, was, of course, somewhat different. There was no immediate expectation of democracy, yet authoritarian rulers did not enjoy the traditional institutions and power bases of their metropolitan counterparts, and eventually had to seek forms of legitimacy which owed something to public support.) For reasons that will be examined in later chapters, the democratic expectations were frequently not realized, but the ideal was never completely extinguished. While many Western rulers had retained non-democratic bases for their legitimacy until well into the nineteenth century, including divine right, custom or the moral superiority of the upper class, the legitimate credentials of twentieth-century Third World rulers have usually had some connection with democracy. If they cannot claim a popular mandate, they will at least claim to have removed a non-democratic regime, to be devising ways of establishing a democratic one or to be offering democratic choice through intra-party competition. The pre-twentieth-century European claims to legitimacy based on divine right, custom or social superiority might carry some weight at a purely local level, but they would make little sense in a larger nation state composed of communities with varied cultures and traditions. Even if there is not the drama of a prolonged inter-group conflict followed by a democratic reconciliation, as in Rustow's model, there may at least be a realization that democratic choice, if necessary buttressed by checks and balances to protect weaker groups, offers one of the few means of reconciliation. Group conflicts in the Third World have tended to be less 'prolonged', and are more likely to consist of a series of fluid shorter-term alliances which may eventually encompass the majority of the population. The restoration of democracy in Ghana in 1969 was thus helped by the mending of fences between Ashantis and Akans, first at a military and then at a civilian level, while almost every permutation of alliance between North, East and West has been attempted in Nigeria. Such alliances do not guarantee democracy, but compromise between powerful rival groups will make the achievement of democracy easier.

Concentrating now on the practical rather than the philosophical plane, we have already noted people's experience and knowledge of authoritarianism at home and abroad. Authoritarian governments have generally done little to improve people's material well-being, and have thus done little to win the allegiance of the masses, while they have frequently executed, tortured, imprisoned or exiled the more articulate members of the population who have attempted to resist them. In pre-nineteenth-century Europe, people suffering such deprivations might have conceived of no alternative other than a more efficient or more benevolent form of authoritarianism, but in the twentieth-century Third World they, or at least their leaders, are aware of the democratic alternative and may strive positively to achieve and maintain it.

We thus arrive at a precarious vantage point for observing democracy in the Third World, and one to which we shall need to return in subsequent chapters as we try to understand specific features of the landscape. Where democracy exists, it does not appear to have sprung from the same roots as in the West, although some of the roots have an affinity with their Western counterparts. Thus relations between interdependent elites and social groups are important, though not necessarily in the ways outlined by Rustow and Moore. Public attitudes are important, but less in Almond and Verba's sense of tolerant attitudes towards everyday political life and more in a belief that democracy must prevail because of more recent experience (than most Western citizens have had to suffer) of the alternatives. The luxuries of extensive economic development, to make politics less of a life and death struggle, and steady consolidation of the polity as political crises are resolved one by one over a long period, are not generally available, but the lessons learnt from other countries' experiences and the willingness, in some cases, of wealthier countries to offer assistance at crucial moments, as in the eventual rejection of the Latin American military juntas, may give a boost to democracy which Western countries in their formative years did not enjoy.

Even these somewhat shallow democratic roots are by no means universal in the Third World. One does not have to look far to find their opposites in group intransigence (as in Lebanon or Sri Lanka), antipathy towards democracy as a compromise between good and evil (as in much of the Middle East), or Western actions which aid authoritarianism rather than democracy (as in Central America). But where the soil is less barren and where the commitment of political actors is substantial, who is to say that institutions will not eventually develop to make the aspiring democracies more secure, despite their different origins from those in the West?

Democracy and the end of empire

Experience of colonial rule is a factor common to the vast majority of Third World states, although it is not exclusive to them. 'Western' and Old Commonwealth countries, such as the United States, Belgium, Norway and Australia, also emerged from the tutelage of foreign powers, but the gap between the foreign masters and the elites in these dependent countries was generally much narrower, in terms of ethnicity, culture and economic position, than was the gap between European colonial masters and aspiring elites in Africa, Asia and Latin America. And below the elites were societies which were radically different from the metropolitan societies over which the Europeans ruled.

Decolonization in the Third World was therefore much more a leap into the unknown than it had been in Norway or Australia, where institutions modelled largely on those of the departing masters might be expected to serve the needs of the new nation without undue strain. Transferring the letter and spirit of the 'Westminster model' to Australia, where the level of economic development was relatively high, education was almost universal and most people shared a common language and culture, was a very different matter from transferring such a model to Nigeria, with its economic underdevelopment, mass illiteracy and cultural heterogeneity. The more gradual pace of decolonization also gave the older colonies an advantage. They were able to experiment with metropolitan institutions, such as elections and legislatures, long before independence, and to introduce their own adaptations, such as federalism or appointed ceremonial heads of state, as part of an evolutionary process, instead of unwrapping them after independence with little notion of how they would work.

The timing of the transfer of power was also significant. Supporters of Dahl's thesis, that democracy will be built on firmer foundations if contestation precedes participation, will note that the West and Old Commonwealth countries became self-governing for practical purposes before the

First World War, when demands on the state were fewer than today. The 'crises' of 'identity' and 'penetration', to move to Binder *et al.*'s terminology, had largely been resolved, while the 'crisis of distribution' in meeting mass demands was still on the distant horizon. Most African and Asian states, in contrast, gained independence after the Second World War when expectations of social welfare and economic intervention were more widespread as nationalist politicians and their followers sought to emulate the all-embracing role of the state now common in the West, yet the basic problem of establishing effective legitimate authority throughout the land was not yet resolved. Indeed, the colonial powers often raised people's expectations further by promoting welfare and development in the terminal years of colonialism in the belief that this would make for more viable post-independence governments. The establishment and survival of democracy in the Third World thus required not only the rapid adaptation of institutions alien to indigenous society (or the rapid discovery of alternative institutions for those bold enough to make such a search) and the establishment of legitimate bases of authority in culturally heterogeneous societies, but also the ability of political structures with limited administrative experience and expertise to cope with a range of public demands in societies with very limited economic resources.

If the end of empire cast most Third World countries adrift on a voyage into the unknown with similar limited means of coping with the hazards ahead, there were still great variations in the circumstances in which the different countries found themselves. Our concern in this chapter is with the relationship between, on the one hand, the extent to which democracy was or was not established and, on the other, the nature of colonial rule, the processes of decolonization and the legacies these left. This leads us to two main sets of questions. First, in what ways did colonial rule itself encourage or discourage democratic development, directly or indirectly? Second, what was the process of the transfer of power? Was there a 'preparation' for independence, or did it come about as a result of irresistible nationalist pressures or the collapse of the metropolitan power? If there was 'preparation', how comprehensive was it, and what were the objectives and priorities? Was democracy high on the lists of priorities of either the colonists or the nationalist 'heirs apparent', or were there greater concerns with a swift, peaceful transfer of power to any group that appeared capable of sustaining stable administration?

The impact of colonial rule

The impact of colonial rule varied according to its timing, the nature of the societies being colonized and the policy choices of the colonial powers. I set out some of these variables, the cases approximating to them, and implications for democracy in Table 3.1. The variables of the timing of colonization, the depth of colonial penetration, the nature of the centre of power and relations between colonizers and indigenous peoples are to some extent interdependent. Thus pre-democratic colonization, that is colonization which took place at a time when the colonial powers themselves had no pretensions to internal democracy, occurred in the sixteenth and seventeenth centuries when limited administrative and technical knowledge made deep colonial penetration of societies difficult. In contrast, the scramble for Africa occurred in the nineteenth century, when material advancement had facilitated both political pluralism in Europe and technological opportunities for deeper control over the colonies, through such means as the railway, the telegraph, the steamship and the Maxim gun.

> He stood upon a little mound,
> Cast his lethargic eyes around.
> And said beneath his breath:
> 'Whatever happens we have got
> The Maxim Gun and they have not' . . .
>
> We shot and hanged a few and then
> The rest became devoted men.

                                                    (Belloc 1970: 184)

Questions of racial assimilation versus exclusiveness also became more clear-cut when improvements in communications and health enabled more Europeans to bring their wives and families to the colonies, where previously the absence of European women had made for more inter-breeding, though without any acknowledgement of the equal status of the participants. By the nineteenth century, a choice was available between the British policy of an arm's length relationship with the indigenous populations or the French policy based on the belief that there could be no higher social goal than to bring Africans and Asians within the ambit of French culture. Yet despite the interdependence of some of the variables, Table 3.1 indicates enough permutations to suggest that each group of countries had distinctive features which had some bearing on their ultimate prospects for democratic development. Some tentative hypotheses about the implications of the variables for democracy are suggested in the right hand column.

The timing of colonization

The colonization and subsequent liberalization of a territory by a pre-democratic country, as in Latin America in the sixteenth and seventeenth centuries, would suggest poor prospects for democracy. There were few democratic examples for nationalist politicians to emulate, yet there was no aristocracy comparable with that in Europe, with legitimacy based on heredity. Heper sees a link between the origins of the Spanish Latin American states, in which neither democratic norms nor deference sustained governments, and their continued problems in searching for democracy in the twentieth century. In the absence of shared norms on which to build

Table 3.1 Variations in colonial rule

Variable	Spanish Latin America	Brazil	India	British East and West Africa	British Southern Africa	French Africa	Possible implications for democracy
1 Timing of colonization							
(a) Pre-democracy	+	+					No democratic foundations
(b) Democratic era			+	+	+	+	Democracy seen as ultimate destination
2 Depth of colonial penetration							
(a) Shallow			+	+	+	+	Outcomes depend on strength and norms of indigenous institutions
(b) Deep	+						Society weak in relation to state, therefore possible authoritarianism
(c) Destructive		+					Society weak, democratic legitimacy difficult to establish

3 Main centre of power		
(a) Metropolitan rule	+	Consensus between colonial and indigenous elites may facilitate peaceful transfer of power
(b) Settler rule	+	Settlers may resist majority rule
4 Relations between colonizers and indigenous populations		
(a) Attempted assimilation	+	Nationalism blunted; opportunities for consensus
(b) Racial exclusiveness	+	Conflict between 'nationalists' and 'collaborators'
(c) Racial laissez-faire	+	Conflict between a variety of ethnic groups

+ indicates the presence of the variable.

effective institutions, power passed to *caudillos* (personal rulers) building support through patron–client networks. The continued absence of effective institutions to filter public demands, as new social groups emerged, made repression more common than democratic accommodation (Heper 1991: 199–203). Such generalizations obviously cannot explain all the varied political outcomes in Spanish Latin America, from the relative democratic stability of Uruguay to the prolonged violence of Guatemala and El Salvador, and Stephens illuminates some of the subtler light and shade by looking at such post-independence variables as the relative significance of labour-intensive agriculture, economies based on mineral extraction and the behaviour of such institutions as were established (Stephens 1989).

Brazil was different again in that, although it gained independence from a non-democratic power, its tropical location precluded extensive European settlement. Portugal was therefore able to transfer a hierarchical and authoritarian model of government that was the antithesis of democracy, but was at least more conducive to the development of stable institutions than was the disorder of Spanish Latin America. As Huntington has suggested, stable authoritarianism may evolve into stable democracy more easily than unstable authoritarianism, as democrats use the institutions they have inherited to pursue new ends (Huntington 1984: 210). A contrast could be made between the relatively orderly and controlled, if prolonged, transition from military government to democracy in Brazil in the 1970s and 1980s, and the more confrontational relationship between military rulers and civilian politicians in Argentina and Chile. Whether one believes that these differences will ultimately make for a superior form of democracy in Brazil depends largely on how far one supports Huntington's emphasis on stability as a precondition for democracy, as opposed to those who take the more populist view that democracy depends on the masses capturing and transforming the political structure to achieve greater participation and social equality.

Where colonization was embarked on by metropolitan powers with democratic political systems, albeit on a restricted franchise, the contribution of the colonial powers was more ambiguous. The political structures they set up in Africa, Asia and the Caribbean were certainly not democratic, at least until concessions were made on the eve of independence, yet they could not hide their domestic democratic politics completely from their colonial subjects. Indigenous education, which economic development required, could not easily avoid some exposure to the culture of the metropolitan society, and higher education often required residence in the metropolitan country where democracy could, for good or ill, be observed at first hand. The educated elites were bound to contrast the ability of the British and French to choose their own governments with their own inability to do so, and in many cases they sought to build power bases at home to bring about the desired changes. They were also able to seek allies in the metropolitan countries in the open political systems that prevailed there, in a way which would have been unthinkable for any eighteenth-century Latin American visitor to Lisbon or Madrid. While official governmental acknowledgement of the goal of democratic self-government might have been slow in coming, nationalism built on knowledge of, and contacts with, democratic institutions and individuals in Europe had a longer history. The colonial powers were also unable to envisage handing power over to any form of government other than a democratically elected one, once the case for independence had been conceded. None of this guaranteed that democracy would be sustained after independence, but it did make it likely that democracy would remain a point of reference, and at least an ultimate ideal to which people aspired, in a way that it was not in post-independence Latin America.

The depth of colonial penetration

Crawford Young brings out some of the significant variations in the depth of colonial penetration (Young 1988: 37–40). The Spanish and Portuguese colonizers destroyed many of the indigenous civilizations, although administrative and technical knowledge in the sixteenth and seventeenth centuries did not allow them to build elaborate power structures of their own, and the societies which eventually revolted were dominated by Creole elites who had little conception of democracy, or of reversion to earlier values. In Asia, in contrast, the colonial state was superimposed on existing structures, and its imprint was less dislocative and comprehensive than in Latin America or subsequently in Africa (see especially Manor 1990: 20–38). Africa was the most extreme example of deep colonization. The scramble for Africa in the nineteenth century coincided with the development of strong states in Europe, aided by the technical and administrative developments of the industrial revolutions. The colonial powers were thus able to provide professional bureaucracies, greater resources and permanent military forces to maintain their authority. At the same time they had articulated a clearer racialist ideology, with a strong belief in European and Christian superiority.

It is tempting to draw immediate inferences for democracy from these different levels of colonial penetration. The elites which replaced Spanish rulers in Latin America ruled with an intolerance of dissent, and of democratic participation, which is common to settler communities, and indigenous civilizations had been too shattered to resist them, whereas the fate of democracy in Asia depended more on the fertility of the indigenous social soil, which the British had left relatively undisturbed. Hindu India, with its traditions of dispersed power and compromise between elites, was able to sustain a pluralist system after independence, whereas the more authoritarian culture of Pakistan was less conducive to democracy. Africans, like the Latin Americans, had had their traditional political structures largely uprooted, even though the colonial presence was a much briefer one and memories of an earlier culture were fresher, and had little practical alternative but to build an independent state which was modelled on the metropolitan power. By the second half of the twentieth century that meant democracy based on universal suffrage.

Such a simplified analysis runs the risk of treating the depth of colonial penetration as merely an independent variable. The relative shallowness of penetration in eighteenth-century India was not due only to a technical inability to adopt the solutions favoured in nineteenth-century Africa, but also to a recognition of a culture which Europeans treated with some deference, in contrast to their general attitude towards African civilization. One could argue that history had given India a substantial start over Africa in building political institutions. The relationship between the depth of penetration and democracy is anyway an ambiguous one. Colonial penetration ensured that the formal post-independence political structure was modelled on Europe, if only because clearly defined national frontiers cut across the boundaries of the earlier political kingdoms, but the incongruence between the formal democratic structures and political reality soon became apparent. This could be attributed partly to practical inexperience of democracy, of which there had been little under colonial rule, but it also reflected an imbalance between state and society, compared with Europe. Whereas in Europe, and especially Britain, the state had evolved to meet the needs of dominant social groups, and its power was constrained by them, in Africa the state had been imposed to ensure the subordination of indigenous groups. The authoritarian governments which discarded nominally democratic constitutions soon after independence were not merely imitating their colonial predecessors but were filling a vacuum that would have been filled in Europe by political parties, pressure groups and a variety of other autonomous bodies.

The strength of the state in relation to society in Latin America following the destruction of pre-colonial structures has, on the face of it, facilitated similar authoritarian tendencies, but post-independence history has been much longer, and the variety of democratic and authoritarian outcomes at different times and places should caution against attributing too much to events of over 200 years ago. There may be the common factor of the difficulty in establishing a legitimate centre of authority once the old structures had been swept away, but time has allowed new social, economic and political structures to evolve in a way that has not yet been possible in Africa. Depending on circumstances, these can facilitate outcomes as varied as the long-standing ritual of two-party competition in Uruguay and the crude authoritarianism of General Pinochet in Chile.

Centres of power

When the colonies were ruled by men who served on brief tours of duty but who regarded the metropolitan country as 'home', the granting of independence was largely a matter of negotiation between two parties – the nationalist movement and the colonial power – though the situation was sometimes complicated if there were ethnic or religious minorities which the nationalist movement could not or would not embrace. Negotiations for independence might involve lengthy disputes over the protection of minority rights, but there was no question of minorities demanding the right to rule over the majority. When control of the colonies was largely in the hands of settler populations whose ancestors had migrated from Europe, as in Spanish Latin America and British Southern Africa, the situation was more complicated. Minorities might insist on the right to rule over majorities on the grounds of administrative experience, wealth, superior education or racial superiority. In Spanish Latin America and South Africa this right was conceded, and the struggle for democracy based on equal citizenship has been a prolonged and often violent one, as it was in Zimbabwe where the settler minority took power despite the opposition of the metropolitan country. Even if the principle of 'one adult, one vote' has been conceded, conflict may continue as the minority races strive to defend their economic advantages, as in Central America.

Countries without settler populations from the metropolitan power would appear to have an easier road to democracy, and the few Third World countries which have achieved anything approximating to liberal democracy have been of this type. Yet the absence of European settlers may also indicate a relative absence of wealth available for exploitation, and we have seen that poverty generally militates against democracy. At best, the absence of settler colonial rule, or settler rule after independence, relieves a country of a major liability in the building of democracy, but more positive influences will have to be present for democracy to thrive.

Relations between colonizers and indigenous populations

We have noted the contrast between the British practice of retaining a sharp distinction between colonists and indigenous populations, and the French attempts at assimilation. The latter practice was applied to every level of society, from giving African primary school children a similar education to their French counterparts, to allowing the colonies to elect deputies to the French Parliament. Munslow has argued that the French system made for less of a split between older urban elites and the petty bourgeoisie, and that political parties in French Africa were able to develop one-party regimes with more extensive popular support than their counterparts in English-speaking Africa (Munslow 1983: 226). One can see that, in theory, nationalism might be blunted and a consensual atmosphere conducive to democracy might develop if all citizens see themselves as part of a wider French Community, in contrast to the conflict between nationalists and alleged collaborators in English-speaking Africa, but former French colonies have not been noted for their democratic achievements. Algeria and the states of Indo-China only gained independence after bloody conflicts, and many French-speaking states in tropical Africa have been wracked by military coups. It may be that attempted assimilation, like deep colonial penetration, weakens or destroys autonomous centres of power. Such centres can be troublesome and destabilizing, as the Ghanaians found in Ashanti and the Nigerians in the north, but they may also contribute to a pluralist system which eventually becomes institutionalized, while the French system makes for a more authoritarian conformity, or for violent reactions against such conformity.

The Latin American system is best described as one of neither assimilation nor exclusiveness, but of 'racial *laissez-faire*'. The number of female European immigrants was much less than the number of males, so there was inevitably much inter-breeding. While the distinction between ethnic groups was less clear-cut than within the British Empire, a pecking order developed within which those with the lightest coloured skins were generally the most socially privileged. In countries which lacked many of the other preconditions for democracy, these distinctions made the search for consensus in society even more elusive.

The transfer of power

The discussion of the conditions most favourable to democracy suggests a number of hypotheses about the kinds of transfer of power which are most likely to achieve that end. These are set out in Table 3.2. Most of the hypotheses are not mutually exclusive, but the different hypotheses do reflect the different analytical perspectives from which Third World politics are viewed.

Hypothesis 1, on the need for adequate preparation for independence, could be linked to the 'modernization school' fashionable in the 1960s, which saw democratic development largely in terms of following in the footsteps of the West, and which therefore required a rigorous tutelege from the colonial masters. Hypothesis 3, on the need for politicians and parties with mass bases, again implies an expectation that Third World countries could tread a similar path to the West in their formative years. Hypothesis 2, on the need for consensus between colonial rulers and nationalist politicians, places the emphasis more on actual political behaviour and the choices arrived at, and is closer to the more recent 'public policy-making' approach (see especially Philip 1990). Hypothesis 4, on maintaining stability and containing mass participation which will otherwise lead to the system being unable to cope with unsatisfiable demands, is closer to Huntington's emphasis on 'order' as a precondition of democracy (Huntington 1968). Hypothesis 5, on the need for consensus between the main groups in the political system, or at least their leaders, takes us back to Rustow's thesis that democracy is not necessarily sought as an end in itself, but emerges because rival groups, which have an interest in preserving the existing nation state, find that there is no alternative but to reach an accommodation (Rustow 1973). Finally, there are those who seek democratic salvation through economic success, though in different ways. Hypothesis 6, on the need for a high level of achievement on such indicators as per capita income, industrialization, literacy and longevity, harks back to Lipset's work in 1959, which belongs to the 'modernization school'

Table 3.2 The transfer of power and democracy: some hypotheses

	Latin America	Old Commonwealth	India	West Indies	British and French Tropical Africa	Portuguese Africa	Zaire
1 Democracy requires careful, long-term preparations involving colonial rulers and nationalists		+	+	+			
2 Democracy is helped by consensus between the colonial power and nationalist politicians over the transfer of power		+	+	+	+		
3 Democracy requires politicians with effective power bases		+	+	+			
4 Democracy requires the transfer of power to politicians who can contain mass demands	+	+					
5 Democracy is helped by consensus between groups (or their leaders) within a colony		+	+	+			
6 Democracy is helped by high level of social and economic development		+					
7 Democracy is helped by economic autonomy							

+ indicates the presence of the condition.

to the extent that he saw few barriers in the way of Third World countries treading the same path to democracy as the West. Hypothesis 7, on the need for economic autonomy, and on the incompatibility of democracy with economic dependence on the West, belongs to the 'economic dependency school', as espoused by such writers as Frank (1984) and Amin (1987).

The task in this chapter is not to go over the merits of these different perspectives on democracy again, but to discuss the extent to which the political actors involved in the transfer of power were willing or able to move the incipient independent nations closer to the conditions in which democracy was said to be more likely to prevail.

The preparation for independence

The countries which made little preparation for the independence of their colonies are easy to identify. The Spanish and Portuguese Empires in Latin America collapsed as the strengths of the metropolitan powers ebbed, with little attempt at any orderly transfer of power. Portugal was equally unwilling to yield its African Empire in the twentieth century, until a combination of guerilla warfare in the colonies and the collapse of the authoritarian regime in Lisbon left it with little alternative. Power in Indonesia and Zaire was abandoned rather than transferred, as the maintenance of a Dutch or Belgian Empire became too expensive, and the French departed from Guinea in haste after a referendum had rejected continued membership of the French Community. In none of these countries has democracy emerged, at least until several generations after independence.

Where attempts at 'preparation' have been made the results have been more varied, as indeed have been the attempts. It is often difficult to establish whether particular policies were adopted with specific objectives of preparing a country for independence, or whether they were means to other ends, such as facilitating economic exploitation through building an economic infrastructure or expanding education, or alleviating the suffering of the poor through improved welfare provision. The pronouncements of metropolitan politicians did not always clarify the situation. There were some such as Malcolm MacDonald who, as early as the 1930s, saw self-government as the ultimate destination, but with little notion of any time-scale within which specific preparations would have to be made (Hargreaves 1979: 3). Others, such as Churchill, vowed not to preside over the liquidation of the Empire, yet allowed the forces of dissolution to occur under their noses, as concessions were made step by step.

We have noted the lack of any preparation in the Spanish and Portuguese Empires. The French were late in conceding the principle of complete independence, having clung to the myth that the colonies were an extension of metropolitan France until the late 1950s, by which time they had learnt lessons from costly wars against nationalists in Indo-China and Algeria who did not regard themselves as extra-metropolitan Frenchmen.

The interval between conceding the principle of independence and the formal transfer of power was very brief, but earlier attempts to socialize citizens into the French way of life may have done something to enhance the prospects for democracy by providing educated cadres and stimulating at least some economic development.

The extent to which there was any real preparation for dismantling the largest empire of all is a matter of dispute. Hargreaves (1979), Flint (1983) and Low (1988) all insist that such preparation to dismantle the British Empire did take place. According to Flint, new attitudes were emerging in the Colonial Office by the eve of the Second World War, influenced by the rise of Nazism, the riots in the West Indies in 1938, the appointment of Malcolm MacDonald as Colonial Secretary and the publication of Lord Hailey's *African Survey*. The riots and *Survey* suggested a need for immediate social and economic solutions – hence the 1940 Colonial Development and Welfare Act, which allocated £120 million to the colonies over the next ten years – but the rise of Nazism and MacDonald's ideological preferences implied the need for a democratic Britain to offer the long-term prospects of democratic self-government abroad, and not merely material development. The need to persuade the anti-colonial Americans to join in the war, and to dispel notions about a Japanese 'liberation' of Asia, no doubt helped to strengthen the arguments of 'decolonizers' within the Government and the Colonial Service.

What sort of democratic blueprint was available? Britain did not seriously consider the idea of restoring power to 'traditional' authorities, which would have been of doubtful practicability, given the incongruence between the boundaries of the 'traditional' territories and the existing colonies, and the fact that many traditional functions had been compromised by their incorporation into colonial administration, yet the 'Westminster model' was seen as unsuitable in a radically different setting, and colonial peoples were expected to work out their own form of democracy (Flint 1983: 400–1). If the world had moved at a rate that suited British politicians and administrators, social and economic development might have proceeded apace to produce strong educated elites and articulate but moderate citizens, while nationalist demands for independence would have remained muted until most of Africa and Asia had achieved a level of development comparable with that of the Old Commonwealth. In the event the pace of nationalist demands outstripped the pace of development.

The case of India has been largely ignored so far, though we have noted that Britain treated Indian civilization with greater deference than was accorded to Africa. India was never humiliated with the title 'colony', and was administered separately from the Colonial Office. The question of its independence remained a matter of controversy between British politicians until the 1940s, but the logistics of maintaining control over such a vast sub-continent after the war, against the wishes of a deep-rooted and well-organized nationalist movement, quite apart from any moral arguments, made continued British rule untenable. And once the Indians had succeeded in achieving independence it became increasingly difficult to contain nationalist demands, whether by force of argument or force of arms, in other parts of the Empire.

The riots led by ex-servicemen in Accra in 1948, in what had previously been regarded as a model colony, gave an early warning that Africa might offer resistance similar to India. The nationalist upsurge in Africa hastened the transfer of power, and rendered arguments about the social or economic 'readiness' for independence increasingly academic. Indeed, some sceptics question whether there ever had been any real plan for decolonization. Davidson argues that it was merely a matter of European powers reacting to events, such as the Suez Crisis and the Mau Mau uprising in Kenya, and that there was little contact between colonial administrators and nationalist politicians (Davidson 1988). Pearce, too, sees no clear plan for decolonization, only judicious but limited land reform, with a Colonial Office 'strategy for nation building' drawn up in 1947 largely as a public relations exercise. Like Davidson, he sees the growing strength of nationalism as the driving force behind decolonization (Pearce 1984: 83–6).

Much obviously depends on what one means by words such as 'plan' or 'policy'. Governments can hardly 'plan' a decolonization programme in the way that they might plan an expansion of nursery education, given all the imponderables involved, but it is indisputable that the attempts at social and economic development were seen at least partly as preparations for self-government, if not full independence, and that there was concern with the possible distribution of political power after independence, however inadequate the assessment. This could be contrasted with the virtual absence of such preparations and concern in Zaire and the Portuguese colonies, and the disastrous results that followed. The post-war rise of nationalism may have taken British governments unawares but, as the contrasting French, Belgian and Portuguese policies show, meeting nationalist demands at an early stage was only one policy option, not an inevitable outcome.

Britain's relative speed in shedding its colonies could be explained in both political and economic terms. Politically, Flint suggests that Britain already had plans for decolonization by the late 1930s, when nationalist movements were still insignificant, and that the only differences with the nationalists were over questions of timing and strategy (Flint 1983: 390). Fieldhouse argues that colonies were no longer necessary to secure the position of metropolitan capital as economic conditions improved in the 1950s, so that Britain was able to decolonize before the other (poorer) European powers, with the advantage of being able to handle nationalist demands before they became unmanageable, and to enjoy good relations with the new governments (Fieldhouse 1988: 137–40). One may infer from such arguments that there are virtues in avoiding over-long preparations for independence, just as there are virtues in avoiding undue haste. To suggest that Britain achieved something close to an 'optimum' transitional period would be pretentious, but the undemocratic effects of surrendering power to an unrepresentative minority by withdrawing too soon, as in

South Africa, or of surrendering it to revolutionary forces by going too late, as in Portuguese Africa, were generally avoided by Britain.

Consensus between colonial powers and nationalist politicians

It may seem fanciful to suggest that there is ever much common ground between colonial rulers and nationalists. Where was the consensus between Churchill and Kenyatta, or Macmillan and Makarios? Yet we can attempt to demonstrate the importance of relative consensus by noting the converse cases of its absence. If, as in the examples in the previous section, the colonial power can see no moral reason for conceding independence and will only do so under duress, or if it wishes to transfer power to an unrepresentative minority, post-independence politics are more likely to be characterized by armed struggle than democratic consensus. Flint's suggestion of common ground between Britain and nationalist politicians does not imply so much a general convergence of values as, at the very least, a rejection of notions of colonies being retained indefinitely because the people would never be fit to govern themselves, because the colonies were already integral parts of the metropolitan power, or simply because the metropolitan power could not afford to let them go. Such a minimal agreement is clearly not a sufficient condition for democracy, but experience suggests that it may well be a necessary one.

Mass power bases and mass containment

Hypotheses 3 and 4 in Table 3.2 offer apparently conflicting recipes for democracy. The earliest decolonizations involved creating elitist political structures which offered very limited scope for mass participation, as in Latin America and, to a lesser extent, the Old Commonwealth, if only because such participation had not yet been conceded within the metropolitan country.

The attitudes of post-1945 decolonizers were more ambivalent, and subject to varied interpretations. On the one hand there was the popular image of the man in the bush, simple and uneducated, but deserving of protection from the upstart nationalist politician, for whom a little learning was a dangerous thing, and who did not represent the real aspirations of the people. Thus Colonial Secretary Oliver Stanley expressed concern about the gulf between politically minded Africans and 'the vast bulk of African cultivators living under tribal conditions', while his successor Arthur Creech Jones denied that any African political party could bridge the gap between the aspirations of the rural masses and the political rituals of Accra (Hargreaves 1979: 34, 450).

On the other hand, there was the practical consideration of to whom to transfer power, since 'traditional' rulers could not command the allegiance of people throughout the modern nation state, and there were no obvious leaders to represent the man in the bush other than nationalist politicians. The colonial ideal might have been the emergence of a relatively conservative party which was able to win power by appealing to the moderate sentiments and limited political horizons of the illiterate peasants, and then exercise power with similar moderation, but parties and politicians of this sort were in short supply, except possibly in Northern Nigeria. Votes were not won easily by self-effacing politicians who offered only minor departures from the colonial status quo. Where such politicians existed, they were generally outflanked by those who demanded 'self government now', and promised material benefits to alleviate poverty. If these 'radical' politicians could boast of a spell of imprisonment or exile for their beliefs, that enhanced their reputations still further.

The academic debate between 'modernizers' like Almond, who saw democracy in the West sustained by political parties with mass bases to channel participation, and who thought that they saw the beginnings of similar developments in the Third World, and 'institutionalists' like Huntington, who emphasized the need for strong institutions which would moderate mass demands to prevent the disorder that would result from unfulfilled expectations, came too late to have much influence on actual colonial policy. Instead we find politicians and administrators attempting to smooth the transition to independence in a pragmatic way, without always appreciating the dynamics of politics in the territories they ruled. Flint suggests that Britain deliberately sought political leaders with 'mass bases', in preference to more 'traditional' leaders (Flint 1983: 400–1), and one could argue that the French practice of allowing colonies to elect deputies to Parliament in Paris encouraged many parties to model themselves on France, but we need to be careful in using terms like 'mass bases' and 'participation'.

The parties which led the colonies to independence were highly visible throughout the land, and often appealed to people across social divides that had rarely been bridged before. Austin, for example, refers to the 'primary school teachers, clerks in government and commercial offices, petty traders, storekeepers, local contractors [and] not very successful businessmen with a one-man, one-lorry transport enterprise or a small import–export trade' who formed the backbone of the early Convention People's Party (CPP) in Ghana (Austin 1964: 16). This party attracted mass support at election time and provided upward social mobility for some of its members and their immediate followers, and it might (like parties the world over) have raised voters' hopes as to how they would prosper once the party had won power, but the notion that the CPP and other nationalist parties stimulated 'mass participation' beyond the ritual of electioneering is more difficult to sustain (see especially Pinkney 1988: 38). In most of Africa and Asia outside India, the time interval between the creation of nationalist parties and the accession to power of their leaders was so short that any 'mass organization' was weakened almost as soon as it had been created, as party leaders were able to use the machinery of state, with all the resources that this implied, rather than the party, to decide who got what, when and how. If there were 'participatory pressures' on politicians, it was not so much in the sense of 'mass bases' channelling demands upwards (by the time of independence the party structures were often too ramshackle to channel such demands) but in a more general sense of people seeing a gap between their initial expectations and their actual condition, and having no wish to sustain politicians in power who had failed to meet their expectations. Since opposition parties had generally been proscribed or bought off, ruling parties were faced at best with growing public unrest and disorder, and at worst with displacement by the military.

It was generally the parties which had enjoyed a much longer life before independence, as in India and the West Indies, and which had therefore generated a greater degree of support and legitimacy for both themselves and the pluralist systems over which they ultimately presided, which proved most resilient. In tropical Africa, in contrast, the party structures were much more fragile, and many sank as they reached the rougher waters of post-independence politics and were unable to maintain public support as they tried to cope with growing austerity.

Was the general failure of democracy in tropical Africa the result of Britain's insistence on politicians building 'mass bases' which led to 'the politics of ethnic reality', as Flint (1983: 411) asserts, or was it the result of the shallowness of the power bases in reality? The equation of competitive party politics in Africa with 'tribalism', and thus with a zero-sum game in which one set of constituents only gains material benefits because others are losing them, has frequently been asserted by leaders of one-party states and military governments, but the reality has often been more complicated, with parties needing to build coalitions of diverse groups in order to win a majority. The shallowness of the power bases was probably more serious than the alleged tribalism, and revealed itself as ruling parties were brushed aside by the military. While nationalist and international pressures may have left the colonial powers with little alternative but to concede independence more hastily than they would have wished, a major effect of this was to leave new nations with fragile political structures that made the survival of democracy difficult. A country with a more developed party structure, such as India, was able to fare better, despite its greater poverty.

Huntington's emphasis on containing participation in order to achieve stability, which in turn is seen as a precondition for democracy, leaves room for argument about cause and effect. Democracies such as India and Jamaica have survived challenges to authority which might well have destroyed more authoritarian governments showing less willingness to compromise or conciliate. Participative pressures that demand more from governments than economic or administrative circumstances enable them to deliver, whether in Allende's Chile or Nkrumah's Ghana, are clearly a threat to democratic stability, but whether any transfer of power in a world aware of the ideal of universal suffrage, in an age of mass communications, can explicitly limit participation is another matter. More important than the volume of participation may be the need to provide and maintain channels through which it can flow with a minimum of disruption. This has been attempted within the framework of some one-party states, but the safety valve of allowing people to vote their rulers out, no matter how inadequate the alternative on offer, may in the end offer a better recipe for stability than greater authoritarianism. In the end, the system which is best able to help the articulation of mass demands may also be the system which is best able to prevent such demands from threatening stability.

Democracy and consensus between groups

The consequences of dissensus between major groups in society are clear enough. Britain's attempt to set up a Central African Federation (from what are now Malawi, Zambia and Zimbabwe) in the 1950s failed because Europeans and Africans could not agree on their respective rights, and attempts to include Chinese-dominated Singapore in a Malaysian federation met with a similar fate. Authoritarian governments may be able to maintain their rule over large dissident groups; democratic ones could not do so without ceasing to be democratic. For the colonial power or nationalist successors seeking to build democracy, the challenge is to establish means of reconciling the aspirations of different groups within a given territory, or to decide when and whether democracy can only be saved by conceding the secession of parts of the territory, as in the partition of Ireland and India, and the eventual abandonment of the Central African Federation.

There are few instruction manuals to help the would-be democratic de-colonizer, but with hindsight we can note the relative success of countries where government depends on the support of a multiplicity of small groups, in contrast to the failure where two major groups confront one another, as with Protestants and Catholics in Northern Ireland, Greeks and Turks in Cyprus, Christians and Muslims in the Sudan and Chinese and Malays in the enlarged Malaysia. In less polarized countries there is at least scope for constitutional engineering to minimize confrontation. The relative success of federalism and checks and balances in India could be contrasted with failure in the Nigerian First Republic, where the creation of three large states rather than several small ones heightened confrontation between north and south.

The economics of democracy

The desirability of stimulating social and economic development in the years before independence was hardly disputed, at least by those colonial powers which envisaged independence as the ultimate goal. Whether such development was seen as merely a means of improving people's material and spiritual well-being, as a means of ensuring the establishment of a viable nation state or as a means of enhancing the prospects for democracy is less clear. We have noted the way in which the 1940 Colonial Development and Welfare Act led to increased investment in the colonies over the next decade. Forty per cent of the revenue was spent on education, health, housing and water, and in the West Indies the state surpassed the churches in the provision of social welfare (Edie 1991: 30–3). In the Gold Coast (Ghana) there was a ten-fold increase in state welfare expenditure in the decade before independence, compared with a mere doubling in the previous 35 years, and even in the Congo (Zaire) there was a rapid expansion of health care and primary education (Young 1988: 55–6). Even if one puts the least charitable interpretations on such expenditure, it could hardly be seen as an attempt at maintaining economic exploitation, though such exploitation obviously continued independently of welfare programmes. Flint dismisses the notion that the British were planning the 'development of underdevelopment' by arguing that such a goal would have implied strengthening the indigenous bourgeoisie, rather than seeking political leaders with a legitimate 'mass base' and emphasizing social and economic development to precede political advancement, in line with Lord Hailey's recommendations (Flint 1983: 401–9). Even the argument that increased welfare provision was an attempt to appease nationalist politicians is unconvincing, since the nationalists offered little serious challenge outside India until the 1950s.

Trying to interpret what the colonial powers, and especially Britain, were trying to do is more difficult than interpreting what they were not doing. Increased welfare provision obviously existed alongside continued economic exploitation through unequal trading relationships and the eviction of colonial subjects from their own land so that they could be employed by expatriates and settlers for minimal wages (see especially Heavey 1991: 136–51). It may be that there was little consistency in colonial economic policy, with the compassionate missionary, the unscrupulous trader and the well-meaning administrator all having an imprint. A vague notion of 'nation building' made little attempt to anticipate any conflict between democracy and stability, and Low notes the paradox that economic development often implied more authoritarian, rather than democratic, measures, such as imposing better cropping patterns, cattle inoculation and anti-erosion terracing (Low 1988: 45).

When the nationalist tide began to flow more strongly, especially after Indian independence and the Accra riots, political pressures became more important than social or economic. This did not mean any decline in economic or welfare provision, but it did mean the abandonment of any notion that independence would only come when the colonial powers judged that such provision was sufficient for the new nations to be launched. Given the acknowledged ability by this time of nationalists to undermine colonial authority, whether through civil disobedience in India or Mau Mau violence in Kenya, the growing disapproval of the principle of colonialism in the metropolitan countries and the wider world, and the high cost of maintaining the colonial military and administrative apparatus, the alternatives to an accelerated drive to independence were limited.

The prospects of the independent countries sustaining democratic political systems were not helped by the inheritance of social and economic structures that, despite the belated investment of the 1940s and 1950s, left the new nations with predominantly illiterate, rural populations, and with few of the opportunities for building centres of economic power independent of the state. If democracy was to thrive in such conditions, which became worse as the terms of trade deteriorated in the 1960s, such an outcome would have been contrary to the accepted wisdom of most political scientists on the conditions conducive to democracy.

Alongside the modernization theorists' view, that economic development helps to promote democracy, is the dependency theorists' view that such development is unlikely to occur because development in the West implies the exploitation and thus the 'underdevelopment' of the Third World. That such development and underdevelopment have frequently gone together is beyond dispute, as wealthy countries, which have had a head start in developing their industries, leave poorer ones with few opportunities for entering their markets, and thus leave the poorer countries as predominantly suppliers of primary produce to meet the needs of the rich. Yet there is room for argument about whether this is a universal tendency. The conclusion of dependency theorists, that democracy is impossible under such conditions of poverty and exploitation, and that it can only be realized by achieving economic autonomy, is more difficult to accept, since the countries that have come closest to achieving such autonomy, such as Albania and Cuba, have not so far shown many democratic tendencies. While economic autonomy may be a desirable end, it is likely to require considerable authoritarianism to cope with the austerity which it implies, at least in the short term. If democracy was weakened, or rendered impossible, by a transfer of power which 'failed' to promote economic autonomy, one could argue that such a failure was not just the fault of the colonial powers and the economic interests they served, but was also a consequence of the pressing demands of nationalists and world opinion, which gave greater priority to immediate political independence than to any long-term considerations of the requirements of either democracy or material well-being.

Conclusion: the prospects for democracy at independence

To compile a retrospective Independence Day balance sheet, listing the assets and liabilities which might contribute to the realization or non-attainment of democracy, would be a formidable task. To establish whether such assets as existed were subsequently squandered by the profligacy of political actors, or whether the assets lost their value on account of circumstances beyond the control of indigenous politicians, would be an even more formidable task. In the concluding section of this chapter I

merely summarize some of the more obvious factors that might have contributed to democracy at the time of independence, before proceeding to
look at subsequent changes in the 'balance sheet' in the next chapter. To
pursue the analogy, Independence Day was perhaps treated more like 'pay
day', with the recipients wanting to celebrate with the apparently ample
assets in hand, rather than scrutinizing the overall balance sheet with a view
to ensuring a secure future. I am thinking here not just of economic assets
in the narrow sense, though many of these were squandered with gay
abandon on projects that made little economic sense, but of the sort of
assets and liabilities suggested in Table 3.2, which might either facilitate or
undermine democracy.

In the early years of independence the tendency of politicians and, to a
lesser extent, political scientists was to focus on the apparent assets. Especially
in the countries granted independence willingly after 1945, the apparent
consensus between nationalist politicians and the colonial powers on the
desirability of liberal democratic constitutions (hypothesis 2 in Table 3.2)
seemed to augur well for the future. Why should Ghana, Nigeria or Kenya
not follow the same path as New Zealand or Canada? Why should anyone
have been expected to anticipate the descent into civil war in Nigeria or
brutal authoritarian rule in Uganda? One could, perhaps, question the depth
of democratic commitment on the part of some of the nationalists, who
might give a lower priority to democracy if it clashed with other objectives,
such as 'order', 'socialist planning' or a paternalistic conception of what
was good for society, but a more serious problem was the liabilities, which
were easy to overlook in the post-independence euphoria. If we turn to our
other hypotheses about the conditions conducive to democracy, four of the
conditions appear to have been generally inadequate, and one appeared
only fitfully on the assets side. The 'preparation' for independence (hypothesis 1) involved varying degrees of planning but in few cases, if any, was
a level of socio-economic development achieved (hypothesis 6) that could
facilitate substantial elite or mass autonomy from the state, and thus greater
political pluralism. There were cases, such as Zaire, where events went to
the opposite extreme and state structures disintegrated to the extent that
there was no structured means of regulating political competition.

The inadequate social and economic foundations might have been
overcome if sufficient consensus had existed between groups in society as
to how to distribute the limited resources available (hypothesis 5). There is
no intrinsic reason why even the poorest communities should not maintain
such a consensus, but the culturally heterogeneous territories which existed
within the new nations were more likely to produce irresolvable conflicts,
or conflicts that could only be resolved by authoritarian means. In India,
the fact that each group was a small fish in a big pond may have helped to
ensure a willingness, if not a necessity, to compromise, but otherwise it
has generally been in the smallest states, such as Botswana, the Gambia,
Mauritius and the West Indian islands, that consensus has been relatively
easy to achieve. Elsewhere, uneasy power sharing in times of relative prosperity has frequently collapsed under the strain of greater austerity. In

much of Africa and Asia the cleavages have been along ethnic or religious lines, though mass resentment at elite privileges may add fuel to the flames once elite wealth fails to 'trickle down' sufficiently from patrons to clients. In the long-standing independent Latin American states the conflict is more obviously along class lines, with elites frequently unwilling to redistribute enough of their wealth to satisfy the poor in a way that is possible, or at least easier, in Western countries, where the volume of wealth available for redistribution is much greater and the plight of the poor less severe. To these problems we can add an economic dependence on the outside world which is different in quantity, and some would say in quality, from that found in Western democracies, which means that governments may have to follow the dictates of powerful interests abroad rather than democratic pressures at home.

Finally, there are the problems of politicians building democratic power bases that help to ensure their responsiveness to the popular will, while at the same time giving them the legitimacy to take unpopular decisions at times of crisis, without too wide a disparity between the demands of the governed and the willingness or perceived ability of the government to meet these demands (hypotheses 3 and 4). Authoritarian governments may deal with such problems in a variety of ways, but in a democratic system it is competing political parties that are usually seen as the means of both channelling demands and moderating them. In countries such as India, Jamaica and Trinidad, parties with strong, deep bases developed well before independence and appear to have performed such functions, however imperfectly, after independence, but in most of Africa, Asia and Latin America this has not been the case. In Latin America, parties emerged long after independence, and often became little more than appendages of the state rather than independent centres of power, while in Africa and Asia outside India, parties emerged only on the eve of independence. Opposition parties had little traditional or ideological loyalty to sustain them, and therefore little *raison d'être* if their supporters were deprived of government patronage, or of even basic amenities in their constituencies, while ruling parties, no longer faced with competition, could easily wither as control of the machinery of state became a more important asset than control of, or participation in, the party apparatus. If the military intervened, in the absence of any other means of changing the government, control of the presidential palace, the broadcasting stations and the main airport were sufficient to give them power. The erstwhile ruling party, without popular support or the resources of the state, would offer little resistance.

In retrospect, we can see that there was little basis for any expectation of the triumph of democracy once the countries of the Third World became nominally independent. Even if our 'balance sheet' had remained constant, there would have been only limited democratic assets on which to draw. In the event the liabilities, both in the narrow economic and in the broader political senses, became greater. It is to the dynamics of this deterioration that we shall now turn.

The eclipse of democracy

Some false dawns

There was never a total eclipse of democracy. There have been Third World countries with a record of continuous pluralist democracy, as we shall see in the next chapter, but they are the exception. What is remarkable is that almost all Third World countries have had at least nominally pluralist political systems at some time in their history, yet the majority did not or could not build on these to establish durable forms of democracy. The eclipses were, in other words, preceded by false dawns, but these dawns differed in character between different countries and regions, and the subsequent 'failure' of democracy may require different explanations, depending on the different bases on which democracy has been established.

At the outset there is a distinction between pluralist systems which 'evolved' as a result of the interaction between forces in society, as in much of Latin America and the Middle East, and those which were 'planted' as part of the colonial transfer of power, as in much of tropical Africa and Asia. In both groups of countries one can suggest similar broad influences to explain the eclipse of democracy: economic, social, institutional, behavioural, military and external. But these influences generally worked in a different way in the countries where pluralism had evolved from in those where it had been planted. Before looking at the dynamics of this, let us sketch briefly the processes by which the false dawns broke.

In Latin America, we have noted, colonial rule was abandoned long before the development of the concept of liberal democracy, and there were therefore no democratic constitutions 'planted' at the time of independence. Political systems fluctuated between authoritarianism and general disorder until social changes, resulting mainly from economic development, led to new groups demanding participation in the political system. This is a process familiar to people in Western Europe, but in these new nations, unlike the countries of Western Europe, there were no old-established aristocracies enjoying some 'traditional' claim to legitimacy and a degree of deference from lower social classes. In the absence of these assets, ruling elites had to rely more heavily on force to defend their positions, and groups challenging them had to rely more on violence to advance theirs.

Even today we can see legacies of this conflict in some Central American republics, where members of elites resort to rigged elections and the employment of armies to defend their positions, while the masses resort to guerilla warfare, but further south uneasy accommodations were arrived at in many countries by the inter-war years or earlier, as elites began to feel secure enough to concede demands for universal suffrage and free elections. The story is a complex one, with many variations between countries, and is analysed succinctly by Stephens (1989). She draws attention in particular to the broader, more stable democracies established in Argentina and Uruguay, where industrialization was achieved relatively early and the export economy was based on non-labour-intensive agriculture, and the less stable initial democracies of Chile and Peru, where industrialization came later and the export economy was based on minerals. The economic structure of the latter countries made for a greater polarization between elites and working classes organized into radical mass parties. Brazil offered yet another variation, with exports based on labour-intensive agriculture, and the state, rather than 'clientistic' or 'radical mass' parties, shaping 'the political articulation of the subordinate classes' (Stephens 1989: 287). Here, the initial democracy was 'restricted' but relatively durable. ('Restricted' democracy can be taken to mean that even if most of the formal trappings of democracy exist, such as universal suffrage and competitive elections, elites will veto attempts to challenge their privileges beyond a certain point, whether by harassing or banning radical parties, or by calling on the military to intervene if such parties wield power in an unacceptable way.)

In no case did the initial establishment of democracy mark the end of the story. Although the detailed histories varied between individual countries, there were common problems of the absence of widespread consensus on what constituted a legitimate basis of government. Any democratic arrangements therefore depended heavily on *ad hoc* truces between contending groups, which might be broken with any change in the relative strength of each group, or by shifts in policy such as moves towards greater egalitarianism or state control, which other groups might find unacceptable. Authoritarian rule, whether civil or military, might thus return. Until the 1964 coup in Brazil, this alternation between authoritarianism and democracy, whether full or restricted, was a common feature of South American political life. Democrats might have preferred to do without the authoritarian phases, but there was always the hope that, as in the West, social and economic development would eventually make democracy secure. What happened subsequently in Brazil, Argentina, Chile and Uruguay shattered such illusions, as much more brutal and more comprehensive forms of authoritarianism engulfed these countries.

The Middle East also produced various forms of evolved democracy. Generalization is again difficult, with differences between states under direct Western colonial rule, such as Algeria, Libya and Tunisia, where the existence of an alien regime helped to polarize conflicts between nationalists and colonial rulers, and states which had emerged from the disintegrating Ottoman Empire and had come under varying degrees of European control or influence. Such control was, however, different from that in the colonies in tropical Africa, in that these states were regarded from the outset as candidates for independence – lodgers in the imperial household rather than long-term subordinates below stairs. In these states, as in Latin America, many traditional structures of authority had been weakened or destroyed, and means had to be found of accommodating new groups that emerged as a result of social and economic changes.

> The irrigation engineer and the local government official stood jux-
> taposed to the prominent local landowners. The village primary school
> teacher threatened the values, status (and indeed financial position)
> of the traditional village teacher of the Koran. The salience of agri-
> culture in the economy, the limited industrialization and lack of
> absorptive capacity of the economy tied the graduates of the educa-
> tional institutions to a career with the state apparatus, either the army
> or bureaucracy.
>
> (Cammack *et al.* 1988: 38)

In such a fluid situation, 'traditional' elites were unable to rule on their own, and by the mid-twentieth century many Middle Eastern countries had established what Pool (1991) calls quasi-democracies. Elected parliaments played a significant role in decision-making, but they were built on a narrow social base, and elections were frequently rigged by kings and prime ministers. Elite privileges were preserved by such processes, and underwritten by foreign policies which invoked close collaboration with the West and the establishment of foreign military bases. This quasi-democracy had few attractions for the new middle strata of teachers, bureaucrats, technicians and engineers produced by the expansion of education, or for the reformist army officers who shared many of the values and backgrounds of these groups. (Pool 1991: 11–14). While democracy in countries under more direct colonial tutelage was often seen as desirable in itself, quite apart from the political outcomes it might have produced, as a result of the socialization processes noted in the previous chapter, democracy in the Middle East was more easily equated with the sustaining of privileges and the surrender of Arab interests.

Social changes had not produced the working class movements demanding mass participation found in much of Latin America, but a 'modernizing' middle class that saw salvation in terms of land reform, nationalization, social welfare and closer links with the Eastern bloc. Perceptions of 'democracy' were not, as in tropical Africa, based on ideals learnt at English-speaking educational institutions or the experience of living in Europe or North America, but on the culture of the West, which was seen as the source of many of the people's ills. The limited social and economic development experienced in the Middle East thus led not to an expansion of the embryonic democratic forms, but to the seizure of power by young army officers who then presided over authoritarian, if frequently left-wing, governments, which did not even feel the need to make the customary promise to return to democratic norms in the foreseeable future.

The emergence of 'planted' democracy requires less explanation. We have seen that any mutually agreed transfer of power between colonial rulers and nationalists after 1945 could hardly have taken place on any basis other than the acceptance of a liberal democratic constitution. For the colonial powers, 'readiness' for independence implied a belief that people were capable of operating a democratic polity, in addition to enjoying the social and economic assets that the post-colonial afterlife was deemed to require. Hence there was a reluctance to grant independence to Kenya, Malaysia or Zimbabwe until political conflict based on violence had largely subsided. For their part, the nationalist 'heirs apparent' generally accepted the democratic ideal, and had everything to gain from the legitimacy which success in a free election would confer on them, especially if the result of such an election was in little doubt.

Virtually all the colonies that achieved independence by negotiation after 1945, as opposed to those that took it by default or by revolutionary war, thus started life as democracies to the extent that they enjoyed universal suffrage and had had at least one free competitive election, often supervised by the departing colonial power. But, unlike the democracy achieved in the false dawns in Latin America and the Middle East, democracy in these former colonies owed little to the configuration of forces that normally leads to an ability and willingness, if not necessity, to make the compromises which a plural system, however fragile, requires. Levels of social and economic development were generally low, and there were few strong social groups able to mount a serious challenge to the incumbent elites. Mass movements could hardly have been expected to emerge in such a setting, and there were few political institutions with sufficient historical depth or current strength to ensure that political conflicts flowed through the regularized channels democracy requires, given the late emergence of political parties, electoral processes and legislatures. If the 'democratic balance sheet' described in the previous chapter had remained constant, or even improved on the credit side as a result of economic growth or prudent political judgement, it is conceivable that planted democracy might have flourished despite its shallow roots, as indeed it did in a few countries, but for the most part worsening economic conditions, the indifference of politicians and their constituents alike to democratic values and procedures, and the growing confidence of armies in their ability to topple governments, whether out of moral indignation or a lust for the fruits of office, ensured that the eclipse of democracy was witnessed in most of Africa and Asia.

Table 4.1 The undermining of democratic forms, 'evolved' and 'planted'

Variable	Undermining in 'evolved' democracies	Undermining in 'planted' democracies
Economic	Greater class conflict with economic development	Economic decline
Social	Conflict over the extent of inclusion or exclusion	Lack of social cohesion
Institutional	Institutions lacked autonomy from the state	Institutions failed to function effectively
Behavioural	Fear of mass pressure led to undemocratic behaviour by elected politicians	Mass indifference facilitated undemocratic behaviour by elected politicians
Military	Widening ideological divide between the military and ruling politicians, actual or potential	Military realization of their ability to exploit their position
External	External responses to ideologically unacceptable rulers	Limited efforts by external powers to defend democracy

The undermining of democracy

Tables 4.1 and 4.2 present some hypotheses on the reasons why the initial, and sometimes the second and third, attempts at democracy failed. Many of the variables involved can be seen as the mirror image of those that were suggested in earlier chapters to be conducive to democracy. Thus economic development can lubricate the wheels of democracy while economic decline can intensify a crude struggle for power; consensus between dominant groups and the construction of effective institutions can contribute towards effective democracy, while irreconcilable conflicts and the absence of effective channels for mediating conflict can contribute to praetorianism. But the forces making for the rise and decline of democracy are not completely symmetrical. The creation of democracy, by its nature, requires a process of steady building rather than a 'big bang', whereas its destruction can come much more suddenly through an economic crisis, a careless decision by political actors or a military coup. The root causes of these events may, of course, have been festering for some time, but their actual occurrence still depends largely on man-made choices. Table 4.1 suggests that although similar variables – economic, social, institutional, behavioural, military and external – can be used to explain the eclipse of democracy in both 'evolved' and 'planted' democracies, this apparent similarity masks wide differences in the aspects of the variables which are important. I shall examine the arguments in more detail presently, but for the moment I look at them in broad outline.

Economics is important in the evolved democracies in the dynamic sense that economic developments such as industrialization, the exploitation of mineral resources or changed relationships with trading partners may give rise to changes in the relative resources and demands of different social classes, which come into sharper conflict with one another. In the planted democracies, in contrast, it is more likely to be economic decline, possibly following a deterioration in the terms of trade or the failure of attempts at industrialization, that undermines both the ability of politicians to satisfy their constituents, and the already limited commitment of the population to the existing order, once the material benefits dry up.

Social changes may undermine evolved democracies on account of the unacceptability of new political demands which are being voiced. Universal suffrage may be acceptable to elites, but not the inclusion of trade unions or peasant cooperatives in the political process, with demands for greater equality or social welfare, and attempts to advance or resist such causes may prove impossible within democratic channels. In the planted democracies, the social problem is less of confrontation between distinctive classes than of lack of social cohesion to provide either a solid base on which ruling coalitions can build, or a society which provides democratic counterweights against attempts at authoritarianism.

Institutional weakness is a problem in the evolved democracies in that institutions frequently lack autonomy from the state, and are thus easily captured with little resistance by opponents of democracy, whereas the problem in many planted democracies is that institutions have failed to function at all, even after attempts to sustain them through state resources, and there are thus inadequate links between formal state structures and the population as a whole. *Political behaviour* in the evolved democracies has frequently taken the form of elected politicians short-circuiting the democratic process out of fear that mass pressure will sweep away their offices and privileges, whereas in the planted democracies it is often the passivity or indifference of the masses which makes undemocratic elite behaviour possible.

The *military* may destabilize the evolved democracies because of a widening ideological divide between army officers, on the one hand, and elected politicians, actual or potential, with more populist power bases, on the other. In the planted democracies, the military threat is less the result of an ideological divide, since there are not such clear-cut social cleavages, than the consequence of soldiers coming to recognize their ability to intervene in politics to their own advantage as fewer and fewer people have the will to defend what is left of the democratic structure. Finally, the threatened *external* response in the evolved democracies is largely positive, in that outside governments or institutions may take steps to subvert elected but ideologically unacceptable rulers, while in the planted democracies the problem is less often that of subversion than of inability or unwillingness to come to the aid of elected politicians, as in Nigeria in 1966 and Ghana in 1972.

Having asserted baldly that the variables listed above are the most important ones in explaining the eclipse of democracy, we can now look at the arguments in more detail. Some of the refinements are shown in Table 4.2.

Economic explanations

I have hinted that the eclipse in the evolved democracies in the 1960s and 1970s was qualitatively different from what had gone before. Previously there had been alternations between precarious democratic governments and army-led governments which intervened, partly out of self-interest and partly to restore order, but which were generally modest in their objectives and narrowly selective in their persecution of political opponents. The military regimes which overturned pluralist systems in much of South America and South Korea in the 1960s and 1970s, in contrast, favoured a much more radical break with the past in terms of economic policy and a much more brutal suppression of a much larger number of political opponents. Explanations of this phenomenon have been offered by both functionalists and Marxists. Both are agreed that the transition from a predominantly rural, primary producing economy to the beginnings of an industrial economy imposes social and political strains. Huntington and Nelson (1976: 168) draw attention to the conflict between the goals of economic growth and participation in the 'later stages of modernization'. In nineteenth-century Europe participation was contained because the expectations of the masses were lower in the absence of more developed economies to emulate, and of structures such as mass parties, popular pressure groups and welfare-minded bureaucracies, which might be expected to deliver material benefits. In contrast, Weiner points out the way in which elites in 'late developing countries' have created an institutional framework in imitation of the existing developed countries, only to find that such institutions become strained as economic change produces a growing articulate working class. Because the institutions were created as imitations rather than in response to indigenous demands, they lack durability and are liable to be removed by military coups (Weiner 1971: 176).

From a different ideological standpoint, radical Latin American scholars have developed the 'bureaucratic authoritarian model' to explain both military intervention and what follows it. The political system is seen to pass from a populist phase in which multi-class coalitions of urban and industrial interests, including the working class, use the state to promote industrialization around consumer goods, to a bureaucratic authoritarian phase in which the coalition consists of high-level military and civilian technocrats working with foreign capital. Electoral competition and popular participation are now suppressed, and public policy is concerned with promoting advanced industrialization. Such a process is said to come about because the market for simple manufactured goods has been satisfied and the market dictates a 'deepening' of industrialization through the domestic manufacture of intermediate and capital goods by highly capitalized enterprises,

Table 4.2 Explanations of the eclipse of democracy

Explanation	Arguments	Countries/regions most relevant
Economic	1 Early stages of economic development involve greater inequality; this makes government by consent increasingly difficult	Latin America, South Korea
	2 Changes in the economic structure are to the (short-term) disadvantage of the mass of the population; they can only be overseen by authoritarian governments	Latin America, South Korea
	3 Economic changes produce a more articulate working class that places new demands on the political system, which governments cannot or will not meet	Latin America, South Korea
	4 Economic decline in already poor countries leaves fragile governments with fewer resources to distribute, and leaves the public indifferent to their fate	Tropical Africa
Social	1 A growing range of conflicts was difficult to handle after independence	Tropical Africa
	2 The social structure provided few democratic controls	Tropical Africa
	3 The bulk of the population was largely indifferent to democracy	Tropical Africa
	4 Narrow pluralism was discredited; new middle-class radical nationalists, including army officers, rejected Western institutions	Middle East
Institutional	1 Parties failed to adapt from opposition to government	Tropical Africa
	2 Bureaucracies lost their 'legal-rational' role without gaining a 'democratic' one	Tropical Africa
	3 Institutions lacked autonomy from the state, and therefore offered limited resistance to authoritarian attacks	Latin America
Behavioural	1 New rulers saw little need to respect people's 'rights'	Tropical Africa
	2 New rulers failed to deliver material benefits	Tropical Africa
	3 Therefore populations were largely indifferent to the removal of governments by undemocratic means	Tropical Africa
	4 Elected politicians chose to use undemocratic methods	Latin America, Turkey
Military	1 Soldiers acquired a greater sense of corporate identity	Tropical Africa, Pakistan
	2 Soldiers acquired greater confidence in their ability to intervene	Tropical Africa
	3 Soldiers perceived threats to their immediate interests	Ghana, Bangladesh
	4 Officers developed ideological beliefs which became increasingly distant from those of ruling politicians	Latin America, Middle East
External	1 The United States aided armies which were willing to challenge ideologically unacceptable governments	Latin America

often affiliated to multinational corporations. Brazil after 1964, Argentina after 1976, Chile after 1973 and Uruguay after 1975 are all presented as examples (see especially Collier 1979: 19–32; O'Donnell 1979; Cammack 1985; Im 1987: 239–41). The political implication of such a process is that since a mass electorate is unlikely to vote for policies that will reduce living standards in the immediate future, only an authoritarian government will be able to impose it and, in the absence of traditional elites enjoying any legitimacy or coercive power, only a military takeover can ensure that capitalist development takes precedence over popular demands.

The bureaucratic authoritarian model has been criticized on the grounds that it is difficult to fit the facts of individual countries to the processes described, and that anyway the policies of the governments concerned have varied from the extremes of free-market economics and political suppression in Chile to the more interventionist and pluralist policies in Brazil. In yet other cases, such as Colombia and Venezuela, democratic regimes have achieved economic restructuring without bureaucratic authoritarianism, presumably because elites were able to obtain popular consent (see O'Donnell 1986: 9).

Both the functionalist and bureaucratic authoritarian schools clearly have a point. The growth of an entrepreneurial class, and an urban labour force wrought by economic development, is likely to make for new political pressures with which the formal political structures may find it difficult to cope. Cammack offers a more modest perspective in referring to 'the political economy of delayed and dependent capitalist development' in South America, in which military governments in Argentina, Chile and Uruguay have (or had) a common desire for the transformation of 'the dynamic of the state apparatus of class relations' (Cammack 1985: 28). If the rise of populist, participatory politics was not to the army's liking, it needed to seek alternative arrangements and civilian allies to help it pursue new directions. No doubt some of the earlier reasons for military intervention, such as dissatisfaction with the incompetence of civilian politicians, continued to play a part in the downfall of democratic systems, but whatever titles one gives to the new non-democratic regimes, their severity had implications for subsequent political developments. If future polities failed to settle their conflicts within the democratic arena, they would be aware of the bleak alternative which might lie in store.

In the planted democracies, the general pattern was one of economic decline, in countries where governments were already fragile and ruled over citizens who had only limited attachment to democratic institutions. There might be good instrumental reasons for supporting democratic governments as long as they continued to provide material benefits, but many governments were left stranded as these benefits began to dry up. The case of Ghana might be regarded as typical of much of tropical Africa. Between 1955 and 1960, under favourable world economic conditions, Ghanaian gross domestic product rose by 5.1 per cent per year. In the 1960s it grew at a lower rate than the growth of population, and in the 1970s it fell by

3.2 per cent a year (Bequele 1983: 223; Kraus 1985: 165). Ghana's dependence on world economic forces, and especially on the prices of exported
cocoa and imported oil, might lend support to Bretton's view that 'Political
institutions [in Africa] are facades to retain the loyalty of the masses, while
the socioeconomic substance – money, financial wealth and economic
opportunities – serve as the infrastructure for the effective government'
(Bretton 1973: 94).

  Planted democracy did not necessarily give way to brutal authoritarianism in the way that evolved democracy often did. Military governments
frequently emerged as low levels of performance and legitimacy left government vulnerable to even the most ill-organized and inarticulate soldiers
but, in societies of limited economic development and limited class polarization, they seldom offered radically different ideologies or policies. Some
of these military governments degenerated into arbitrary personal dictatorship, as in the Central African Republic, Equatorial Guinea and Uganda,
but for most of the people the differences compared with civilian governments were barely visible except to the most politically aware. In other
cases, notably in Côte d'Ivoire, Cameroon and much of East Africa, ruling
parties ended any nominal liberal democracy by snuffing out such opposition as existed and establishing one-party states. Some of these continued
to permit intra-party elections to the legislature and thus claimed to be
upholding democracy, but if most power was concentrated in the hands of
a non-elected president, and the raising of major national issues was not
permitted in parliamentary elections, it was a very limited form of democracy. In yet other cases, the partial disintegration of political authority
described by Chazan (1988) was a significant development, although it is
difficult to envisage communities detaching themselves too far from the
state where there are long-standing expectations of state provision of not
only law and order, but also an elaborate economic infrastructure to
facilitate the marketing of crops and the importation of essential supplies.
Generations of economic dependence cannot be wished away.

  The main hope for a second bite at the democratic cherry in countries
that began as planted democracies was not so much a revolt against
authoritarian excesses, though such excesses undoubtedly existed, but a
realization that authoritarianism did not offer any better solution than
did democracy to problems of everyday hardship. (The other alternative of
detachment from the state was more of a reaction to events than a consciously pursued policy.) If a minority of intellectuals or thwarted opposition politicians found authoritarianism positively distasteful, and not merely
another form of failed politics, there was the possibility of a nucleus around
which pressure for democratic restoration might develop.

Social explanations

Many of the social changes that led to the eclipse of democracy are implicit in what I have said about economic change, such as the emergence of

new groups with new demands which placed strains on political systems in Latin America, but in some cases the course of economic change was severely constrained by the prevailing social structures, and in others it was social structures that remained relatively constant, but provided rocks on which attempts at establishing democracy might founder. The evolved, limited democracies of the Middle East belong to the first category and the planted democracies of much of tropical Africa and Asia to the second.

We have already noted the rise of new groups such as teachers, bureaucrats, engineers and 'modernizing' soldiers in the Middle East not so much as a result of market forces but as a consequence of government policies. At other times or places, the growth of such groups might have augured well for democracy, but in the Middle East, unlike the countries which had imbibed some Western values under close colonial tutelage, liberal democracy was seen as a more alien concept, especially if it failed to achieve the desired ends. In this case, the end was a more egalitarian, nationalist, state-directed society, and the existing elitist, exclusionary pluralism stood in its way. If radical groups could not gain entry into politics by persuading existing elites to broaden the basis of participation, and elites were just as hostile to Western notions of democracy as their challengers, then political change required the intervention of the military and the demolition of the limited democratic edifice. As in Latin America, though in different circumstances, the main social factor which undermined initial attempts at democracy was conflict over which groups should be included in the political process, and on what terms.

In the planted democracies, the problem was less one of inclusion or exclusion of distinctive social groups than of a general lack of social cohesion. Political structures had changed rapidly in the brief run-up to independence, because of the largely uncritical acceptance of the need for liberal democratic constitutions, yet social structures could hardly be expected to change at the same rate. At least three arguments can be put forward.

First, Low refers to 'the plethora of localised agitational propensities' in tropical Africa, which the colonial powers always had sufficient coercive power to crush in the last resort, but which had become increasingly assertive with the rise of nationalism, which itself implied confronting those in authority. The events that led Nigeria into civil war might be seen as an extreme version of such confrontation, but lesser challenges, such as those from Ashanti and Ga groups in Ghana and the north–south conflicts in Benin, were more troublesome to governments attempting to operate relatively open systems than they would have been for colonial governments for whom the maintenance of order was the first priority. Low thus argues that the emergence of authoritarianism in Africa was partly due to a desire to 'hold the lid on' these conflicts (Low 1988: 47–8).

Second, Munslow notes that extra-constitutional checks and balances, found in the West in the form of powerful economic institutions, newspapers and educated citizens organized into pressure groups, are not found in tropical Africa. It was therefore difficult to follow the spirit of a

'Westminster constitution', especially when people's main experience of politics had been under undemocratic colonial rule (Munslow 1983: 223). One could argue that in some cases it was the strength rather than the weakness of economic institutions, especially expatriate ones, that threatened democracy, but experience does suggest that when initially democratic governments tried to strengthen their positions, whether out of a genuine fear of threats to order or a desire to monopolize the fruits of office, by imposing preventive detention, rigging elections or buying support through corrupt dealings, there were few articulate or effective groups to stand in their way.

Third, there was no obvious reason why the bulk of the citizenry, any more than in the Middle East, should have cherished or rushed to defend liberal democratic values once they were under threat. While many pre-colonial communities had organized their affairs in largely democratic ways (though many had not), there is a wide gulf between such local democracy within a relatively homogeneous face-to-face community, and attachment to a form of democracy with such refinements as freedom of expression and association, secret ballots or independent judiciaries, all of which had been imported quite recently. Chazan argues that, even in the 1980s, the upholders of democracy in Ghana came largely from the middle class, while commoners continued to voice populist concerns and propound statist ideas. The advocates of democracy had propounded liberty, but were not concerned with equality (Chazan 1988: 119). The dilemma for democracy of the masses taking an instrumental view of it, that it is good as long as it contributes to material well-being but is not worth going to the barricades to defend if it does not, is not of course a purely Third World dilemma, as witness much of Europe in the 1930s, but it can be a more acute dilemma if there are few other elements in society to help tide democracy over lean times. In these planted democracies, the initial demise of democracy was not the result of dramatic changes in society, as in much of Latin America and the Middle East, but more a coming to terms with reality. In retrospect, the prospects for democracy at independence were not as good as many people had viewed them at the time. Society offered little respite if material conditions deteriorated or if politicians tested democratic structures to destruction.

Institutional explanations

Political 'structures' are easily recognizable. A legislature, a political party or a pressure group either exists and has its own organization, or it does not. 'Institutions' are more elusive, but Huntington's definition of 'stable recurring patterns of behaviour' (Huntington 1968: 196) points us in the right direction. A parliament may exist as a structure, but if it meets only infrequently and then only to approve what the government tells it to approve, or if it flits unpredictably between different activities such as raising peasants' grievances or voting to condemn dissidents to death, it is hardly an institution. For it, or for a party or a bureaucracy, to be an institution, it would have to perform a distinctive role which had an important effect on the working of the political system. In the Third World, structures can be created that have the same names as their Western counterparts, such as parties or bureaucracies, but their institutional roles, if any, are often different and unpredictable.

The 'crises and sequences in development' approach, adopted by Binder et al. (1971), suggests that structures created at particular stages of socio-economic development may, instead of performing the institutional roles expected of their counterparts in the West, precipitate crises in which violent unconstitutional change is likely. In simple terms the thesis is that non-Western countries adopted structures such as elections by universal suffrage, mass parties, pressure groups and the development of welfare-oriented bureaucracies at a relatively early stage in economic development, and in an environment in which (in contrast to the early years of industrialization in the West) internal and international communications facilitated a rapid transmission of information and demands. The information made for an awareness of living standards and political rights in more developed countries and thus fed into growing public demands on authority. The structures came into being for a variety of reasons. They were badges of nationhood and symbols of legitimacy in largely new nations which could not resort to traditional aristocratic bases of legitimacy, yet they reflected neither the reality of elite power nor the achievements of the masses in extracting democratic concessions – they were a baby, as it were, for whom no one acknowledged parentage and who might grow into a wayward adolescent in the absence of parental affection. Economic development would not by itself precipitate a political crisis, it is argued, but if this development is accompanied by the opportunity for pressure via the ballot box, mass movements or the bureaucracy for a redistribution of resources which is not to the liking of ruling elites or the army, then the subsequent crisis can be explained by both the fact that the existence of the political structures has facilitated such pressures and the fact that the base of the structures is too insecure (insufficiently 'institutionalized') for them to resist counter-attack from elites wanting to protect their interests. Thus, in South Korea in 1972, 'The popular sector was politically excluded; competitive elections were abolished; strikes were prohibited; the organization of labour unions was severely restricted; and basic human rights were violated arbitrarily' (Im 1987: 239). The need for such repression can be gauged from the threat a pluralist political structure had posed in the previous year:

> The opposition party candidate, Dae Jung Kim, included popular democratic demands in the New Democratic Party's platform. His campaign theme was the realization of the populist era based on a populist economy. According to Kim, popular democracy would be in opposition to the developmental dictatorship of the Park regime, and a populist economy would be based on popular welfare, fair

distribution of the fruits of economic growth, and employee share-owning system, agrarian revolution and new taxes on the rich.

(Im 1987: 254)

Similarly in Argentina, and more especially in Chile, political structures that had facilitated popular participation, in a way which would not have been possible during the early stages of industrialization in Europe, proved too much of a threat to elites, and seemed too brittle to facilitate any compromise between elites and populist demands.

If there is a general argument that the importation of Western political structures can precipitate conditions conducive to military intervention, there is also a particular argument that the similarity of the imported product to the Western equivalent is only superficial. In Brazil, Cohen argued that military autocracy was not due mainly to economic forces but to a democracy 'imposed from above', which discouraged stable political competition. This was apparently the result of a more positive state role in economic development that was common in the earlier industrializing countries, which could afford to adopt a more *laissez-faire* approach. Parties and pressure groups developed from the top down in response to state activities rather than from the bottom up in response to popular demands, and this left the opposition weak and discouraged stable political competition (Cohen 1987). In functionalist language the problem was one of a weak 'political sub-system' – the area of voluntary participatory bodies such as mass parties and pressure groups, which normally reinforce a democratic system. Without it, a largely passive population is left at the mercy of elite manipulation.

In the planted democracies, the institutional problem is not presented so much in terms of the shadow of a strong state or of elites reacting to what they saw as mass threats to their survival. Threats to order and stability there may have been, but not generally the threat of lower social groups usurping power. The literature more frequently presents the problem as one of weak institutions which failed to provide adequate channels through which political demands could flow and political decisions be executed. Parties and bureaucracies are particularly singled out for their inadequacy, though legislatures could also be cited as playing generally marginal roles compared with their Western counterparts. Pressure groups are often presented as being of two diametrically opposed types. First, there are groups of little significance which lack such sanctions as withdrawing electoral support or organizing effective campaigns of non-cooperation, on account of the people's limited commitment to 'secondary' groups. Trade unions may thus lack the discipline and organization for mounting effective strikes. Second, there are the groups that act less as 'channels of communication' than as dangerous 'tidal waves' which can leave a chain of devastation in their wake, as with multinational corporations that seek to subvert governments or to set their own terms for dealing with them. In neither case do the groups contribute much in terms of institutionalization.

Political parties have been criticized for their failure to adapt from being nationalist movements to parties of government (Alam 1986: 56) and for failing to realize the need for force to back up rhetoric in their early years in power, only to go to the other extreme later, with the result that the military stood out dangerously as one of the few groups which had not been cowed, and which now provided virtually the only 'alternative government' in the absence of any 'loyal opposition' (Liebenow 1985: 129, 134–5). Governments lacking a strong party base might have turned to bureaucracies, but these were seen to be equally inadequate in adapting to the post-colonial order. There was the perennial problem in poor countries that bureaucracies could not easily be 'depoliticized', not only because under colonial rule bureaucracy and government had been virtually synonymous, and because administrative decisions, such as the location of a new school, or the allocation of an import licence between competing firms, took on a greater political significance (Munslow 1983: 225), but also because many bureaucracies could not even retain the roles and effectiveness which they had previously enjoyed, once the colonial power had departed. Rothchild and Chazan speak of a more formal hierarchy, with greater bureaucratic regulation and abstract administrative norms, under colonial rule, in contrast to the more personalized and patrimonial arrangements after independence, with a need for more personal incentives and sanctions from the ruling class (Rothchild and Chazan 1988: 57).

Perhaps the contrast is overdrawn, but the different basis of bureaucratic power after independence is inescapable. Not only did the new bureaucracies lack the ultimate coercive power of the metropolitan nation and the experience and expertise of its officials, but the new structure might well have been viewed differently by the populace. The new bureaucrats were people from the same political culture as their clients, and therefore more susceptible to indigenous political pressures, or even to what some people would call 'corruption', rather than to 'abstract administrative norms' (see especially Price 1975: 160, on Ghana). As political parties atrophied, politicians came to lean more heavily on bureaucracies in formulating and propagating policies, and bureaucracies thus lost much of their distinctive institutional role. If, as Liebenow (1985: 134–5) argues, the new nationalist governments were less even-handed than the colonial bureaucracies in dealing with conflicts between groups and individuals, this partiality was likely to permeate the bureaucracy as well. Two potentially important groups of institutions for mediating conflict, parties and bureaucracies, were thus reduced to (or perhaps confined to) a relatively subordinate status. And if conflict could not be mediated adequately through such institutions, it was more likely to manifest itself in a more 'raw', less democratic form, with a power struggle involving ruling politicians relying on patronage rather than consent, and groups in society relying on bribery and intimidation rather than votes, with the army stepping in as the final arbiter. It is not, of course, argued that political structures ought to have functioned in the same way as their Western counterparts. There are a variety of ways in which political pressures and decisions can be channelled and processed, but the problem in many of the planted democracies was that the 'traditional' and colonial institutions had been left behind, yet no adequate alternatives had emerged.

Behavioural influences

If we allow for political outcomes depending on an element of human choice rather than more impersonal forces, there is again a distinction between the processes at work in the evolved and the planted democracies, although both may have the ultimate effect of aborting democracy. In the evolved democracies, the growth of mass demands for greater participation and equality, whether actual or perceived, which was associated with social and economic development, created a dilemma for both the advocates of change and elected politicians. Excessive public demands or shows of militancy might provoke a repressive reaction. Ruling politicians, whether initially committed to democracy out of conviction or expediency, might take decisions that not merely maintained 'order' or responded to pressure, but also brought an end to democracy itself.

Chalmers argues boldly that the imposition of military-dominated regimes in Latin America has been the product not of the general characteristics of the state, society and culture, but of particular historical crises and the choices men made during those crises (Chalmers 1977: 38). Valenzuela argues that in Chile a political crisis preceded (and presumably contributed to) the socio-economic crisis, with naive 'democrats' preferring to allow the military to destabilize the system rather than working for compromise within traditional mediating institutions (Valenzuela 1978). Without being so explicit, other literature also stresses the failure of political actors to reach consensus rather than the adequacy or otherwise of the structures for doing so. Loveman emphasizes the variety of groups in Chile that were willing to destroy the whole political structure if that was the price to be paid for destroying the Allende regime (Loveman 1988: 261–2); Sunar and Sayari note the incompatible courses pursued by the main parties in Turkey, with the ruling Democratic Party determined to exploit the authoritarian structures it had inherited, and the opposition Republican People's Party determined to politicize the army as a means of challenging authority (Sunar and Sayari 1986).

In the planted democracies, the problem has been explained less as one of a mass threat to order than of mass indifference. At best, democracy was a distant ideal.

> In 1969 – and very possibly still today – the legitimacy of the Ghanaian state in the eyes of its ordinary rural citizens appeared to depend on its long-term conformity to the model of representative democracy. But it was also clear that the prudential and moral requirement

of obedience to whatever was currently the government was a much
more definite and salient precept for all but the most politically
engaged than any vague conception of how the polity ought legit-
imately to be organized.

(Dunn and Robertson 1973: 314)

Young suggests that since the colonial claim to legitimacy in Africa had
been based on conquest rather than election, there was limited resistance to
authoritarianism after independence. Single parties and military governments echoed the colonial approach by claiming legitimacy on the basis of
trusteeship and good government, weaving together radical and populist
language and exclusionary political institutions (Young 1988: 27). This might
suggest an exceptionally docile or gullible population. There was certainly
little attachment to abstract notions of liberal democracy, since the bulk
of the population had had no experience of such a phenomenon, and this
made the piecemeal dismantling of democratic institutions, through rigging elections, harassing the opposition or muzzling the media, easier than
it would have been in other countries, but ignorance of the works of John
Stuart Mill did not make people any more docile when they faced hyper-
inflation and shortages, yet witnessed the opulent lives of politicians and
their favourites. It was the failure of democratically elected governments to
deliver the expected benefits that provoked greater public discontent, but
when governments responded to this discontent by resorting to greater
authoritarianism, as in the crushing of the rail strike in Ghana in 1961 or
the urban discontent in Western Nigeria after the removal of the Action
Group from power, public resistance was relatively weak. This can be
explained partly in terms of the nature of predominantly rural, illiterate
societies in which the organization of resistance was difficult, but the
absence of deeply held democratic values made life easier for politicians
choosing to adopt authoritarian methods to crush democracy. Economic
crises should not, of course, be accepted as the only reason for the resort
of politicians to undemocratic methods. Many might have found accountability to the electorate irksome anyway, and have modified the political
system to enhance their own wealth and prestige – the relatively prosper-
ous Côte d'Ivoire was no more democratic than the economically declining
Ghana by the late 1960s – but a combination of economic decline and mass
indifference to liberal democracy was generally a lethal combination.

Military explanations

The military are often portrayed as victims of circumstances when (initially) democratic governments are toppled. Governments have relied on
them increasingly to suppress dissent because government by consent has
broken down, it is said, and the military have thus become 'politicized'.
Alternatively governments have failed to deploy sufficient force to crush

illegal protest, and the military have little option but to intervene to restore order. To blame the army for the eclipse of democracy would be like associating fires with the presence of the fire brigade.

The fragile condition of many Third World governments was undoubtedly conducive to military intervention, but there was no inevitability about this process. Some poor countries, such as Cameroon, Kenya and Malawi, managed to extinguish pluralist politics with little explicit help from the military, while wealthier countries, such as Greece and Uruguay, where democracy appeared to have been institutionalized, succumbed to military government. Much clearly depended on the choices made by both soldiers and politicians, but certain general trends can be discerned.

In the evolved democracies, there was often a clear divergence of ideology and perceived corporate interests between army officers and elected politicians. In much of the Middle East we have seen how young army officers who belonged to the 'modernizing' professional classes overthrew the narrowly based elected governments, which had been subservient to the West and hostile to social developments that would have threatened their dominance. In Latin America the situation was more complex, with a wealth of variations between individual countries, but certain features of civil–military relations stand out (for a more detailed discussion see Pinkney 1990: 28–34). First, armies had a long history in countries which had been independent for over a century, and therefore had time to develop a sense of corporate identity and a notion of which political actions advanced or threatened their corporate interests. Second, the position of army officers as relatively privileged men in a well-established institution, used more for defending elite interests than fighting foreign foes, made them natural defenders of the status quo, unlike their radical counterparts in the Middle East. This did not imply unquestioning subservience to civilian elites, and there were cases of officers declining to support conservative causes, as in Peru in 1968, but the trend was none the less a right-wing one. Third, training in, or under the influence of, the United States during the Cold War helped officers to equate radical popular movements with communism, which was seen as an alien threat to Latin America, especially after the Cuban Revolution. As political conflict became more polarized, with left-wing governments perceived as a threat to established interests in Brazil and Chile, and guerilla movements challenging authority in Uruguay and Central America, the ideologies and interests of army officers pointed not to attempts to arbitrate between competing groups or to remain aloof from politics, but to attempts to intervene in such a way as to crush democracy where it produced, or seemed likely to produce, reforming governments.

Of the planted democracies, the South Korean army shared its Latin American counterparts' fear of communism and equation of most popular movements with communism, largely as a result of the way in which the army had been built up, with American support, to contain the threat from North Korea and China. The army terminated South Korea's brief experience of pluralism in the early 1960s, but in most of Africa and Asia armies occupied more free-floating social and ideological positions in societies where social and ideological divisions were less tightly drawn. The political alternatives in these countries were not generally those of diametrically opposed radical and conservative governments, but of rival elite groups. Armies had not had a century in which to develop a distinctive sub-culture that might give them notions as to how society should be ordered or what their role should be within it, but they had had enough time to develop a sense of corporate interest. Thus a budget that reduced the amenities enjoyed by Ghanaian officers in 1972 led to swift military retaliation and the suspension of democracy for eight years, while an attempt by a populist government in Bangladesh in 1975 to pare down an over-large army, find an economically more productive role for it, and place it under the control of provincial governors in a decentralized structure, also led to a coup (Rizvi 1985: 224).

Whereas in the evolved democracies military intervention was a cause of the eclipse of democracy in the sense that, in the polarized situation produced by social and economic forces, army officers intervened largely because of the ideological gulf between themselves and elected politicians, or politicians likely to be elected, in the planted democracies military intervention was generally part of an intra-elite squabble. The timing of intervention had less to do with a critical point in ideological or social conflict than with a growing realization on the part of officers that they could exploit their positions. The retirement of expatriate officers and the ending of agreements, formal or informal, that the former colonial powers would defend civilian governments enhanced the prospects of a successful coup, and every success in neighbouring countries helped to build up an army's self-confidence and sense of anticipation. Many of the coups were, of course, directed against governments which had long since abandoned democracy, but in Nigeria in 1966, Ghana in 1972, Sierra Leone in 1968 and Pakistan in 1977 it was democratic systems, however imperfect, that were overthrown. The unpopularity and ineffectiveness of the elected governments made the task of the military easier, but in the end it was the perceived interests of military men, together with the elements of chance that invariably accompany such conspiracies, that brought democracy to a halt.

External influences

It is in the evolved democracies that the clash between the wishes of elected governments and their supporters, and the interests of external powers, especially the United States, has been most marked. Muller produces evidence to show that the breakdown of democracy in Latin America owed more to United States subversion than to dependent development. Thus United States aid to pro-coup armies in Brazil, Chile and much of Central America brought about the breakdown of democracy, whereas other countries, such as Jamaica, Trinidad and Tobago, Costa Rica and Venezuela also experienced economic development and the emergence of import-substituting industries without such a breakdown (Muller 1985). But this raises questions as to why the United States should choose to subvert some governments rather than others. The strategic position of the country may be one factor, as in Nicaragua where there was a fear of Cuban influence gaining a foothold on the Central American mainland, but it might also be the case that social and economic development in Brazil, Chile and Central America produced a polarization conducive to the rise of strong left-wing groups that was not found in the other countries. If that were the case, we would have to see external intervention as an added threat to democracy rather than a primary cause. The curtailment of democracy in Argentina and Uruguay without any apparent foreign assistance suggests that many of the necessary anti-democratic ingredients, including a right-wing army, were already present. In the Middle East, it was more often the Eastern bloc that had an interest in overthrowing the elected yet elitist and pro-Western governments in the 1950s and 1960s, but beyond moral support for the conspirators and indications that they might be treated favourably in the event of successful coups, the external influence was marginal.

In the planted democracies there is little evidence of external powers from either East or West wishing them ill, though the countries acquired more enemies when their politicians became more authoritarian, or were replaced by authoritarians. Foreign exploitation or lack of adequate aid may, of course, have made democracy more fragile, but these were not new problems. At worst, external powers contributed by default to the demise of democracy. It is possible that aid to build a more solid infrastructure, or even 'first aid' to avert immediate crises, might have saved the elected governments of Balewa, Bhutto and Busia, but the short time intervals between independence and the ending of democracy suggest that there were more fundamental weaknesses which could not easily have been remedied from outside. Indeed, Busia led a country (Ghana) in which democracy had already been given a second chance after an authoritarian interregnum, and attempts to build second and third republics in Balewa's Nigeria were no more successful than was the first attempt. To lose one democratic constitution may be a misfortune. To lose two or more might suggest not so much carelessness as defeat in the face of impossible odds.

Conclusion

The six variables that contributed to the eclipse of democracy can be seen partly as independent variables and partly as different perspectives from which to view the same phenomena. If, for example, one examines the transformation of Ghana from a pluralist system in 1957 to a one-party state based on uncontested elections by 1965, or the more sudden move from multi-party competition to military dictatorship in Chile in 1973, any one of the variables (except perhaps the military in Ghana) could be taken as a vantage point from which to view democratic disintegration. There would be room for argument about which variable was the most important, or about whether attempts to assign 'importance' are useful, since the variables might be regarded as part of an integrated whole. There are certainly close links between the economic, social, behavioural and external factors in the evolved democracies. Observers with a preference for economic determinism might see sharpened social conflict as a natural outcome of particular 'stages' of development, as a more articulate disadvantaged group challenges elite privileges, while current rulers abandon such democratic norms as exist (the behavioural factor), or the military intervene if they have no confidence in the ability of civilian politicians to achieve the desired outcomes. At the same time, external powers take a greater interest in these affairs as the political and economic stakes become higher. Similarly in the planted democracies, there is nothing particularly remarkable about a juxtaposition of economic decline, the crumbling of already fragile institutions when they fail to deliver material benefits, political behaviour characterized by arbitrary rule on the one hand and mass indifference on the other, and soldiers waiting like vultures to swoop on the decaying political system.

If that were the whole story, not only would democracy have been eclipsed in all countries with the social and economic characteristics outlined, but the eclipse would have occurred in similar ways in broadly similar countries, and over a similar time span. Yet this is clearly not the case. Some countries retained pluralism through two-party alternation, as in the West Indies, some through one-party domination by consent, as in India and Botswana, some through intra-party competition, as in East Africa, and at least one (Papua New Guinea) through a loose multi-party system. Where democracy was eclipsed, it was sometimes through elected politicians becoming authoritarians and sometimes through military intervention, which itself took varied forms. In Uruguay the eclipse was total but brief, in Brazil partial but long, in Chile total and long, and in Ghana and Nigeria intermittent with democratic interludes.

Those who reject determinism might place more emphasis on the decisions of individual actors, but these are always constrained by economic, cultural and institutional factors: a poor government cannot easily expand social welfare; a government dependent on the support of a narrowly defined social group cannot easily make concessions to that group's adversaries; a presidential constitution cannot easily facilitate power sharing. The unique history of each country, set against certain common historical developments in the region in which it is situated, will again help to ensure a diversity of outcomes. Thus the relative subordination of political institutions to the 'strong states' which antedated them in Latin America, or the problems of social cohesion in African states where the boundaries of 'traditional' kingdoms had been replaced by arbitrary European-imposed frontiers, weakened attempts at democratic development, but the extent of these handicaps and the skills with which political actors overcame them were not the same in any two countries. Uruguay's party system was much more resilient than Brazil's in relation to attempts at state domination, and the Gambia made light of its (possibly less serious) artificial boundaries compared with Nigeria. Any one of our variables could be singled out and shown to be different in its nature and impact in any one Third World country, as compared with all the others. But taken together the variables placed considerable impediments in the way of democratic development. If we are to explain why such impediments were eventually removed in many countries, or in a few cases brushed aside so that democracy was never extinguished, we are left with another large area of enquiry.

The survival of democracy

For democrats in a few Third World countries, the main problem has not been one of achieving a transition from authoritarianism to democracy, but of preserving a democratic structure which has survived continuously since independence. These countries include Jamaica, Trinidad and Tobago, the Gambia, Botswana, Mauritius, India and Papua New Guinea, together with some very small islands where the small population facilitates something akin to the Ancient Greek city-state style of democracy. There is also the case of Costa Rica, which achieved independence much earlier, but which has enjoyed a record of continuous democracy since 1948 and which has much in common with the 'continuous democracies'.

What is it that marks the continuous democracies off from the larger number of countries which have experienced authoritarian rule? Is it a matter of chance, with such factors as bungled military coups or the presence of the right leader at the right time enabling democracy to survive, just as a child who avoids typhoid at an early age may eventually grow into a centenarian, or do these countries possess distinctive features that mark them off from the others? Most of the literature focuses on explanations of democracy in individual countries, and little attempt has been made to develop a comparative framework for the continuous democracies as a whole. In Table 5.1 I bring the explanations together under a few broad headings in a search for common ground.

Table 5.1 can be related to the preliminary search for the conditions conducive to democracy set out in Table 2.1. The inter-elite relations emphasized by Rustow and the interactions between social groups emphasized by Barrington Moore find little place in countries where social divisions are generally less clear-cut; and the sequences in development emphasized by Binder *et al.* receive little prominence, largely because we are looking at a more limited time-scale compared with the evolution of Western countries from rural economies to modern industrial societies. But

Table 5.1 Conditions for the survival of democracy

Conditions	Arguments	Problems
Economic development and equitable distribution	1 Greater wealth makes competition for resources less desperate (Lipset)	Little attention is paid to the extent, pace and direction of economic growth
	2 Where pluralism depends on clientelism, adequate resources must be available (Edie)	Juxtaposition of clientelism and pluralism is exceptional
	3 Greater inequality may lead to social unrest (Crowder)	Greater equality may lead to destabilizing pressures on the political system
	4 Spending on social welfare and economic infrastructure promotes social satisfaction (Close, Crowder, MacDonald, Mitra, Wiseman)	Egalitarianism and social welfare are often associated with authoritarianism
Political culture	1 Importance of tradition of free debate; consensus, elite continuity	Pre-independence traditions are often difficult to carry over
	2 Importance of ethnically heterogeneous elite (MacDonald)	Cultural diversity may lead to compromise, but not necessarily to democratic values
	3 Importance of cross-cutting cleavages (Payne)	
	4 Importance of cultural diversity, with no single group able to dominate (Manor, Mitra)	
Political behaviour, political choices	Democracy is helped by: 1 Conciliatory style of individual leaders, and the support they command (Crowder, Wiseman)	Moderation, social awareness and conciliatory leadership may be a reflection of society, rather than positive political choices
	2 Policies which produce widespread social benefits, rather than prestige projects (Crowder)	
	3 Elite and mass support for moderation, especially when crises threaten the system (MacDonald, Manor, Payne)	Moderation may inhibit democratic choice
	4 A will to preserve democracy on account of awareness of the alternatives (Wiseman)	Countries with experience of authoritarianism have often failed to restore or retain democracy
	5 A realization that democracy makes for more competent, responsive governments (Wiseman)	Administrative efficiency may be a cause of democracy rather than a consequence

Table 5.1 (Cont.)

Conditions	Arguments	Problems
	6 The projection of clear opposition alternatives	Voters may not vote for distinctive party programmes
Political institutions, pre-independence foundations	Democracy is helped by: 1 A long preparation for independence (Manor, Payne)	Some countries have maintained democracy without a long preparation for independence
	2 Political institutions which are strong, but subject to constraints (Manor, Mitra), especially: (a) Competent, honest bureaucracy (Wiseman) (b) Well-established, deep-rooted political parties (Manor, Payne)	Are strong institutions a cause or consequence of democracy?
Individual freedom, rule of law	Democracy is helped by freedom of association and expression, and an independent judiciary (Crowder, Edie)	Legal rights may be offset by extensive government or party patronage
Extent of electoral choice and public participation	Democracy survives largely because it is limited by: 1 Limitations on the range of choices between parties and policies (Edie, Payne) 2 Limited public participation beyond electoral activity (Crowder, Edie) 3 The unlikelihood of power passing to the main opposition party or a radical third party (Edie, Crowder, Hewitt, Wiseman, Payne)	Controversy over whether the limitations enhance or restrict democracy
Role of the armed forces and external powers	Democracy is helped by: 1 Absence or weakness of armed forces, making military coups unlikely 2 Socialization of the armed forces into democratic values 3 Indifference of foreign powers to political outcomes	Difficulty in proving such socialization Foreign indifference may reflect a country's economic weakness (or strategic unimportance) which may not augur well for democracy

many of the other conditions for democracy explored in Table 2.1 emerge in the literature on continuous democracies. Economic development and political culture are important, though the distribution of economic benefits takes on a greater importance, and the behaviour of political actors is often presented in the form of freely taken choices rather than a mere reflection of political culture. Political institutions are important, not just in the general sense of filtering public demands and facilitating compromise, but also in the extent to which they facilitate or constrain freedom of expression and association, the rule of law and political choice and participation.

In sum, the literature on continuous democracies is more concerned with 'micro' than 'macro' conditions. This may be partly a reflection of the more empirical concerns of the authors, as compared with grand theorists such as Lipset, Dahl and Rustow, but it may also reflect the dependence of Third World democracy on precarious sets of delicate relationships rather than spectacular historical developments, such as industrialization or interactions between social forces. Value judgements will, as ever, colour any assessment of what has happened, and students of continuous democracies are no more united than other political scientists in their perceptions of the democratic ideal. A minority, including Edie, see elite democracy, limited electoral choice and limited participation as constraints to be overcome in the pursuit of a more participant, egalitarian democracy, while the majority, whether directly or by implication, take a more Huntingtonian view of democracy as something that is primarily concerned with electoral competition, and is more likely to degenerate into anarchy or authoritarianism than to become a democratic utopia if increased participation, populism or the pursuit of 'unrealistic' demands for radical change are not kept in check. Bearing in mind the primary concerns and ideological standpoints of the authors, let us now consider their explanations of the survival of democracy. The headings below correspond with the headings in Table 5.1.

Economic development and equitable distribution

The literature on continuous democracies does nothing to refute Lipset's assertion that, other things being equal, increased national wealth is likely to enhance democracy, as competition for resources becomes less desperate. Although they are by no means the wealthiest Third World countries, Botswana, India and Trinidad are all said to have found the preservation of democracy easier as a result of increased national wealth, or at least improvements in the physical quality of life (MacDonald 1986: 17–18; Crowder 1988: 456). Using Sivard's ranking of countries on the basis of such indicators as gross national product per capita, education and health, most of the continuous democracies are in the bottom half of the world 'league'. Sweden is top on these indicators and Ethiopia bottom, in 141st place. Of the continuous democracies, Trinidad is 44th, Costa Rica 52nd, Jamaica 56th, Mauritius 67th, Botswana 87th, Papua New Guinea 98th, India 117th and the Gambia 121st (Sivard 1983: 36–40). None of these countries is anywhere near to the exclusive top 28 which have been immune to military coups since 1945. Put another way, they are within the block of countries in which, on the basis of relative 'underdevelopment', military intervention is possible though obviously not inevitable. At the extremes, there are clearly correlations between wealth and democracy. Few people would expect Norway or Sweden to succumb to dictatorship, or expect democracy to blossom in Ethiopia or Bangladesh, but between these extremes the relationship becomes more blurred, with democracy faring better in the poverty of India and the Gambia than in Libya or Iraq, and with non-economic influences taking on a greater significance.

Much depends on the way in which the wealth is distributed, and on the ways in which political actors channel it. Edie speaks of a 'dual clientism' in Jamaica, where two-party competition is preserved because both government and opposition are able to trade patronage for votes, and failure to dispense sufficient patronage can lead to electoral defeat (Edie 1991: 7, 17). While she deplores the narrowness of this clientelistic politics and looks forward to a more egalitarian society, she acknowledges that even the limited pluralism of Jamaica could give way to authoritarianism if the economy fails to provide an adequate resource base for dispensing patronage (Edie 1991: 7). The egalitarian element in democracy comes out in much of the literature. Crowder noted the greater concentration of rural wealth in Botswana and the consequent dispossession of farmers who were forced to migrate to the towns, where many became shanty-town dwellers and often remained unemployed (Crowder 1988: 472). This led to increased support for the (presumably anti-democratic) Marxist section of the opposition but Crowder, like Wiseman, noted the counteracting egalitarian impact of government expenditure as a means of consolidating public support for the political system. There were a few prestige projects (which are often associated with payoffs to narrow elites and foreign backers), there were improvements in communications, health, social services and rural water supplies, and the foundations of a system of universal primary education had been laid. Such policies were made easier by Botswana's growing wealth from mineral resources after independence, which made it one of the richest countries in Africa (Crowder 1988: 456; Wiseman 1990: 33–73), but the consolidation of democracy owed more to the way in which the wealth was used than to its mere existence. Similarly in India, Mitra refers to steady and substantial improvements in the physical quality of life, with reduced infant mortality, increased life expectation, expanded education, land reforms and labour legislation (Mitra 1992: 10–11).

How far can one generalize from these particular examples? The case of democracy in Jamaica being sustained by clientelism, which is in turn dependent on the economy generating sufficient resources, appears to be an exceptional one. Clientelistic systems, such as the notorious case of Bolivia, are more frequently authoritarian than democratic, with clients having to cling to the coat-tails of ruling politicians and bureaucrats rather than threatening to vote for the opposition. Payne suggests that the unusual practice of allowing the loyal opposition to dispense a sizable portion of state largess provides an insurance against the penetration of the political system by a radical third party, so that social discontent is channelled against the ruling party rather than the system as a whole (Payne 1988: 142–3). Such arrangements imply that the existence of a 'loyal opposition' has been institutionalized. We have yet to explore the reasons for this, but such institutionalization is clearly not the general rule in the Third World.

The relationship between democracy and the growth and distribution of wealth may offer more fruitful grounds for generalization. The wealthiest Third World countries, including Singapore, Taiwan, the Middle Eastern oil producers, and even Nigeria during periods of oil boom, have not been the most democratic, and the wealth has often been used by elites to consolidate their authority, but poverty is even less conducive to democracy, as witness the fate of countries such as Afghanistan, Bangladesh and Ethiopia, which have struggled to maintain any coherent political structure. Given a modest degree of economic growth, it is tempting to perceive a link between welfare-minded political systems and democracy, as the masses see something tangible in return for their votes and, in time, make their votes conditional on such benefits, but the democratic achievements of Botswana and India have to be set against the breakdown of pluralism in Sri Lanka, which also had an egalitarian record, and its failure to emerge in Singapore. In each case, non-economic factors upset the delicate balance between a state that is strong and confident enough to maintain institutionalized political competition, and a state that is either weakened by ethnic conflict or is so strong that it can suppress competition.

Sivard's figures suggest a correlation between social provision and democracy. We can take the relatively high levels of literacy, life expectancy and safe water provision, and low levels of infant mortality, as evidence of policies that imply concern with welfare provision and are likely to improve the lot of the poorest citizens. Using these indicators, we find in Table 5.2 that in eight continuous democracies the 'world ranking' enjoyed by these countries in terms of these 'social indicators' is generally higher than their ranking on 'economic and social' indicators as a whole. Trinidad, Costa Rica, Jamaica, Mauritius and India have higher rankings on all four 'social' indicators than on the general 'economic–social' ranking. Botswana has a higher ranking on two social indicators, Papua New Guinea on one and the Gambia on none. These could be contrasted with countries such as Argentina and Libya, which are wealthier but have experienced prolonged periods of authoritarianism. Both have a lower ranking on three of the four social indicators than they have on 'economic–social' standing as a whole. It may be that the existence of democratic answerability is the cause of governments paying attention to social requirements, but it is at least as plausible to argue that political systems which are able and willing to make such provision are more likely to enjoy democratic legitimacy in the eyes of the population than those which divert resources into prestige projects

Table 5.2 Economic and social standing and social indicators in continuous democracies

Country	Average economic–social ranking	Literacy ranking	Infant mortality ranking	Life expectancy ranking	Safe water ranking	Number of social rankings higher or lower than average economic–social ranking	
						Higher	Lower
Trinidad	44	27	37	38	27	4	0
Costa Rica	52	34	35	38	39	4	0
Jamaica	56	40	25	38	37	4	0
Mauritius	67	60	41	64	61	4	0
Botswana	87	107	78	104	81	2	2
Papua New Guinea	98	104	93	98	113	1	2
India	117	107	109	92	87	4	0
Gambia	121	126	139	136	119	0	4

Average economic–social ranking represents average rankings of gross national product per capita, education and health.
Source: Sivard (1983: 36–9)

or self-enrichment. Any quantitative analysis does, however, need to be treated with caution. El Salvador and Guatemala have extremely poor records on democracy, yet, like most of the continuous democracies, their ranking on all four of the social indicators is high relative to their development as a whole. Empirical observation suggests that there is a much greater sense of social injustice in these countries, reinforced by the uneven distribution of wealth along ethnic lines, which cannot be captured by statistics alone.

The importance of the pace and direction of economic growth is little more than hinted at in the literature, but it seems clear that rapid growth, as in the oil-producing states, does more for the political power and bank balances of elites than for democratic development, since growth is not accompanied by corresponding social changes or changes of political attitudes. Even if growth is accompanied by a greater social revolution, as in South Korea or, more haltingly, in much of South America, the short-term effects may be to produce demands for greater participation and redistribution than elites are willing or able to concede – hence the emergence of bureaucratic authoritarianism and its variants. The more modest pace of growth found in the West Indies, the Gambia, Botswana and India seems more conducive to democracy, though we still have to explain why the stewardship of politicians in these countries helped, or at least did not hamper, the wealth-creating processes in the way that it did in Ghana or Uganda.

The relationship between democracy (or its absence) and economic dependency figures prominently in much of the general literature on Third

World politics, but has a surprisingly small place in the literature on continuous democracies. Payne (1988: 142–3) writes of clientelistic politics being shaped by the neo-colonial Jamaican economy, but no thesis appears to have been advanced to the effect that international capitalism is more indifferent to changes of government, or the democratic re-election of existing governments, in these countries than it has been in Chile, Nicaragua or Guatemala. It may be the case, however, that democracies in these countries have the advantage of being insufficiently rich to be of major concern to the outside world and, perhaps partly for that reason, political conflict is less polarized than in wealthier countries such as Chile or South Korea. The consequences of a particular government being re-elected or displaced are thus of less significance to the outside world, which will have little incentive to subvert the democratic process.

Political culture

The cultural features of the continuous democracies do not, at first sight, fit any discernible pattern. The West Indian islands, the Gambia, Botswana and Mauritius are all small states within which it might be more difficult to regard people from outside one's own ethnic group as 'alien' in the way that groups from the opposite ends of large countries such as the Sudan, Nigeria or Zaire often find themselves with little in common. At the other extreme democracy has survived alongside cultural heterogeneity and geographical extensiveness in India. The 'cultural' explanations of democracy vary between the countries, though without necessarily being incompatible.

Crowder emphasized the long tradition of free debate, consensus and elite continuity in Botswana (Crowder 1988: 466), while MacDonald and Payne indicate the ways in which political alliances cut across ethnic cleavages in the West Indies, with elites uniting across ethnic divides to resist radical challenges in Trinidad (MacDonald 1986: 18, 214) and political affiliations in Jamaica cutting across divisions of class, race and generation (Payne 1988: 153). Mauritius, which in 1982 became the first African country to change its government directly though a free election, is another small but ethnically heterogeneous country in which class and ethnic loyalties criss-cross one another to prevent 'zero-sum politics' (Wiseman 1990: 65–73).

These findings are almost like echoes of Almond and Verba's explanation of democracy in much of the West, but the cultural diversity of a giant country such as India presents more complicated problems. While ethnic conflicts may be kept in check in smaller countries by the nature of face-to-face relationships, and with the help of small political elites moderating conflicts when they recognize the danger signals, India presents democrats with a much greater challenge. Yet the challenge to a would-be authoritarian would be equally great. Manor and Mitra both suggest that cultural diversity is so great that no single group is able to dominate the others. Authority is unavoidably dispersed, and a tradition of accommodation and compromise has emerged. Manor suggests that 'Indian culture' gives only a limited role to politics, with the implication that the pursuit of political power is not the sole, or main, preoccupation of elites, while Mitra suggests that government at the centre provides 'just one of many centres' (Manor 1990: 21; Mitra 1992: 10).

Political culture offers a tempting explanation of continuous democracy (and many other political phenomena), but it has often proved to be a slippery concept, and one that may be more useful in describing a situation than explaining it. Crowder's emphasis on traditions of free debate and consensus seem especially vulnerable, since similar traditions could be ascribed to pre-colonial culture in much of Africa. But a willingness to share power within one's own group does not guarantee a willingness to seek consensus with other 'alien' groups within a modern nation state and, even without the dimension of inter-ethnic conflict, the higher political stakes in a modern polity may encourage a more naked pursuit of self-interest. The other 'cultural' explanations of democracy hinge largely on either the ethnic criss-crossing of alliances at elite and/or mass level, as in the smaller countries, or inter-group bargaining based on interdependence, as in India (something perhaps closer to the consociational democracy model). No one would deny that these phenomena generally help the democratic process – though bargaining between groups can involve an elitist carve-up of resources, as in Malaysia, rather than a response to democratic pressures – but there is a danger of regarding democracy as an inevitable outcome of certain cultural conditions instead of seeing these conditions as a reflection of political choices taken within the constraints of particular political structures and economic pressures. Why have Guyana, Sierra Leone and Malawi not followed the same paths as Jamaica, the Gambia and Botswana? Perhaps there are some significant cultural differences, but practical opportunities and obstacles would have to be taken into account, as well as attitudes to society.

Political behaviour and political choices

Is it the wisdom of politicians, and the people who elect them, that has helped to preserve democracy? Crowder extolled the virtues of Seretse Khama in Botswana as a good listener, a man who commanded respect in both traditional and modern society and who had experience of rural development problems, and we have already noted the emphasis of the rulers of Botswana on policies which produced widespread social benefits, and thus commanded mass support, rather than prestige projects for the benefit of narrow elites (Crowder 1988: 463–6). The willingness of both elites and masses to acknowledge the need for 'moderation', when crises threaten the foundations of the democratic system, is well documented. MacDonald notes the way in which the middle classes of different ethnic groups in Trinidad united behind the Williams Government and its policy of 'capitalist development' in the face of challenge from the Black Power movement, thus defusing ethnic tension (MacDonald 1986: 18). Payne suggests a similar retreat from the brink in Jamaica, following the 1980 election in which 600 people were killed and in which a coup had been attempted (Payne 1988: 149). Manor implies an emphasis on moderation in India, with the argument that the limited extent of reform helped to preserve the liberal order (Manor 1990: 37).

Not only is there a willingness to show restraint in the heat of a crisis, but there is said to be a positive will to preserve democracy on both ascetic and practical grounds. Wiseman suggests that the will to preserve democracy in Africa is helped by the experience of the authoritarian alternative, which has failed to provide stability, development, efficiency or human rights, and in the particular case of Botswana he indicates the greater efficiency of democracy where, for example, drought relief was more readily forthcoming from a government that did not want to lose the votes of the victims (Wiseman 1990: 46–7, 182–3). On a somewhat different note, Hewitt refers to the importance of the existence of opposition groups offering clear alternatives as a means of sustaining democracy (Hewitt 1990: 18–19) – a point to which we shall return.

The 'political behaviour' arguments offer the opposite side of the coin to the cultural ones. How far are political actors taking autonomous decisions, and how far is their response to events a reflection of the values of society? Some societies, such as those in Central America or the Middle East, may have less of a tradition of moderation and consensus than others, but it would be foolish to ignore the fact that alternative choices could have been taken in relation to economic development and crisis resolution, which could have produced non-democratic results. Whether we should share the authors' enthusiasm for moderation as a means of sustaining democracy is a more subjective question. Supporters of Black Power in Trinidad or a more thoroughgoing socialist programme in India might see 'moderation' as a constraint on democratic choice, just as Edie (1991) sees two-party hegemony in Jamaica as a restriction on, rather than an enhancement of, democracy.

The argument that the preservation of democracy is helped by a positive will, on account of an awareness of the less attractive alternatives, is one I have pursued elsewhere (Pinkney 1990: 155–6), but it would seem to be more applicable to countries which have actually experienced home-grown authoritarianism than those which have enjoyed pluralism since independence. Even if we allow for knowledge of events in neighbouring countries, one might have expected Ghanaians, Nigerians and Ugandans to have taken greater care not to allow a restoration of authoritarianism when given a second chance, as compared with West Indians or Batswana, whose knowledge of authoritarianism was less direct. The failure of the former countries to avert a second authoritarian coming might suggest that political will alone is insufficient.

The question of the existence of a distinctive opposition alternative takes us into a different territory, and one that is easily overlooked. A democracy which merely offers Buggins' turn or, as the Ghanaians say, the same taxis with different drivers, may be useful as a safety valve to check the abuse of power implicit in indefinite one-party, personal or military rule, but it denies voters any real political choice. Hewitt suggests that India was offered such a choice in 1989, with an opposition manifesto which covered state–centre relations, decentralization, electoral reform, the de-politicalization of national radio and television, and the alleviation of poverty. Whether the contents of any party manifesto have a great impact on the choices made by voters is an open question in any democracy, but it may at least reflect an alternative set of interests, beliefs and priorities that voters can grasp. In the continuous democracies outside India, the question of what is being contested in the democratic arena emerges less clearly, and outbreaks of political extremism are seen as aberrations to be avoided. Perhaps these countries are small enough to subsist on a relatively parochial diet of political conflict, with rival individuals competing largely on the basis of personal competence rather than ideology, but if this is the case they may offer only limited lessons for other, larger countries seeking to institutionalize democracy.

Political institutions and pre-independence foundations

We have looked at the impact of preparations for independence, or lack of them, in previous chapters, and the literature on the continuous democracies confirms many of the propositions already examined. The advantage of a long preparation for independence in Jamaica is emphasized by Payne: a generation of Jamaicans was, he argues, socialized into democratic values. Many of the political leaders were educated in Britain, and genuinely believed in multi-party democracy (Payne 1988: 153). In India, Manor mentions, the relatively restrained use of imperial power enabled indigenous social groups to flourish and the Congress party to establish broad and deep support long before independence. The institutional structure at party and state level was, he says, strong without being overbearing (Manor 1990: 21–32). This is leading us towards the Huntingtonian argument that successful democracy depends more on effective institutions than on large numbers of people adhering to democratic values or seeking democratic participation. Political parties are thus singled out as vital institutions by Manor and Payne, while Wiseman emphasizes the contribution of a competent, honest bureaucracy to democracy in Botswana (Wiseman 1990: 35–6).

The argument that institutions are generally more durable if they have deep foundations in pre-independence history is difficult to refute, though one could dispute the phrase 'preparation for independence'. If the imperial power consciously 'prepared' nationalist politicians or indigenous administrators for independence at all, this was only done very late in the day, but countries such as India and Jamaica did enjoy the advantage of relative freedom to develop their institutions at an earlier date than many others. This might, however, be due to an acknowledgement by Britain that these countries were already more 'advanced' than the African colonies, which takes us back to culture and economic development. Outside India and the West Indies we cannot easily explain the durability of democracy in terms of the length of preparation for independence. Indeed, the preparation was much shorter in the Gambia and Botswana than in countries such as Ghana and Nigeria, which succumbed to authoritarianism within a decade of independence. Institutional strength in the former countries may, paradoxically, have been helped by the relative shallowness of nationalist movements, which left older elites and bureaucracies more intact and able to provide continuity. If other forces helped the continuity of democracy, these institutions could then help to reinforce it, even if the democracy in question was too conservative for many tastes.

To the institutional support provided by parties and bureaucracies, we can risk stating the obvious by adding the importance of an independent judiciary and the rule of law. Crowder (1988: 462) mentioned freedom of speech and of the press, as well as free elections, in Botswana, and Edie accepts the importance of open media and a free and impartial judiciary in Jamaica, but both authors are careful to qualify the advantages of these formal structures by noting other forms of elite control, including restrictions on trade union rights and the nomination of ruling party candidates to prevent the opposition from taking control of local authorities in Botswana, and the clientelistic processes already described in Jamaica (Crowder 1988: 462; Edie 1991: 47–8).

The extent of electoral choice and participation

Democratic choice may be limited not only by the limited quality and quantity of policy alternatives on offer, but also by limited prospects of the ruling party losing office, or the limited scope for public participation beyond the electoral process. Payne suggests that the convention of government and loyal opposition sharing in the distribution of patronage in Jamaica is an insurance against the penetration of the system by a radical third party (Payne 1988: 142–3). Edie goes further in arguing that the two-party system actually deprives people of political choices (Edie 1991: 47). Crowder noted the limited scope for participation in Botswana, where rural voters continued to support traditional elites (Crowder 1988: 472–6). Edie sees participation as being restricted to electoral activity in Jamaica, and even here the contest is between personalities and leaders rather than between party programmes. The parties themselves have close (presumably un-democratic) links with business and the technocratic elite (Edie 1991: 49). Changing the government through the democratic process is a common occurrence in the West Indies, an occasional one in India and Mauritius and, according to Wiseman (1990: 63), an unlikely one in the Gambia and Botswana.

There is, of course, nothing intrinsically undemocratic about voters choosing to re-elect the same party at regular intervals, but cynics might explain the willingness to tolerate the opposition in terms of its remote prospects of winning, or the expectation that it would make only limited changes to the status quo if it did win. Where ruling elites have seen the threats to their policies or their privileges as more serious, as in Sierra Leone, Nigeria and Pakistan, they have been less willing to tolerate free elections or the results they have produced. A more central question is whether one should see these limitations on choice and participation, self-imposed or imposed from above, as necessary restraints to ensure the orderly functioning of the democratic process, with the prospect of addi-tional democratic increments when the system is strong enough to absorb them, or whether such limitations indicate the limited circumstances in which elites are willing to tolerate pluralism.

Answers to such questions can only be speculative. The fact that elites in some countries are willing to tolerate even limited choice and participation should not be overlooked, bearing in mind the intolerance, ballot rigging and repression which occur in much of the Third World even when the prospects of an opposition victory are much more remote than in Bot-swana or the Gambia. It may be that social forces or the underlying political culture have reached a stage where repression would be socially unaccept-able or costly in terms of resources and political principles, but the social structures and political cultures of the continuous democracies are not obviously different from those of neighbouring countries where authorit-arianism has flourished. In relatively new states, it is difficult to avoid turning to the attitudes of individual rulers and their immediate followers as explanations of the survival of democracy. Lacking the megalomania, fear, greed or even inferiority complexes of the leaders who have turned to authoritarianism, they have allowed pluralism to continue. Perhaps the democratic leaders would have been more tempted to tamper with the pol-itical process if the initial opposition threat had been electorally stronger or more extreme, but the pluralist process may eventually become so institu-tionalized that rulers cannot suppress opposition even if they want to. The ability of Jamaica, Trinidad and India to survive major political crises with the democratic process intact might suggest that an important threshold has been crossed.

Is electoral pluralism only possible because of limited party differences and limited participation in the political process as a whole? Such a view would fit neatly with Dahl's prescription of contestation before participa-tion or Huntington's emphasis on order. Raise the political stakes or the range or intensity of expectations, one might argue, and power holders will be reluctant to relinquish power, while non-elites will be less willing to accept the legitimacy of decisions based on electoral pluralism alone. Look at the gap between the aspirations of the 'haves' and 'have nots' in Latin America, and one can understand the reluctance or inability of political actors over the years to accept free and fair elections. Extreme polarization certainly makes democracy much more difficult, yet it may itself be blunted by continuous democracy. We have noted that many of the continuous democracies are culturally heterogeneous. Black Power was for a time a subject of intense political conflict in Trinidad, and India has faced a range of ethnic and religious conflicts which might have involved an authoritarian clampdown elsewhere, yet the existence of a deep-rooted democratic structure helped each political system to return from the brink. Once again democracy may play a part in determining the nature of political conflict as well as responding to it.

The armed forces and foreign influence

The military coup is a common means of ending democracy in the Third World. If there is no military, there can be no military coup. The absence of an army in the Gambia, in Botswana in the formative years before 1977 and in Costa Rica since 1948 might thus be an important explanation of the survival of democracy, though one would still have to explain why each government took the exceptional decision not to create, or to dispense with, an army. It might be a reflection of such variables as the perceived stability of the country, the modest aspirations of its rulers or its remoteness from any international conflict, all of which would in themselves augur well for democracy, in contrast to Middle Eastern countries with internal instability, megalomaniac leaders and positions of strategic importance.

Where armies do exist but do not interfere with the democratic process, it is tempting to assert that they have been socialized into values of military professionalism and respect for democracy, but if the main evidence for such an assertion is the non-occurrence of coups, we are only going round in circles. In the early 1960s it was fashionable to argue that the rigours of previous training under the British and French would rule out the possibility of coups in tropical Africa, and this seemed a plausible argument until coups began to occur. It is, of course, possible that soldiers witness the effective working of the democratic process and conclude that elections are a better means of changing the government than coups, but in that case non-intervention is a consequence of democracy rather than a cause. It is generally true that armies do not intervene when the democratic process is working relatively smoothly, unless provoked by outside powers as in Guatemala in 1954, but the converse does not apply so consistently. Armies removed Prime Minister Balewa in Nigeria, President Margai in Sierra Leone and Prime Minister Bhutto in Pakistan when their legitimacy was in dispute, yet they remained in barracks during constitutional crises in Jamaica, Trinidad and India. This may be because democracy was more firmly established in the latter countries, but can one say with certainty that the outcome might not have been different if key army officers had made a different assessment of the situation? Was democracy secure, or was it just lucky?

Foreign intervention, like military intervention, is more often seen as a means of subverting democracy than sustaining it. From Hungary to Chile, and Guatemala to Iran, actual or emerging democracies have been brought down through foreign-inspired coups or invasions. The absence of foreign influence in a country may reflect its strategic unimportance, which is generally good for democracy. Countries at international crossroads, such as Egypt, Pakistan, South Korea and Panama, are unlikely to have as much freedom to develop their own political institutions, and often suffer the burden of inflated armies demanding more resources and influence. But foreign indifference may reflect a paucity of economic resources, which is generally bad for democracy, though probably not as bad as being someone else's military base.

Conclusion

Is it possible to offer general explanations for the survival of democracy in our varied countries? There is room for argument about whether apparently common features are causes, effects or symptoms, but at least four variables suggest some common ground: the minimal disruption associated with the transfer of power at independence, the qualities of national leaders, the limited degree of political polarization and the existence of state structures that were strong enough to maintain stability without being strong enough to suppress dissent.

The conventional wisdom is that a lengthy transition to independence, as in India and the West Indies, during which a strong institutional structure can develop, is conducive to stable democracy. It is difficult to refute such a contention, but it is easy to overlook countries such as Botswana and the Gambia at the opposite extreme, where preparations for independence were much more hasty than in countries with a longer history of nationalist agitation, such as Ghana and Nigeria. The former countries were almost 'free riders' who gained independence unexpectedly easily after the independence of the larger colonies had made the preservation of an empire less tenable. Yet their brief preparation for independence gave them the advantage, at least in retrospect, of not having nationalist parties that seriously challenged the older traditional and bureaucratic elites, and elsewhere propelled to the top politicians who were inexperienced in government yet intolerant of opposition. Paradoxically, there appears to have been greater political continuity in the extreme cases of the very long preparations for independence, where politicians and parties had had time to establish effective power bases, and the very short preparations, where older elites were sufficiently confident of their authority to permit dissent. It is in the intermediate cases that democracy often fared worst, with nationalist politicians who had built up their parties in the 1950s, relying on patronage rather than institutionalized support, then resorting to authoritarianism to retain control as the resources for patronage dried up.

Allied with the 'right' circumstances for the transfer of power was the quality of the leaders who took over the reins after independence. Enjoying the following of parties that were either deeply rooted in society or had not needed to overreach themselves in appealing for mass support was undoubtedly an advantage, but the qualities of a Nehru or a Seretse Khama, or of the broader party elites of the West Indies who commanded public respect and were committed to the democratic ideal, were important in nurturing democracy in its early years.

Limited political polarization is likely to help the democratic process in any country by making the contrast between winning and losing less stark. The question of why polarization is limited is a difficult one to unravel. The smallness of the countries, other than India, may help by making adversaries less remote, as does the inability of any one group to win power without cooperating with others, but the nature of political competition also depends on the perceived interests of different groups and the resources for which they are competing. I have suggested that the 'developmental position' of the continuous democracies, in between the most industrialized and the poorest Third World countries, has provided governments with sufficient resources to offer something in return for votes, but without the divisive effects of the sharper class divisions that frequently go with development, as in much of South America. The 'right' geographical boundaries, ethnic mix and economic conditions may thus make democratic development easier, but much will still depend on governments using the resources in what is seen to be an equitable way. Statistics and empirical studies suggest that the leaders of continuous democracies have been more socially concerned and probably less self-seeking than authoritarian rulers, but the evidence is more impressionistic than conclusive. It may be argued that democratic constraints leave rulers with little choice in these matters, but in cases where democracy is not deeply entrenched we return to the importance of political leaders setting the standards that help to sustain democracy.

On the power of the state and political institutions, there is again the argument that the ingredients which can sustain democracy can also destroy it if they are over-abundant. The general point is made effectively by Heper in his observations on weak institutions in Spanish Latin America and strong institutions in Turkey, both of which have done democracy more harm than good (Heper 1991: 196–201). Without a broadly and deeply based dominant party and a strong bureaucracy, India would have disintegrated long ago, but if these institutions had been even stronger they might have been more tempted to pursue authoritarian solutions. In the case of India, a culturally diverse society that contained many 'non-political' centres of power helped to keep such tendencies in check. In the smaller continuous democracies, a comparable balance between state and society can be observed. President Nkrumah had advised Ghanaians to 'Seek ye first the political kingdom and all other things shall be added' – a recipe for a strong, and ultimately authoritarian, state. It is difficult to imagine the leaders of Botswana or the West Indies offering such advice, since they have never been in a position to offer 'all other things', given the constraints of societies which contain more autonomous centres of power.

In the end a search for a 'cause' of the survival of democracy may prove fruitless. Just as we may believe that we have unearthed a cause, nagging doubts set in as to whether it is really a symptom or a consequence, or whether a comparable phenomenon elsewhere is not compatible with authoritarianism. Yet we do seem to have located a combination of circumstances, arising from historical or political accident or political will, that helps to reinforce democracy. One has only to look at their opposites to emphasize the point. A major break in political continuity at independence, incompetent or self-seeking leaders, extreme polarization, abject poverty and a state too weak to regulate political competition or so strong as to suppress competition are all inimical to democracy. A country able to avoid these eventualities in its formative years may, but is by no means certain to, see democracy prosper. The extent of political choice in terms of parties, personnel and policies may be too narrow for many tastes, and mass poverty and domination by economic elites may continue to exist alongside the electoral process, but at least the structures are in place on which future democrats may be able to build.

The dynamics of transition 1: the seeds of challenge to authoritarianism

We now move from the question of why some countries have remained democratic to the question of why a much larger number have made the transition from authoritarianism to democracy. Events in these countries are central to an understanding of Third World politics for at least two reasons: they comprise the vast majority of the Third World's population, and the movement of these countries from authoritarianism to democracy, though still incomplete in some cases, has been achieved with a speed that has little parallel in the West. The collapse of authoritarian regimes in Eastern Europe after 1989 may have helped to make democracy more fashionable, and helped to accelerate the transition in the Third World, but the democratization process in the Third World was well under way before the demolition of the Berlin Wall, and needs to be seen as a process with its own dynamics. In Latin America, few countries could boast of democratically elected governments by the mid-1970s. By the 1990s, there were few governments there which were not so elected. In Asia, South Korea, Pakistan, Bangladesh, Thailand and Nepal had similarly moved from military or personal rule to pluralism, and by 1992, 25 of the 41 states in tropical Africa had held competitive elections or were preparing to do so (*The Economist* 22 February 1992: 21–3). Whether democratization has worked well is a matter on which we must postpone judgement but, to paraphrase Dr Johnson, it is remarkable that it has worked at all.

The term 'transition' is open to criticism on the grounds that it may imply a recognizable process with a beginning and an end, and with an interaction of different forces in between. It might also imply the resolution of conflicts between distinctive groups or individuals, who can be categorized easily as pro- or anti-democratic. Politics in the real world are clearly more complicated than that, with democracy and authoritarianism often a matter of degree, and with the pursuit of, or resistance to, democracy frequently emerging as a secondary consideration for political actors pursuing other goals. Were General Franco's immediate successors in 1975 authoritarians who had to be bullied into accepting democracy, or were they democrats who were merely awaiting the right conditions for democratic restoration? Did Spanish communists who favoured competitive elections really give a high priority to pluralist democracy? Have all heads of one-party and military governments been implacable opponents of democracy, or have they been victims of circumstances in which democracy failed to work? Was President Stevens of Sierra Leone a democrat because he won power through a competitive election despite an attempt by the military to thwart him, or an authoritarian who revealed his true intentions once he was in power? And beyond the formal political structure there are innumerable groups in society for whom democracy may be of only marginal interest, but who may support or oppose moves towards greater democratization according to whether or not it is seen to enhance their wealth, status or security.

It is difficult to discuss the move from authoritarianism to democracy without the concept of 'transition', however. Countries are not, except occasionally in a very formal sense, authoritarian one day and democratic the next. The intervening period is likely to be a matter of years, even if we cannot easily plot the exact beginning and end. If our purpose is to understand why many non-democratic regimes have become democratic, or been superseded by democratic regimes, we need to seek an understanding of three processes, as set out in Table 6.1: the sowing of the seeds of challenge to the authoritarian regime, the articulation of interests and the resolution of conflicts between the main contenders. These are not presented as separate sequences in a process, but more as parallel processes that enable us to view democratization from different perspectives. Thus the challenge to authoritarian rulers is not necessarily confined to early rumblings of discontent within the ruling junta or to an early show of public defiance. Even after bargaining has opened between authoritarians and would-be democrats, new events such as a failed military adventure or a rise in unemployment may add to the pressures on the government. Similarly, the process of 'resolution' is not to be seen as a final 'summit conference' that ushers in the new order, but as a process that may continue intermittently from the first serious cabinet revolt to the final counting of votes in a contested election.

Pridham suggests a distinction between 'functionalist' and 'genetic' schools of transition theory, with the former approximating to our seeds of challenge, emphasizing environmental factors, and the latter approximating to our articulation of interests, emphasizing political variables and the scope for choice by political actors (Pridham 1991: 6–7), but exclusive reliance on one of these approaches would clearly leave many questions unanswered. Using the three perspectives of Table 6.1 we can highlight three sets of variables which are given prominence in the literature. The seeds of challenge are concerned with the forces that may weaken an authoritarian government, irrespective of the political structure over which it presides.

Table 6.1 Elements in the transition to democracy

Focus of study	Questions	Variables involved	Areas of academic debate
Seeds of challenge to authoritarianism	How does the political system respond to the forces of change, and to political events?	1 Economic change 2 Social change 3 Cultural strain 4 Policy success or failure	1 Relative importance of (a) Socio-economic forces (b) Political choices 2 What is the relationship between economic liberalization and political liberalization?
The configuration of interests	How does the political system respond to the pressures of groups with different demands and resources?	1 Specific political structures 2 Government and opposition 3 Elites, counter-elites, masses 4 Specific groups in society 5 External powers and groups	1 What opportunities and limitations do different forms of authoritarianism present? 2 Respective roles of formal political structures and forces in the wider society 3 'Top-down' versus 'bottom-up' explanations of democracy
The resolution of conflicts	How are the conflicts, implicit above, resolved within the political arena, and at what costs, or benefits, to the actors involved?	1 Ability of some groups to persuade or coerce others 2 Extent of conflict/consensus/order 3 Nature and extent of changes sought or achieved 4 Speed of change	1 How genuine have the transitions to democracy been? 2 Do any particular 'types' of transaction achieve distinctive results?

The collapse of the Soviet Empire, a change in the price of oil, rapid economic growth, the humiliation of a military defeat or the rise of an educated middle class could all have the effect of undermining the power base of an authoritarian government in different ways. (One might also add the unquantifiable influence of 'contagion'. The restoration of democracy in country A may not directly alter the relative resources of authoritarians or democrats in country B, but it may raise the morale of democrats and increase their expectation of success. Just as in earlier times a military coup in country A often had the effect of inspiring soldiers in country B to attempt a similar venture, so the movement to democracy may create new political currents, which sweep along weaker countries that would not have made the transition as easily without external stimulation.)

The study of the articulation of interests throws light on the actual demands being made and the interests being pursued. The demands and interests will vary according to both the formal political structure – is the authoritarian regime military, single party, personal or traditional? – and the underlying society – are there influential professional groups, a large landed elite or a significant industrial proletariat? The study of resolution enables us to weave together the underlying forces and the main interests in the political system, and to examine the ways in which various advantages and opportunities are exploited. In this chapter I shall look at the seeds of challenge to authoritarianism, and then consider the articulation of interests and the resolution in the two following chapters.

Social and economic forces and political choices

Table 6.2 suggests that academic debate on the forces which have undermined authoritarianism has focused on the relative importance of socioeconomic, as against political, forces, and on the relationship between economic and political liberalization. At first sight this seems a well-worn academic terrain, and one that has been occupied by many of those seeking explanations of the initial emergence, survival or eclipse of democracy, but the protagonists who occupied distinctive positions in the earlier debates have often chosen different positions from which to view the transition to democracy, and with good reason. It is plausible, if not universally accepted, to explain the emergence of liberal democracy in the West in terms of industrialization, to relate the collapse of fragile African democracies to economic downturn, or to develop theories of 'bureaucratic authoritarianism' in Latin America on the basis of a 'deepening' of industrialization, but the countries which have undergone, or appear to be undergoing, transitions to democracy do not conform to any obvious set of economic patterns. A few, such as South Korea, have witnessed major social changes as a result of sustained economic growth, and one can see a rough parallel between the demands for greater freedom and political participation from a more educated, urban population and comparable demands

Table 6.2   Economic pressures for democratic transition

Nature of economic change	Possible conflicts generated	Possible outcomes
Industrialization	New social groups demand increased participation	Government concedes greater freedom and participation, rather than meet the cost of repression
Erosion of state-supported sectors with greater austerity and/or free-market ideology	New business groups develop as independent centres of power, and often cooperate more with foreign interests; poorer groups losing employment and welfare benefits become more discontented	Government seeks new power bases to compensate for the loss of clients; democratic concessions may be made to meet mass demands
Weakening of old economic elites with changes in the structure of the economy	Competition for political influence between old and new elites makes for a less monolithic political structure	Old and new elites both seek allies in the political structure, including the army
Economic collapse	Government loses its ability to dispense patronage, and therefore loses much of its support	Authoritarian regime is easy to topple; competitive elections may be promised as a means of reviving the government's legitimacy, but incoming governments will have little base on which to build

in the nascent Western democracies in the nineteenth century. But most of the countries experiencing democratic transitions in the 1980s and 1990s have done so in periods of economic stagnation or decline. Economic decline may have its compensations, and Karl (1990: 16) argues that it may be conducive to democracy in the sense that it dampens unrealistic expectations and makes utopian solutions of political extremists appear less plausible in the sober light of austerity, but it would take a bold political scientist to build a theory of democratic transition around economic decline. There certainly appears to be a 'floor' of low economic development below which the emergence of democracy is unlikely.

Certain kinds of reasons and preconditions for military withdrawal are unlikely to surface if a society has a low level of development. In many parts of the world freedom from hunger will enjoy a higher priority than civil rights. Since strong government, including military regimes, is often – rightly or wrongly – regarded as the possible solution to economic misery, sufficient pressures for less authoritarian forms hardly eventuate.

(Sundhausen 1984: 552)

The belief that 'strong government' does offer a solution to economic misery may be strained if the performance of authoritarians is manifestly no better than that of the shaky democratic regimes which many of them had superseded, and such a performance may provide an opportunity for would-be democrats to mobilize support. As Rustow suggests, intractable economic problems may make it prudent for authoritarians to depart, and leave the solutions to someone else (Rustow 1990: 76–9). Continued poverty, rather than the rise of wealthier, articulate social groups, has thus pushed authoritarian rulers in countries as poor as Benin and Togo to permit free elections, but it is uncertain whether such moves represent a transition to any durable form of democracy or merely the retreat of one group of authoritarians who have lost their power base while another group wait in the wings until the democrats prove equally ineffective in dealing with the intractable problems. In relation to military government, Welch makes a useful distinction between disengagement related to short-term negative trends which may make for only a transitory civilian regime if its policies fare no better, and long-term disengagement related to positive economic trends (Welch 1987: 23). On this argument, democratic successions would prove more durable in Brazil and South Korea than in Argentina and Central America, whose prospects, in turn, would be brighter than those of most of tropical Africa.

What of the argument that economic development, rather than decay, is a force that will undermine authoritarianism? The former has been less in evidence than the latter in recent years, but the experiences of Spain and Portugal, and more recently South Korea, might suggest that the right combination of favourable economic circumstances in relation to the outside world, and internal policies which, at the very least, do not hamper economic growth, may give rise to social forces with which authoritarians are increasingly unable to cope. Cummings offers a particularly powerful argument in relation to South Korea. Rejecting the more fashionable thesis that democratization depends heavily on the vagaries of behaviour by political actors, he argues that behaviour should be placed in the context of the social structure and world economic structure (Cummings 1989: 27–32). Frequent use of the word 'crisis' by Cummings might cast doubt on whether democratization was related to economic 'development', but if 'crises' did occur they were the product of a dynamic rather than a stagnating economy. The components of the crises are not entirely clear, but the argument is that repression was becoming increasingly expensive (because of the rise of a more articulate urban population with industrialization?). 'Bureaucratic authoritarian' policies that had promoted growth were now in conflict with both the indigenous businesses, which were excluded from the mercantilist favours that the government was dispensing, and the interests of the United

States, which was being excluded from much of the home market through protectionism and which faced competition in world markets from a low-wage economy. Economic liberalization, it is argued, would benefit the excluded indigenous firms and the United States economy, while political liberalization would force an elected government to concede wage demands and thus raise labour costs to the benefit of American competitors (Cummings 1989: 27–32). Thus a combination of internal and United States pressures has forced authoritarians to depart.

Readers who are hard to please might raise at least five questions about such a thesis. (a) Is the concept of 'bureaucratic authoritarianism' as straightforward as it appears if it can be used to characterize anything from a highly interventionist government in South Korea to a free-market one in Chile? (b) How did the businesses excluded from the government's favours manage to influence events? (c) Are democratic governments necessarily more sympathetic to wage demands than authoritarian ones? (d) Did the United States policy-makers really have such a sharp perception of their own interests? (e) Are economic and political liberalization complementary in the way that Cummings implies? The pursuit of some of these questions would divert us too far from our immediate concerns, yet it seems clear that authoritarians who preside over periods of economic growth will eventually find that they have facilitated the creation of forces they cannot easily control, as new or strengthened groups demand a larger share of the national cake, or resist attempts to reduce their share. In relation to unrest in Brazil, another country which has experienced substantially increased, if unevenly distributed, national wealth, Cammack places the emphasis on economic factors as the driving force for democratic pressures. 'The nature of the conflicts and the attitudes of the state are best understood in each case in the light of current patterns of capitalist development and the popular demands they provoke' (Cammack 1991: 542).

It is, perhaps, the phrase 'attitudes of the state' that offers an opening for those who place the emphasis on politics rather than economics. States in authoritarian countries come in varied shapes and sizes, as we shall see when we come to look at specific political structures. Here I merely note that certain types of authoritarian regime might be more vulnerable than others to the forces of economic growth. The military government in South Korea derived its strength more from one of the most developed armies in the world than from any power base in society, and thus proved brittle when it came to responding to popular demands, whereas the Brazilian military government at least had a party base, even if it was largely of its own making. The authoritarian (or semi-authoritarian) governments in Singapore and Taiwan have been sustained by what were originally nationalist parties, and have been able to respond more easily to the pressures in society resulting from economic growth, without so far having had to surrender power in contested elections. But even within the context of a particular type of authoritarian regime, whether it be military, single-party or hybrid, some analysts would argue that political choices, rather than economic forces, are crucial in setting the democratic transition in motion. Weiner (1987: 863) urges us to focus less on 'conditions and prerequisites' and more on 'the strategies available to those who seek a democratic revolution', and emphasizes especially the importance of winning over a sufficient section of the military by showing the moderate or right-wing credentials of potential successors (Weiner 1987: 864–6). At a more specific level, Rustow suggests that particular political decisions or errors can be the catalyst that stimulates the demand for democratization, as with the prosecution of unsuccessful wars by the authoritarian governments of Portugal, Greece and Argentina (Rustow 1990: 76–9). In each case the competence of authoritarian governments, whose legitimacy was already in doubt, came into question.

The balance in recent literature on transitions is certainly more on the side of political manoeuvring than economic forces, and such manoeuvring clearly influences the timing and courses of transitions, yet the fact that few authoritarian regimes have been left unscathed by pressures for democratic transition in recent years might suggest that there is more to the process than a range of political decisions by varied actors scattered across the globe. Improved communications have certainly helped, so that oppressed people in one country can quickly become aware of victories won by fellow-sufferers elsewhere, but the inability of governments to control the consequences of economic changes, whether they be inadequate food supplies in tropical Africa or the growth of large-scale manufacturing in South Korea, often provides the context within which pressures for democracy emerge. In an earlier age the failure of authoritarians to meet people's material wants may have mattered less, as attitudes to authority varied from deference to fatalism, but in a more secular world the juxtaposition of a population in which diverse groups are demanding diverse benefits and a government that has diminishing control over its own economic destiny can put apparently secure authoritarian governments in a vulnerable position.

Even apparently 'political' decisions might be traced partly to economic constraints. Was Portugal's decision to hold on to its colonies by force an autonomous political decision, or the action of a poor European power which could not afford to follow the decolonizing path of its wealthier neighbours? Were the Greek and Argentinian decisions to invade Cyprus and the Falklands the political decisions of deranged army officers, or last desperate attempts to regain the support of populations who had lost confidence in their rulers? A major difficulty with the emphasis on economics is not so much that it is misplaced but that the economic circumstances which may give rise to democratic transition are so diverse. Whereas those who seek economic explanations of the rise of liberal democracy, the end of colonial rule or the collapse of communism have the advantage of dealing with a finite range of economic forces in each case, to say that economic factors have played a part in undermining authoritarianism in South Korea, El Salvador, Chile and Benin leaves us with a much wider array of forces, ranging from industrialization through the decline of old plantation elites and the erosion of large sections of the economy, to virtual economic breakdown. In such diverse circumstances, we can keep reminding ourselves that the economic stage in many countries provides the context within which political actors play their parts, but the diversity of economic pressures and opportunities offers scope for a tremendously varied interplay of political forces. In Table 6.2 I set out four of these types of economic pressure, though the types are by no means exhaustive.

First, there are cases of comprehensive industrialization, such as South Korea, which are likely to generate a range of new social forces, as existing elites are challenged by new elites, which do not enjoy many governmental favours, and a growing, increasingly educated, urban population. Both the latter groups demand greater political participation and increased resources. A more old-fashioned authoritarian government with deep roots in society, as in Bismarck's Germany, may be able to keep the democratic demands in check for some time, but a military government which has survived largely by virtue of superior force, and the reluctant consent of older elites who fear something worse, is likely to make concessions rather than fight an increasingly costly and ineffective war of repression.

Countries where economic change is generated by the decline of state-supported sectors, and the rise of new sectors exploiting a freer market, present a more complex picture. First, one could argue that the withdrawal of state support, often as an expression of 'New Right' ideology, is a political and not an economic influence on democratization. In extreme cases such as Chile there is some truth in this, but the extent to which governments, especially in the more economically 'advanced' Third World countries in Latin America, have retreated from economic intervention might suggest that this is not a mere ideological fad but a response to forces they cannot easily control, as foreign debts mount and the economy remains sluggish. Second, the respective timing of the governmental economic retreat and the emergence of democratic transition can vary. The retreat in Chile was at its height when an authoritarian government was in power, whereas in Argentina it gained momentum under democratic civilian rule. In Mexico a more cautious retreat appears to be occurring parallel to political liberalization within the one-party state. We shall pursue the question of the relationship between economic and political liberalization later, but we can note here that if state economic withdrawal begins under an authoritarian government, the businesses that emerge or grow in the freer market will have the opportunity to assert their political as well as their economic independence, for example in cooperating with foreign investors, so that the government's ability to manipulate the economy to maximize its political benefits will be lessened. Such a weakening of authoritarian control may occur simultaneously with the problem of confronting a discontented working class faced with increased unemployment and fewer welfare benefits as a result of free-market policies. The ultimate outcome will obviously depend on the resources and behaviour of a variety of groups, but the opportunity to exploit potential democratic openings is clearly there.

The Central American republics may be taken as examples of economies in which old economic elites, in this case in the form of plantation owners, gave way to newer groups in a more diversified economy. Under the old economic order, authoritarian government was a relatively simple process of elites using the army to crush challenges to the status quo and, when necessary, to take over the government of the country and run it in the interests of the elites. With a more complex economy the military often lacked both the necessary skills of economic management and the ability to negotiate with a range of pressure groups (see especially Black *et al.* 1984: 53–4; Painter 1986: 829–32, 1987: 50). The working-class population, while not as urbanized and articulate as in South America, was also likely to become more demanding as more cracks appeared in a less monolithic political structure. The prospects of the seeds for democratic transition being planted in such a situation are less bright than in the previous categories, since there is no reason why the army should not reach an accommodation with the new elites and continue to repress the masses, as indeed has been the case in El Salvador, Guatemala and Honduras for long periods. But the fact that armies have been involved in government for such long periods is itself indicative of a lack of consensus on how the country should be run – yet another case of 'whenever no other card is turned up clubs are trumps'. If repression becomes increasingly expensive, especially when foreign backers such as the United States threaten to withdraw their support, the search for a democratic opening may be pursued with renewed vigour.

Finally, countries that suffer economic collapse, usually on account of a combination of governmental ineptitude, a worsening of the terms of trade and natural disasters such as drought or crop failure, deprive rulers of their ability to shore up their authority through economic rewards and punishments. Since governments in such countries, which are often poor ex-colonies with heterogeneous populations, have generally enjoyed little public legitimacy from the outset, the loss of the power of patronage leaves them with few means of securing public cooperation (see especially Allen 1992, on Benin). The authoritarian regime is easy to topple, though there is no guarantee that it will be replaced by a democratic one. The main hope for democrats is that if authoritarianism is seen to have failed, free elections may be promised in the expectation of establishing a government with a degree of legitimacy, and thus effectiveness. This was the outcome in Uganda after periods of authoritarian rule under Amin and Obote (Brett 1992: 10), but any emerging democratic government is likely to lead a precarious existence.

One obvious conclusion from this brief survey is not only that economic factors set the context within which political actors can operate, as Cummings argues, but that economic changes, whether in the direction of industrialization, austerity, structural change or collapse, are likely to disturb current political arrangements. If a democratic government is already in power it will face the strain but, if the current rulers are authoritarian it may be their power base that is undermined as old centres of power crumble as groups outside the elite acquire new or additional resources, whether in terms of economic sanctions, organizational ability or increased support from key elements in society. This does not pave the way for an inevitable transition to democracy, but it creates opportunities that would not exist if the economy had remained static.

Political and economic liberalization

The term 'economic liberalization' is generally taken to mean the transfer of economic functions from the state to the private sector, whether directly through the transfer of state enterprises to private ownership, or indirectly through reduced public expenditure or reduced government regulation. The latter might lead to individuals purchasing education, health care or transport from private providers at a free-market price, as government provision becomes increasingly inadequate to meet people's needs, or to activities which were previously controlled by the state, such as the marketing of crops at government-controlled prices, being left to market forces.

The reasons for the liberalization process are largely outside the scope of this study. The process may interact with that of democratization, but its origins are largely independent of it. In the West, economic liberalization was helped by the ideological fervour of the 'New Right', which claimed that state intervention had retarded development by imposing higher taxes on enterprise and diverting resources to less efficient uses, but the process was hastened by the more pragmatic responses of politicians who found difficulty in sustaining public enterprise and social welfare at a time of economic recession. Since these politicians were responsible for much of the aid that had underwritten public enterprise and social welfare in the Third World, there was a growing temptation to say 'do as I do', and to make aid conditional on governmental retrenchment.

The relationship between political liberalization and economic liberalization is touched on in much of the literature, but seldom in a systematic way. Admirers of American capitalism take it for granted that the two are both desirable and complementary (see especially Huntington 1984; Chazan 1988: 132–4, 1989: 350; Diamond 1988: 26–7; Sincere 1991–2: 79–80), while Marxists, at least until recently, argued that democratic rights were meaningless if the means of production, and thus the key political decisions, were controlled by a small ruling class. 'One dollar, one vote' rather than 'one citizen, one vote' would be the norm. Taken to extremes, the market and the ballot box appear to offer conflicting rather than complementary means of deciding on the allocation of resources. We could thus decide on the number of hospitals to be built on the basis of what entrepreneurs were willing to invest and what patients were willing to pay, or on the basis of what voters, or the people representing them, deemed to be desirable. But in the real world opportunities for choice, whether economic or political, are generally constrained by elites whose 'political' and 'economic' powers are difficult to disentangle from one another. For those who genuinely believe in democracy, if only in the vague sense of empowering the people to decide how the nation's resources will be distributed while protecting certain 'individual rights', the balance of argument will hinge largely on whether they have a greater fear of political or economic exploitation. Again we can simplify by offering two extreme propositions:

1 Economic liberalization is complementary to political liberalization because continued state control of the economy encourages the use of political patronage and the diversion of public funds to manipulate or reward selected groups of citizens. The distribution of resources thus depends on the power of the minority who manipulate the system to 'buy' votes or to overrule public preferences, and the citizen is left with very limited choices. The lack of freedom to make largely 'economic' choices is likely to spill over into the political sphere, as citizens have come to accept paternalism, clientelism or authoritarianism. (To these arguments could be added the pragmatic one that Third World states (and many not in the Third World) are often inefficient, if not corrupt, in implementing policies, even if the policies represent the will of the majority. A state-owned railway attempting to implement an integrated transport policy might thus be a greater burden on the community than a railway company seeking private profit.)
2 Economic liberalization, if equated with leaving the distribution of resources to market forces, will remove the protection previously enjoyed by the poorest and least privileged citizens. Decisions which would otherwise be at least partly within the grasp of the majority, on matters such as the extent of social welfare, the redistribution of wealth and the planning of the environment, will be in the hands of a wealthy elite, or of foreign investors.

Such rarefied ideological arguments might not appear to have any immediate relevance to our concern with transitions to democracy, where decisions are more likely to be taken at the margin, and often for non-ideological reasons, rather than between the extremes of complete state control and *laissez-faire*, but it would be helpful to know whether economic liberalization is a stimulus to political liberalization or a consequence of it, or whether both are the result of some common external force.

One immediate question to ask is 'liberalization for what?' In the Third World we are not looking mainly at 'socialist' economies where the state owns most of the means of production, but at mixed economies where the state enjoys extensive powers of patronage and coercion which can be used as a means of channelling resources to favoured individuals and groups. In some countries, such as Nicaragua and Tanzania, these powers have been used in an attempt to reduce the gap between rich and poor, but they have been used more frequently to maintain the privileges of existing elites or to buy off potential challengers, in addition to lining the pockets of individual politicians and their immediate followers. While it might seem attractive to transform these interventionist states with kleptomaniac tendencies into democratic socialist states that use public resources for the common good, the prospects of such a transformation are minimal, if only because of the collapse of the Soviet bloc, and the insistence of potential Western donors and investors on a capitalist economy would leave them with little foreign support.

If a socialist state is not feasible, would it not be possible to retain the same amount of state intervention, but use it to co-opt more representative groups, such as trade unions, social movements and previously underprivileged ethnic or religious minorities, into a corporate, democratic decision-making process? Even in Britain, which is frequently cited as an example of a country achieving industrialization with a night-watchman state, the extension of the franchise coincided with the extension of social welfare and the co-option of a variety of groups into areas of decision-making which had previously been left to market forces. By most definitions, political liberalization in Britain occurred during a period of 'economic socialization' rather than 'economic liberalization'.

When economic liberalization has been attempted in some former British colonies the prospects for political liberalization do not seem to have been enhanced. Schatz, Sandbrook and Stoneman all suggest that the retreat of the state may lead to greater hardship and discontent, and thus to greater repression in response (Schatz 1987: 130–7; Sandbrook 1988: 256; Stoneman 1991: 11), and Uwazurike notes the unpopularity incurred by the Nigerian military government's reliance on market forces, which raised unemployment, though he also refers to the use of the non-market device of a wage freeze (Uwazurike 1990). This should serve to remind us that some governments are selective with the economic areas they choose to 'liberalize' – freedom for entrepreneurs in Pinochet's Chile existed alongside strict restrictions on trade unions.

The curtailment of welfare benefits, and of policies to stimulate employment, might be seen as necessary, if regrettable, attempts at retrenchment in difficult economic times, and as different in kind from attempts to demolish a more elaborate state interventionist structure, as in much of Latin America and South Korea. While this demolition can be explained partly as a pragmatic response to straitened economic circumstances, it also had its roots in conflicting political pressures, many of which cut across the traditional divide between the 'interventionist left' and 'free-market right'. State intervention had evolved not so much as part of a grand socialist design but as a means of politicians rewarding their supporters in political systems where followers frequently lacked the deference, class solidarity or ideological commitment that often sustained the leaders of Western

democracies in their formative years. This is not to say that state intervention in the West did not also involve payoffs to powerful groups, as witness
the generous subsidies given to farmers, but regular free elections did check
the worst abuses of power. In the Third World, authoritarianism has been
more common than representative democracy, or even populism, and there
was less reason to expect that the directions of state intervention would
reflect the popular will rather than the requirements of influential elites.
Thus any 'rolling back of the state', while it may cause hardship by increas-
ing unemployment and reducing social welfare, also represented an attack
on the privileges of elites and, in countries such as Argentina and Mexico
with more developed party systems, on the privileges of party functionaries and their clients. Thus we find writers such as Cammack and Cummings,
whose personal preferences would almost certainly be for an interventionist
socialist state, celebrating economic liberalization as a necessary step towards liberal democracy.

> The general withdrawal of the state, under financial pressure, from
> social and economic intervention undermines the basis of continued
> patronage politics. . . . The accepted principles of liberal democracy
> and current practice of liberal economic doctrines stand in flagrant
> contradiction to the two central strategies – co-optation and repres-
> sion – upon which current Latin American democracy generally con-
> tinues to depend.
>
> (Cammack 1991: 550)

Cummings, as we have noted, saw 'bureaucratic authoritarianism' as ser-
ving exclusive groups in South Korea, so that there was a parallel between
excluded businesses wanting economic liberalization and excluded citizens
wanting political liberalization (Cummings 1989: 27–32). While the former
could presumably have been attempted without the latter, it would have
left any government with a precarious power base.

At a theoretical level there is the long-standing argument that economic
liberalization makes for more diverse centres of power. People whose wealth
and status have been achieved independently of the state, it is argued, will
be in a better position to challenge authority, whether individually or
through political parties and organized groups, than people whose incomes
and prospects depend on the state, whether directly through public employment or indirectly through being at the mercy of the state, for decisions
such as the issue of import licences, the award of contracts, the granting of
planning permission or the distribution of subsidies. While there is much
force in such arguments, it is more difficult to establish whether economic
liberalization in any Third World country has reached the stage where
sufficient people of independent means have emerged as challengers of
authority, or whether such institutionalized political competition as has
emerged owes much to economic liberalization.

Much of the confusion arises when authors mix real-world cases to
describe political systems they dislike with theoretical, and possibly

Table 6.3   Democracy and authoritarianism in interventionist and non-interventionist states

	Interventionist	Non-interventionist
Democratic	*Socialist state* Extensive state intervention reflecting perceptions of needs in society, and possibly the wishes of the majority. State structures are the servant of the citizen. Democracy operates through participation in state structures, and possibly through competitive elections.	*Night-watchman state* Minimal state intervention. Distribution of resources depends on consumer preferences, backed by money, in competitive markets. Market forces are the servant of the citizen. Democracy operates through free elections, and the countervailing power of institutions independent of the state.
Authoritarian	*Clientelistic state* Extensive state intervention reflecting the needs of politicians and elites to retain their power bases. State structures are controlled by the few. Democracy is restricted by the ability of elites to divert state resources to supporters and away from opponents.	*Capitalist state* Minimal (direct) state intervention. Distribution of resources depends on manipulation by capitalist elites in imperfect or monopolistic markets, often supported by the police and armed forces. Democracy is restricted by political inequality stemming from economic inequality.

unattainable, models to suggest the desired objective. A four-fold classification of political systems based on the axes of democracy and state intervention is suggested in Table 6.3. Democratic types are shown at the top and the authoritarian at the bottom, while interventionist states are shown on the left and non-interventionist on the right. We can thus conceive of: (a) an ideal socialist state in which extensive state intervention reflects rulers' perceptions of needs within society, and in which democracy is sustained through popular participation within state structures; and (b) an ideal night-watchman state in which the distribution of resources depends on consumer preferences, and democracy is sustained through free elections and the countervailing power of institutions independent of the state. But in the real world we are more likely to meet 'perversions' of both systems. (The reader may prefer the term 'liberal state' to 'night-watchman state', but it seems misleading to tie liberalism to any particular set of economic arrangements.) The interventionist state is more likely to be clientelistic than socialist, with state intervention reflecting the needs of politicians and elites to retain their power bases, and with democracy restricted by the ability of elites to divert state resources to supporters and away from opponents. Similarly, the non-interventionist state is more likely to be capitalist than night-watchman, with the distribution of resources dependent less on consumer preferences than on manipulation by capitalist elites in imperfect or monopolistic markets, often supported by the police and armed forces. Democracy is thus restricted by political inequality stemming from economic inequality.

In an imperfect world there is nothing remarkable about the preference of some democrats for the capitalist state as the lesser evil to the clientelistic state, or for hoping that the former will eventually grow into a night-watchman state in which market forces become the servant of 'empowered' citizens. Conversely, there are (or were) some democrats (though not nearly so many) who prefer the minimal protection the underprivileged enjoy in the clientelistic state, and hope that this will eventually evolve into a socialist state in which the machinery of state becomes the servant of participating citizens rather than the tool of elites.

Since the 'democracy via capitalism' school is much larger than the 'democracy via clientelism' school, it is the views of the former that require scrutiny. It is one thing to argue that democracy would flourish in a competitive economy in which corporate wealth was widely distributed and no one economic group was able to dominate the rest. It is another to believe that such a utopia is just around the corner from privatization and reduced government expenditure and regulation, or to hail every withdrawal from state marketing schemes, or every self-help scheme among the newly unemployed, as a step along the road to democracy. We have noted that such a rolling back of the state has often led to greater hardship, rather than democracy, in West Africa, and to greater authoritarianism in response to expressions of discontent, while countries on the other side of Africa, such as Kenya, Malawi and Zimbabwe, have for years combined free-market economies with political repression. In Chile, and to a lesser extent Uruguay, economic liberalization reached its zenith under repressive military governments. These examples should remind us that free-market policies are not some 'politically neutral' means of allocating resources, in contrast to the 'politically interfering' policies of interventionist governments. Both are means of allocating resources in which governments are clearly aware of the likely 'winners' and 'losers'. No one would question the self-interest of clientelistic governments in using state patronage to reward their supporters, but is there any less self-interest in using market forces to reward multinational corporations, or weaken trade unions and peasants, if such policies will strengthen a government's power base?

Much of the argument about the relationship between political and economic liberalization has so far been negative. We can acknowledge that groups which have always enjoyed a degree of autonomy from the state, such as the church, the bar and to lesser extent the university, have often provided centres of resistance to authoritarianism, and may be strengthened by the rise of groups with greater economic autonomy (the growth of 'civil society' in modern terminology), but there is a danger of equating the growth of a bourgeoisie with the growth of economic liberalization, which in turn allegedly promoted political liberalization. Such a pattern was discernible in many Western countries, but it may be the growth of the bourgeoisie as a whole, not just the section of it engaged in private trading, that is the important factor (see especially Sklar 1987: 704–6, on Africa). This was almost certainly the case in the Soviet bloc, where a growing middle class created by socialist industrialization demanded political liberalization at a time when there had been little economic liberalization. In tropical Africa it is more often academics and lawyers than entrepreneurs who lead the demands for political liberalization. Their political programmes may include a freer economy, but that takes us to a consequence of political change rather than a cause. Insofar as political and economic liberalization are complementary, the explanation is often to be found in the attitudes of governments on which the Third World is dependent (see especially *Africa Confidential* 6 December 1991: 3–4). Western governments are increasingly making aid and investment conditional on greater use of both the ballot box and the market. The reasons for this are not immediately clear, bearing in mind the record of Europeans as colonial powers and Americans as supporters of military dictators in South America and Asia. At an altruistic level, one might credit the Western governments with a belief in the ideal of liberal democracy, even if they had found practical reasons in the past for supporting authoritarians, including the now defunct excuse that these authoritarians were bulwarks against communism. The preference for economic liberalization reflects the fashion current in most Western countries, though it may also be influenced by experience of dealing with exceptionally inefficient and corrupt interventionist governments.

Conclusion

In attempting to explain the economic bases of democratic transition in the Third World, we are left with few of the certainties that have been linked to the relationship between economics and democracy in the West. All the European countries, together with those settled by Europeans in North America and the Antipodes, achieved both pluralist democracy and industrialization, and relative affluence, even if the chronological relationship between political and economic change, the types of political actors involved and the form of democracy varied. Indeed, one could argue that, if the bourgeois revolution in Russia in 1917 had not been overtaken by the peculiar circumstances of the First World War, which created the widespread disorder that enabled the Bolsheviks to triumph, the pluralist pattern would have spread across Eastern Europe as well at a much earlier stage.

In the Third World there have been fewer transitions to industrialization and economic affluence and fewer transitions to democracy, and the former and the latter have not necessarily gone together. Singapore and Taiwan have achieved few significant democratic developments to match their impressive economic records, and South Korea has moved only fitfully towards democratization, whereas Nicaragua, Senegal and Zambia have moved from authoritarianism to pluralism without any significant economic developments. The relationship of 'economic liberalization' with democratic development remains ambiguous. Few of the countries with extensive state control over their economies have moved far in the direction of pluralism and, other things being equal, one might expect the growth of autonomous centres of economic power to enhance pluralism, but such growth is more likely to be part of a gradual evolutionary process than an immediate response to the demands of the International Monetary Fund or foreign governments.

In the West it is often argued that authoritarianism ceased to be a feasible form of long-term government once an educated, articulate population conferred legitimacy only on rulers chosen by competitive election; and diverse centres of power, autonomous from the state, protected interests and beliefs that no power holder could overrule. For their part, rulers had little inducement to outstay their welcome, as there were ample opportunities to pursue wealth and status outside politics and without dependence on political patronage.

Few Third World countries, if any, are close to this state of affairs. Relative poverty, in societies where there is little consensus on the basis of legitimate government, still gives many advantages to those who win and retain power by undemocratic means. In this context it is often the destabilizing effects of economic changes, rather than the benefits of steady economic growth, that may sow the seeds of democratic challenge. Authoritarian governments may appear immovable in periods of economic calm when faced by populations with little expectation and even less experience, of government based on free choice. But economic changes, whether in the direction of industrialization unleashing new social forces, austerity altering the balance of rewards to clients or economic collapse leaving the rulers impotent, can create a political vacuum that democrats may seek to fill, if only because there are few would-be rulers available who can derive legitimacy from any other source. Unlike in the European autocracies of earlier times, there is no 'king across the water' to offer a legitimate continuation of authoritarianism. A military coup is conceivable, but if this is directed against a civilian autocracy, the incoming soldiers will at least have to pay lip service to the ultimate objective of democratic rule, which thus offers potential openings, and if the coup is directed against an existing military government it might do too little to satisfy people that the old order has been removed. Forces are thus at work which make the demise of authoritarianism a serious possibility, even if no inevitable march towards democracy is set in train. Economic change provides the opportunity. We must now look at the ability of groups in society to exploit this opportunity.

The dynamics of transition 2: the configuration of interests

Before we can attempt to explain the ultimate arrival of countries at the destination of pluralist democracy, we need to map out the jungle of conflicting interests and structures through which they have to pass. Indeed, we require at least four different 'maps' to enable us to view the jungle from different perspectives. We need to examine:

1 The varied types of authoritarian government against which would-be democrats are rebelling.
2 The varied groups in society that may sustain or undermine authoritarianism.
3 The underlying rules and conventions of political conflict, and the political institutions to which they give rise, which may be partially suspended by authoritarian governments, but which can provide guidelines for political behaviour as transition gets underway.
4 The line-up of 'government' and 'opposition' forces, which consist not of exclusive camps but of 'members' and 'supporters' with varying degrees of commitment, and which will seek to attract many unattached 'floaters'. Membership of these groups will, of course, overlap with membership of the groups mentioned in point 2, but I attempt to make a distinction between the roles of sustaining or opposing the government on the one hand, and on the other, the more independent role of groups such as churches or trade unions, which exist primarily to look after the interests of their members or to pursue non-political objectives.

An examination of these variables may help us to pursue the questions raised in Table 6.1: What opportunities and limitations do different forms of authoritarianism provide for would-be democrats? What are the respective roles of formal political structures and forces in the wider society in the process of democratization? And to what extent and for what reasons is democratization a 'top-down' or a 'bottom-up' process?

Table 7.1 Types of authoritarian government and the opportunities for democratic transition

Type of authoritarian government	Prospects for transfer of power	Analytical problems
Military	1 Few institutional barriers to democratization 2 Military governments generally see themselves as only temporary 3 Conflict between 'political' and 'professional' functions may encourage a return to barracks 4 Military governments have a narrower power base of people and groups dependent on authoritarianism	1 Army as an institution is likely to remain intact, and may therefore intervene again 2 Left-wing military governments frequently reject bourgeois democracy 3 Successor government will not necessarily be democratic 4 Is the existence of a military government a cause or a symptom of the nature of political conflict?
One-party	1 One-party regimes often claim exclusive legitimacy and ideological purity 2 Broader power base with a vested interest in retaining power 3 Party leaders may show greater skill than soldiers in devising a viable successor regime	Many Third World ruling parties are less tightly structured or ideologically coherent than those in the totalitarian model
Personal	1 Personal rulers seldom want to surrender power, but have a limited lifespan 2 They may leave few viable authoritarian structures behind	Is personal rule a reflection of political polarization, which might make democratization difficult?

The varied patterns of authoritarianism

Huntington offers a four-fold typology of authoritarian regimes: one-party, personal, military and racial oligarchic (Huntington 1991–2: 582). He places only South Africa in the latter category, and that country had not completed any transition to democracy at the time of writing, so we shall concentrate on the other three categories. Huntington summarizes neatly the prospects of each type being supplanted by democracy, and some of his ideas are pursued in Table 7.1.

Military rulers are the ones best able and most willing to retreat, provided there are sufficient personal safeguards from prosecution for the
soldiers, and institutional safeguards for the resources and autonomy of the
army as a whole, but displaced armies find it easier to return to power than
other authoritarians because the army as an institution is more likely to
remain intact than a displaced authoritarian party, or the entourage of a
displaced personal ruler (Huntington 1991–2: 582–3). This is generally borne
out by experience, though one could make a distinction between right-
wing or largely 'apolitical' military governments with the relatively modest
objectives of restoring order, or retaining or restoring the power of dominant elites, as in most of Latin America, tropical Africa and Southern Asia,
and left-wing military governments which seek a more thoroughgoing
social transformation, as in North Africa and the Middle East. Soldiers in
the former group will often prefer an early return to barracks as the army
faces a growing strain of reconciling its professional functions with the
process of government (see especially Clapham and Philip 1985: 3). This
does not guarantee that the successor government will be a democratic one,
but the impending departure of the military at least creates an opportunity
for democrats. Left-wing military governments are likely to cling to power
for much longer, and to have little time for bourgeois democracy. A
transition to democracy is less likely than a transition to Huntington's
other authoritarian types: one-party rule, through an army-created party to
give the soldiers a greater legitimacy (as in Egypt), or personal rule (as in
Libya). Of the more conservative military governments, those in Indonesia
and Paraguay are the only obvious ones to have gone along a similar road.

One-party and personal rule both present greater institutional and ideological barriers to democratization. Institutionally, there is the problem of
disentangling the party from the state and resisting the anti-democratic
pressures of party functionaries who have a vested interest in the status
quo, and ideologically there is the question of why people who have previously insisted on the party's exclusive right to determine the nation's
destiny should cease to proclaim such a right. Huntington (1991–2: 582–6)
focuses more on countries closer to the totalitarian model than on the
flimsier one-party states of Africa, but even the latter are likely to embrace
a wider range of powerful interests than a government relying on the army
as its main constituency.

Personal rulers are even more reluctant to retire than military rulers or
party politicians. Their departure is more likely to depend on death, whether
from natural causes, assassination or revolution. In the former case the
ruler's successors may seek a democratic transition if no other viable political structure appears to be available. Huntington cites the case of Spain,
though one could argue about how far Franco's rule was 'personal'. In
some cases personal rulers have sought legitimation through the ballot
box in elections or plebiscites of varying degrees of freedom and fairness.
Blatantly rigged elections bring democracy no closer, as with General
Pinochet's first appeal to the people of Chile, but more open ones, such as

his second, may enable the electorate to take advantage of the leader's miscalculation of his popularity and bring his rule to an end.

One danger in focusing on the structural form of authoritarian government is to assume that it is an independent variable. Was it only a matter of chance whether earlier attempts at democracy were suspended by military, one-party or personal rule, or did the outcome depend largely on the country's culture, history and recent political structure? The one-party states closest to the totalitarian model, which are Huntington's main concern, are generally devices for imposing authority on the more economically advanced societies, as in Eastern Europe, where a relatively complex political structure and a relatively plausible claim to legitimacy are considered necessary for effective authority. In contrast, a handful of soldiers can take and retain control of a less advanced country, such as Togo, through a rudimentary political structure with little coherent ideology. The 'non-totalitarian' one-party state, as found in much of tropical Africa, has frequently emerged gradually and by default, rather than through a dramatic event such as a coup, revolution or invasion, and has reflected the failure of democracy to flourish in a hostile environment.

Personal rule is, at first sight, more difficult to explain, since it has emerged in both relatively advanced Third World countries such as Chile, and relatively backward ones such as Zaire, in countries where much of 'traditional society' remained intact, such as Ethiopia under Haile Selassie, and countries where both 'traditional' and 'modern' structures had broken down, such as Uganda and the Central African Republic. Insofar as there is a common thread linking the emergence of personal rule in these countries, it appears to begin with a period of extreme polarization, whether along ideological lines as in Chile (and possibly Spain), or ethnic lines as in Uganda and Zaire. Such polarization makes any institutionalized resolution of conflict, by a party or a disciplined army, difficult, with the result that a leader is able to break free from the political structure that initially put him in power. In some cases the polarization may be exacerbated by foreign support for one faction, as in the case of Somoza in Nicaragua and Batista in Cuba, so that the internal power base becomes less important.

If we treat the type of authoritarian rule as a dependent variable, largely dependent on the type of society the authoritarians are attempting to rule, rather than an independent variable, any discussion of the prospects and nature of a transition to democracy must bear in mind the broader environment. Of the Third World countries cited by Huntington as undergoing democratization between 1974 and 1990, the only ones to begin that process from a starting point of personal rule were Chile, the Philippines and the dubious case of India (Huntington 1991–2: 583). We might infer that the small number of cases reflected not only the reluctance of personal rulers to depart but also the difficulty in establishing any consensus for democracy in the divided countries which had given rise to their emergence. Only two Third World one-party states were cited by Huntington as undergoing a transition to democracy – Grenada and Nicaragua – and observers might dispute the extent of eventual democracy in the former and the extent of initial one-party authoritarianism in the latter.

Why was there such a dearth of transitions from one-party rule to democracy? Huntington's explanation of institutional and ideological barriers has more force in the communist bloc than the Third World, where party structures are more rudimentary and ideologies vary from the vague to the incoherent, but we can acknowledge that many one-party regimes do enjoy limited reserves of legitimacy, which military regimes lack. It is often the case that the ruling party won power initially in a free or semi-free election, and that its leaders are people who have deliberately chosen careers in politics and might therefore be expected to act with some competence in plying their trade, in contrast to soldiers who can claim no electoral base and who become politicians by chance. While party functionaries may grow fat on the benefits of patronage under prolonged one-party rule, soldiers outside a ruling military junta may become increasingly restive as military government puts strains on an army trying to reconcile its formal functions with the burden of government. Other things being equal, we might thus expect an easier transition to democracy from military government than from one-party government.

Huntington's list of Third World countries achieving democratization certainly contains more from the military government category (13) than from any other, but closer inspection requires us to look at geography as well as type of authoritarian regime. Nine of these countries are in Latin America, two in Asia, where only four other countries have experienced military government, and only two in Africa, where military government has been much more widespread. Even these two, Nigeria and the Sudan, subsequently reverted to military rule. Put simply, military government is the typical form of authoritarianism in Latin America, with authoritarianism based on single-party rule virtually unknown outside Mexico, while authoritarian rule in Africa has been evenly divided between one-party and military governments. Asia outside the communist bloc has been closer to the Latin American model, though Singapore and Taiwan have experienced long periods of one-party domination.

In the light of this information, did the majority of transitions to democracy occur where they did because the countries initially had military governments rather than single party or personal rule? Or did they occur because the countries were situated in Latin America, where on most indicators they were more economically advanced than most of tropical Africa, together with South Korea which enjoyed even greater material prosperity, and Pakistan which enjoyed the benefit of a highly professionalized army with a clear notion of its correct role in society? The presence of military governments as the typical form of authoritarianism in these countries might suggest more than a series of historical accidents. Party politics in Latin America had emerged much earlier than in Africa, and party alignments reflected significant social, and not merely ethnic, divisions. Few of the countries (apart from Mexico, which is still a long way from democracy) had undergone the type of popular revolution that might usher in one-party rule or been invaded by other countries where such conditions prevailed. A 'totalitarian' ruling party was therefore unlikely to emerge, but so was the form of 'one-party rule by default' which is found in much of Africa, where weak opposition parties are suffocated by being deprived of the oxygen of state patronage or are too weak to resist a formal ban on their existence. The competing parties sustained by varied groups in Latin America, even in the face of persecution and rigged elections, cannot be eliminated so easily by a civilian government, so military government may be the only means of imposing authoritarian solutions, and thus provide the most common starting point for democratic transitions.

In Africa there is a greater element of chance in whether authoritarianism takes the single party or military form. Some countries have preserved civilian, and generally authoritarian, government since independence, while apparently similar neighbours have been subject to military government. Both are clearly viable forms of government, and whether a one-party regime survives the military challenge will depend largely on the personal inclinations of soldiers to mount such a challenge, which will in turn be influenced by calculations of the current and alternative benefits of the spoils of office, together with the chance elements that determine the success or failure of any coup. As to whether a one-party or a military regime provides the best starting point for a democratic transition in Africa, the arguments seem to be evenly balanced. A few years ago there was little reason to believe that any one-party regime would surrender power voluntarily, given the feebleness of the opposition and the contrast between the spoils of office and the meagre existence eked out by those not enjoying government patronage. The only hope for democracy seemed to be for the military to remove the one-party regime and then set the machinery in motion for free elections, as in Ghana, Nigeria and the Sudan. But the failure of the elected governments to deliver many tangible benefits, and thus to build up any effective bases of support, might suggest inherent weaknesses in the economy or society, and not just in the form of government. More recently the one-party regimes have shown a greater willingness to restore pluralist democracy without the need for the military to remove them first. Senegal and Zambia have already completed this process, and there are now few African one-party states which have not accepted the ultimate aim of pluralism. We shall explore the driving forces for this later in this chapter, but our immediate concern is whether such a regime is any better placed than a military one to facilitate a democratic transition.

Military governments have generally been quicker to accept the need for pluralism and to set the machinery for contested elections in motion, except in cases such as the Rawlings Government in Ghana, where they believe they are fulfilling a revolutionary mission, but there has often been an incongruence between the rules they impose and the reality of political conflict, in matters such as disqualifying unacceptable politicians from office, outlawing 'tribal' parties or, in the case of Nigeria, actually prescribing the number of parties which may exist and the ideologies to which they must subscribe. This may make the democratic system even more brittle than it would otherwise be. In contrast, leaders of one-party regimes may be slower to concede the desirability of political competition but, once converted, whether out of conviction or fear, they may take a more realistic view of the sort of pluralist system that will be able to survive in an imperfect world. President Kaunda's successors in Zambia, for example, may face dire economic problems but they are at least operating within a tried and tested political system, in which inter-party competition has been grafted on to existing features, rather than an untried system devised by the military or their politically inexperienced advisers.

Group attitudes and activities: a political sub-system?

Some of the pioneering students of comparative politics wrote of the existence of a 'political sub-system' beyond the formal structures of executives, bureaucracies, legislatures and elections. They conceded that the term was less applicable to the Third World than to the First and Second, partly because less complex societies did not have a comparable range of groups, which might range from sabbatarians and opponents of blood sports through tenants' associations and light bulb manufacturers to sporting bodies and proprietors of takeaway restaurants; and partly because the word 'system' implied a regular interaction between the groups and the formal political structures. In the Third World, governments do not generally get as involved in the complex range of political and administrative decisions which, in the West, would make for interdependence between the government and a myriad of groups, but it would be foolish to assume that there is therefore a void between governments exploiting the advantages of coercion and patronage, and citizens with no defence except disobedience or violence. Table 7.2 indicates some of the intermediaries between the citizen and the authoritarian government, and their possible contributions to democratic transition.

In the West in the formative years of democracy, one of the main institutions that bridged the gap between formal political authority and the informal world of individuals and groups was the mass political party, which was accessible to ordinary individuals yet also at the heart of major decision-making processes. In the Third World we have seen that parties are much more fragile structures, often used as a ladder that aspiring elites can kick away once they reach the top, or that can be lowered briefly when they need electoral support. At the risk of simplification we can attribute this weakness of parties to the way in which relatively strong states were established at an earlier stage of political development, so that parties were more likely to become creatures of those who controlled the

Table 7.2 Groups in society, political institutions and the prospects for democratic transition

Group or institution	Possible contribution to democratic transition	Possible weaknesses
Social movements	Ability to articulate interests and participate in protests when more formal groups are banned	Extreme demands; limited formal contacts with authority
Intermediate associations	Autonomy from the state; socialization of the people into political participation; strength of bases in society; moderate nature of demands	Limited sanctions
Guerillas	Ultimate sanction of force against recalcitrant authoritarians	Violence makes dialogue with authoritarians difficult; violence may be used as a pretext for retaining authoritarian rule
Constitutions	Opportunities for repairing perceived weaknesses in the political system	Problems of incongruence with the reality of power or values in society
Political parties	Provide a bridge between groups in society and formal political structures	Dangers of: (a) Subservience to the state (b) Parties increasing polarization (c) Parties restoring the status quo *ante*, and its inherent weaknesses

machinery of state than bodies with sufficient autonomy to set the priorities of current or future governments.

Where does this leave the rest of society? By its nature society will be comprised of groups of people with common interests. (Let us avoid the term 'pressure group' lest it give the impression of regular attempts to influence political decisions.) What is interesting from our point of view is the attention given to what are generally termed 'social movements' in Latin America, and the existence of possibly comparable groups in Africa. Many authors use the term but few define it. Cockcroft (1990) writes of the urban poor in Peru protesting against IMF-imposed austerity, slum dwellers and urban strikers in Brazil hastening the end of military government, and shanty-town dwellers leading the first popular uprising against General Pinochet. Munck refers to the 'varied social movements' in Chile, covering producers, consumers, health and education, who fuelled the protests of 1983 and 1984 (Munck 1989: 90–2), and Petras speaks of social movements in Central America encompassing a broad array of social classes and occupational, professional, civil and human rights associations, which 'dominated' the process of redemocratization in the pre-democratic phase. These groups included trade unions, the self-employed, squatters, the professions and universities (Petras 1990: 88). In terms of activities, as well as range of membership, the social movement seems to be equally ubiquitous. According to Grugel the 'popular sector' (which presumably embraced 'social movements') was involved in street and neighbourhood protests in Chile as a result of economic crises, and galvanized political parties into action, while mass participation was important again in the plebiscite that removed Pinochet and in the subsequent election campaign (Grugel 1991: 367–8). The works of Cockcroft, Munck and Petras imply a similar range of activities against authoritarian governments, but what does all this tell us except that 'the masses are revolting'? What is distinctive about social movements, as opposed to other vehicles of protest at other times and places, and are their objectives or their means of advancing them conducive to the process of transition to democracy?

The descriptions so far suggest a certain 'informality' about the organization of social movements, as compared with more tightly structured pressure groups, with no fixed membership, few rules and few contacts with authority, yet their ability to offer the oppressed mutual support, to embarrass governments through what, in other contexts, we would call direct action, and to make governments fear an enlargement of such action if their demands are not met, are signs of strength. If opposition to authoritarianism came mainly from political parties, governments could (and they frequently do) outlaw the parties and detain their key members, but the more spontaneous and unpredictable uprisings of social movements are more difficult to control. But can the undermining of authoritarianism be translated into the building of democracy? Cockcroft describes the aims of social movements as the redistribution of income and opportunity, and the punishment of the military rulers, and notes the absence of any organizational network to bring the groups together as 'the left' did in earlier times (Cockcroft 1990: 25–9). Even if the description of objectives is exaggerated or over-generalized, there is clearly a problem with a 'black and white' view of society, which is hardly conducive to negotiating a transition to democracy, quite apart from the absence of formal organizations to carry out the negotiation. Social movements can shake the foundations of authoritarianism. Whether this then leads to a democratic transition will depend on the willingness or ability of more articulate or better connected groups to support their cause, including intellectuals, political parties, the church, and ultimately members of the elite and the government itself. We shall return to these groups presently, but first we need to consider whether the social movement is a Third World phenomenon or a purely Latin American one.

Sandbrook speaks of the growth of 'intermediate associations' rather than social movements in Africa, including the Association of Recognized

Professional Bodies, which was instrumental in hastening the demise of the second military government in Ghana, trade unions, cooperatives and ethnic unions (Sandbrook 1988: 259–62). Sklar, too, refers to 'the high degree of autonomy for diverse non-party and extra-governmental organisations' (Sklar 1987: 698).

> Rural development associations and co-operatives resourcefully guard against attempts by governments and party officials to circumscribe their autonomy and subordinate them to outside powers. In Zimbabwe, the future of democracy appears likely to turn largely on the question of respect for the autonomy of demonstrably accountable organisations of small farmers. Similarly in Kenya 'peasant-initiated self-help development projects' are rural 'schools for democracy' that might be expected to foster its revival and growth nationally.
>
> (Sklar 1987: 699)

These appear to be more conservative groups than the social movements of Latin America, in societies where class conflict is much less polarized, and the moderate nature of their behaviour and demands may be reassuring for authoritarian rulers who are contemplating democratic restoration, though the reverse side of the coin is the more limited sanctions available if such democratization is not contemplated. But what is important is that on both continents we need to guard against the caricature of the powerful government and state confronting a powerless, unorganized population. The political sub-system may be less complex than in the West, but when authoritarians ban formal political opposition they may find that a varied range of less formal groups can ultimately engineer their destruction.

We have so far concentrated on groups which, for the most part, live within the law of the land even though they sometimes resort to violence against persons or property. We have said nothing about the contribution to democratic transition of 'guerillas' or 'terrorists' who resort to violent resistance as a way of life, and there is little in the literature to suggest that they make any contribution. Violent anti-government groups are more likely to be blamed for the reactions against them, which give authoritarians a pretext for displacing 'soft' democratic governments, as in Argentina and Uruguay, and such groups have usually remained on the margins of politics in any democratic transition. The main exceptions have been in Central America, although one's interpretation of 'if and when' democracy was established may depend on one's ideological standpoint. In Nicaragua, the Sandinista guerillas overthrew the Somoza dictatorship and established a pluralist system (according to some) and the Contra terrorists (aided by the United States government) subsequently forced the Sandinistas into conceding a more genuinely free election (according to others) in which the Sandinistas were defeated. In El Salvador, years of guerilla warfare appear to have forced the government to move from semi-competitive elections confined to right-of-centre parties to competitive elections open to all comers. Similar developments may yet occur in Guatemala, but observers

of a conservative persuasion might argue that the initial democratic openings, and the departure of military governments, had already been achieved
on account of the 'moderation' of other political actors. It is, perhaps, a
matter of degree. Realists would not expect a challenge to an authoritarian
government to be mounted without a degree of violence, whether from
stone-throwing mobs in spontaneous demonstrations or from organized
guerillas in the bush, but in the end it is the willingness to renounce violence,
by government and governed alike, that makes a democratic dialogue
possible.

A chapter on 'the configuration of interests' might seem unduly blinkered
if it ignored the interests of foreign capital and foreign governments, but
I have suggested in earlier chapters that these interests play a clearer role in
subverting democratic governments than in establishing them. This is not
because they are invariably on the side of the authoritarians but because
destruction, through withdrawing aid or investment or supplying arms to
subversives, is easier than the painstaking process of building democracy.
Western governments have certainly made clear their distaste for authoritarian rulers in recent years, and have increasingly made aid conditional on
democratization. This will obviously give advantages to pro-democratic
groups, unless the interpretation put on 'democracy' is an extremely per-
verse one, but it can at best be only an indirect influence on forces already
in motion.

The rules and conventions of political conflict and the role of institutions

A search for 'rules of political conflict' in authoritarian systems might seem
even more daunting than a search for a political sub-system, but no incoming authoritarian can wipe clean the slate of accepted behaviour in society.
Immediate questions, such as whether the deposed rulers are to be executed, imprisoned or allowed to flee into exile, whether some or all political
parties should be outlawed, and whether members of prominent groups
should be co-opted into the government, can all be related to long-standing
notions of how society should be ordered, which are likely to reflect both
an underlying culture and the realities of the distribution of power, which
are not suddenly altered because a new group has stormed the presidential
palace. Authoritarian rulers have shown varying degrees of deference towards the monarchy in Thailand, the chieftaincy in Ghana, the church in
Argentina and the multinational corporation in Chile, in each case revealing
something about the realities of power and the distinctive values of the
society in question.

These values are likely to be reflected in the political institutions that
regulate conflict. Such institutions may be suspended or immobilized by
authoritarians, but their outlines can easily reappear when the authoritarian
tide begins to ebb, and their nature can have an important bearing on the

nature and extent of democratization. Schmitter explains the relative success of democratic transitions in Southern Europe in terms of the varied
forms of democratic system that the histories of these countries and their
neighbours have bequeathed, in contrast to Latin America, where variations on the United States presidential model are the rule (and executive
power-sharing is presumably inhibited) (Schmitter 1986: 3–10). The
'Gaullist' solution in Turkey, where extremist parties are kept at bay by a
relatively strong president, constitutional monarchy in Spain, with its blend
of parliamentary democracy and historical continuity, and parliamentary
republicanism in Greece, where an unpopular monarchy has given way to
a largely decorative presidency, might all be cited as supporting examples
of the varied forms of pluralist democracy. 'Structures', in the sense of
formal bodies such as parties, legislatures and presidencies, can be created
or destroyed at will, but 'institutions' in Huntington's sense of stable,
recurring patterns of behaviour (Huntington 1968: 244–5), can only evolve
in the fullness of time. Welch suggests that institutional development is
helped by either a revolution, which presumably confers legitimacy on
political structures because they have been forged by the popular will, or
by a long period of independence, which leads him to be more optimistic
about the prospects for democratization in Latin America than in Africa
(Welch 1987: 17).

Within limits, differences in structures and institutions can make a difference to the prospects for democratization. Mainwaring has shown how
South American countries that appear similar in terms of socio-economic
development have vastly different party systems, which have made for
different patterns of transition (or non-transition) to democratic rule. In
Brazil's 'top-down' political system, parties have always been heavily dependent on the state, and the state allowed them to continue to function
even after the military had taken over, albeit with attempts by the military
to tilt the party system in their favour. Such continuity also implied the
continued existence of an elected congress and state governors. The transition to democracy was less abrupt than elsewhere, with the military
gradually retreating in the face of a succession of electoral setbacks. The
Chilean system, in contrast, was one of strong, autonomous parties, in a
powerful legislature, less willing to moderate their behaviour for the benefit
of the head of state. This autonomous, polarized system was deemed incompatible with military government, and parties suffered a long period of
suspension. Uruguay is different again, with the main parties largely frozen
in the narrow elitist mould of an earlier generation. Their restoration posed
no immediate threat to the military, but their inability to incorporate new
social groups contributed to the growth of extra-constitutional activity
before the military intervened, and may yet prove to be a weakness under
the restored civilian regime (Mainwaring 1988).

The major problem in tropical Africa is the one highlighted by Welch
regarding the countries' limited experience of politics since the end of colonial
rule. It is more difficult to recognize the existence of accepted, if sometimes

suspended, rules, conventions or institutions that would contribute to the democratic process. Impeccably democratic constitutions have been promulgated, and elites exist whose members claim to support the liberal democratic ideal, but in few cases has a consensus emerged on the constraints within which rulers should operate in practice, and few institutions have emerged which have been strong enough to impose checks on these rulers. Perhaps in time the autonomous groups indicated by Sandbrook and Sklar will offer institutional checks, but immediate experience suggests that the most universally recognized political rule in Africa is still 'winner takes all'.

Government, opposition and 'neutrals'

Our final perspective for viewing the configuration of interests out of which democracy may emerge is the conflict between 'government' and 'opposition'. While the 'social movements' and 'intermediate associations' to which we have referred may pursue demands that are ultimately incompatible with the current authoritarian government, and political institutions may exist which can ultimately facilitate the removal of the government, a transition to democracy still depends on the interaction between an authoritarian government and an opposition that wishes to displace it. In a pluralist system, members and supporters of governments and oppositions are relatively easy to identify, since both will be competing openly for votes. In an authoritarian system the opposition is less likely to declare itself openly, for fear of loss of life or liberty. Even on the government side, political campaigners will be less important than businessmen, bureaucrats, soldiers and policemen, who wield power behind the scenes (though such sources of support are not unimportant in liberal democracies).

There are many ways of classifying the line-up across the government–opposition divide. Huntington classifies the groups according to their degree of commitment to democracy, with democratizers, reformers, liberals and 'stand-patters' on the government side, and radical extremists and democratic moderates on the other. His argument, put simply, is that moderates on both sides offer the best prospects for democracy, and that they must therefore win over more supporters from the other groups, or push them into isolation (Huntington 1991–2: 589–90). An alternative method of classification would be a more 'structural' one. The government side can be seen as consisting of the central core of the small group actually wielding executive power (the cabinet, military junta, or personal ruler and his court) and the wider groups that have a commitment to, or interest in, preserving the status quo, including the dominant elite, the bureaucracy and possibly the army or dominant party. On the opposition side there may be political parties committed to capturing power, often operating underground or in exile, and armed groups acting either independently or as the military wings of parties, together with the 'intermediate associations' or 'social movements' that are likely to be opposed to much that the

Figure 7.1 Sources of initiative for democratization: government and opposition, elites and masses.

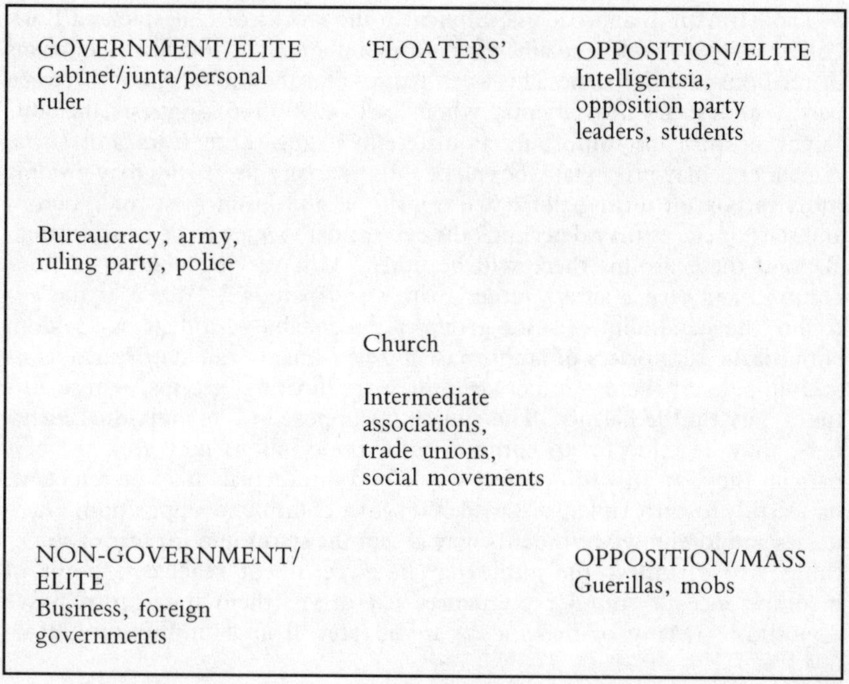

GOVERNMENT/ELITE   'FLOATERS'   OPPOSITION/ELITE
Cabinet/junta/personal   Intelligentsia,
ruler   opposition party
                                              leaders, students

Bureaucracy, army,
ruling party, police

                          Church

                          Intermediate
                          associations,
                          trade unions,
                          social movements

NON-GOVERNMENT/   OPPOSITION/MASS
ELITE   Guerillas, mobs
Business, foreign
governments

government is doing, but are not necessarily committed to democracy or to any specific alternative government.

Implicit in this approach, and in much of the literature on the groups involved in democratization, are four different 'poles' towards which groups may approximate: government/elite, non-government/elite, opposition/elite and opposition/mass. These are illustrated in Figure 7.1. Some groups occupy almost immovable positions at one of the 'poles'. The cabinet, military junta or the personal ruler and his court clearly occupy the 'government/elite' pole, while anti-government guerillas occupy the 'opposition/mass' pole in the opposite corner of the diagram. Between 'government/elite' and 'non-government/elite' will be groups which have been created or adapted to sustain the government, such as the state bureaucracy, the army, the police and the ruling party, but which are not actually a part of the government and could conceivably turn against it. At the 'non-government/elite' pole, many indigenous and foreign businesses and influential foreign governments will normally support the authoritarian government, unless it is anti-capitalist, and at the 'opposition/elite' pole will be found opposition party leaders and some members of the intelligentsia and students (though not necessarily the majority of these). This leaves a variety of 'floating' groups which do not have any automatic allegiance to any of the poles, including the church, intermediate associations, trade unions and social movements.

The 'structural' approach is implicit in the works of Gillespie and Karl. Gillespie (1990: 67–9) explains the nature of democratic transitions in terms of relations among parties, between parties and the military, and between parties and social movements, while Karl (1990: 5–6) suggests that different groups are important at different stages. Elite fears and social movements may precipitate the end of authoritarian rule, parties may become more important during the actual transition, and businesses, trade unions and state agencies may determine the type of democracy to be consolidated. Beyond these groups there will be others with varying degrees of non-commitment (fence-sitters rather than 'stand-patters'?). While at the extremes the standpoint of some groups is predictable – students are seldom enthusiastic supporters of authoritarian governments and state bureaucrats seldom subvert them – in between there are 'floating' groups, whose attitudes may tip the balance. The church, as opposed to its individual members, may be reluctant to commit itself, trade unions may seek the best bargain they can in an imperfect world and intellectuals may be reluctant, or fearful, to turn sullen dissatisfaction into committed opposition. Businesses and foreign governments may accept the status quo for fear of something worse, unless the authoritarian government reaches a point of incompetence or moral repugnance that drives them into more active opposition. (Many of these ideas are adapted from Huntington 1991–2: 604.)

Whichever method of classification one uses, it is clear that authoritarianism breaks down on account of a changed position of some of these groups, either because a group has changed its attitudes or because there has been a change in its strength, possibly as a result of a change in its size or resources. One of the questions raised in Table 6.1 was the extent to which democratic transitions can be explained as processes initiated from the 'top down' or the 'bottom up'. The pursuit of such a question arouses interest because it may throw light on the extent to which the masses are able to determine their own destiny rather than accepting whatever crumbs fall from the elite table, and because it will have implications for the type of democracy that emerges. Will it be an egalitarian, participatory democracy or of the Schumpeterian variety, in which the masses choose which elites shall rule them? Answers, if any exist, will clearly vary between different times and places. (The words 'top' and 'bottom' in the literature are generally used interchangeably to cover both the 'government/opposition' and 'elite/mass' axes. Huntington's main interest is in the respective roles of government and opposition in democratization, whereas most Latin Americanists appear to be more interested in the elite/mass dimension. Our concern in this chapter is mainly with the latter, but in Africa the distinction between government and elite can become blurred in the absence of powerful autonomous centres of power.)

If we begin with the least controversial area, few people would deny that such democratization as has occurred in tropical Africa has been mainly from the top down. Alubo and Uwazurike note the way in which the latest transition in Nigeria has been tightly controlled by the military, who have decided who shall be disqualified from office, which political parties shall be permitted, what may be debated and what ultimately goes into the constitution (Alubo 1989: 111–19; Uwazurike 1990). Duodo has described a transition in Ghana in which the real voice of the people is not heard, with the government choosing the organizations to be represented in the consultative assembly and controlling the drafting of the constitution (Duodo 1991). At a more general level, Sandbrook suggests that 'dominant groups' in Africa may acquiesce to democratization to 'restore legitimacy to the social order', in the hope of providing more regularized, open decision-making and attracting foreign support (Sandbrook 1988: 252–3). Democracy, in other words, provides a more settled environment in which elites may continue to enjoy their privileges. In societies with no large industrial proletariat and little experience of mass participation in political parties, trade unions or social movements, there are few opportunities for upward pressure. The masses might be more enthusiastic about democracy if they associated it with material prosperity, or if they associated authoritarianism with the persecution of the mass of people beyond the ranks of immediate dissidents. But their limited experience of pluralist politics has often been of the few enriching themselves at the expense of the many, while authoritarian governments, although often incompetent, have generally lacked the need or the means to repress the masses on the scale of a Galtieri or a Pinochet. Brutal personal rulers such as General Amin have been the exception, and their disruption of society has left even less scope for the masses to build up resistance than does a more orderly military or one-party government.

In Latin America opinion is divided more evenly. Levine argues that democracy has emerged not just as a compromise between civilian elites weary of authoritarianism and economic failure, and soldiers wanting to repair the army's shattered morale after the strains of office, but because elite demands for democracy are strengthened by the positive support of the masses, frequently transmitted through political parties (Levine 1988). We have noted Petras's view that re-democratization in the pre-democratic phase in Central America is 'dominated by social movements' (Petras 1990: 88). Karl notes the importance of political parties and trade unions in organizing large demonstrations in 1983 which precipitated the downfall of the Uruguayan military government (Karl 1990: 156–7). Grugel argues that it was the 'popular sector' in Chile which galvanized political parties into action and ensured the defeat of General Pinochet in the plebiscite (Grugel 1991: 367–8). At the other extreme, Cardoso argues that the initial resistance to authoritarianism in Latin America was not from social movements but from progressive sections of the middle class, such as priests, academics, journalists and relatives of political prisoners (Cardoso 1986–7). Baloyra asserts that 'factors related to elite conflict appear to be more relevant than any configuration conjuring up a vision of masses rushing to the barricades' (Baloyra 1987: 38). Cummings sees democratization in South Korea as a result of conflict and negotiation among the state, the military and the business elite, influenced by the United States, with the goal of demobilizing the popular sector (Cummings 1989: 33).

In such academic conflicts there is always the danger of the protagonists talking past each other. The proportions of initiative from above and below are obviously matters of degree. If transition to democracy implies giving the masses political influence they did not enjoy before, it is difficult to imagine them remaining indifferent to the opportunities they might exploit to advance their own position, while any transition in which rulers took no initiative would be better termed a 'revolution'. There are also questions of the time-scale and the magnitude of the initiatives taken. If, for example, we accept Cardoso's assertion that priests and academics were spreading subversive words about the government before workers started taking to the streets, does this constitute sufficient evidence that the former activity was significant in initiating the process of transition, or that the latter activity was only possible as a result of it? Grugel, Karl and Petras all take the view that social movements were important at an earlier stage, with political parties following their lead, but does this imply a bottom-up process with opportunistic politicians waiting to seize the opportunity after the masses have provided the initial cannon fodder, or is it a matter of opposition to authoritarianism manifesting itself in different ways as new opportunities, such as the lifting of censorship or the re-admission of political exiles, present themselves? One could salute the courage of the masses in taking to the streets, but still argue that the reality of political power condemns them to be minor actors in the democratization process. Conversely, one could admire the skills of opposition party leaders in negotiating with authoritarian politicians but still attribute their presence at the negotiating table to pressures from the masses.

To a large extent it is a question of 'horses for courses'. If we are seeking to understand democratic transitions, as opposed to revolutions, we are looking for means by which power is transferred, usually peacefully, in such a way as to ensure that sufficient consensus prevails to enable a pluralist system to function. Even if one does not share Huntington's obsession with 'moderation', it seems clear that such a transfer of power will involve a range of compromises, which require a degree of discipline on the non-governmental side. If, as Cockcroft says, social movements demand greater social equality and the punishment of the authoritarian rulers, and lack any organizational network, they are unlikely to be able to negotiate successfully and are likely to be superseded by political parties. There may, of course, be an overlap in membership, but party members who continue to make the same undiluted demands for the rights of the masses as they made as members of social movements are not likely to make much headway.

Conclusion

Implicit in much of this chapter has been the argument that attempts to understand the emergence of democracy through the interaction between groups, and the interests they represent, do not so much require us to choose between competing explanations, but to use a variety of explanations to illuminate the subject. To ask whether the structure of an authoritarian regime is 'more important' than the nature of the groups in society resisting it, in explaining the form and extent of any transition to democracy, is less helpful than to look at both elements and at the extent to which both may be a reflection of a society with its own deeply entrenched political culture (or cultures) and values. These in turn give rise to certain unwritten rules of the political game, even if it is not necessarily a gentlemanly game or one in which the rules are fair as between the strong and the weak. The players may, of course, gain or lose resources by luck or judgement, and this will affect their ability to control events. In the long run, major economic changes may change the society and the rules by which it lives, but democratic transitions are generally processes occupying much less than a decade, so that the economy and society which previously sustained authoritarianism will not be radically different from those within which the transition occurs. Society will consist of a variety of elite and non-elite groups, including political structures, which provide the raw material of political conflict or cooperation, and it is the contrast between these groups, and their values and resources, in different countries that provides the wide variety of attempts at democratic transition.

Even the 'top-down' versus 'bottom-up' explanations of transition turn out to be as much complementary as competing explanations on closer inspection. There may be extreme cases such as the Nigerian army at one end, laying down the conditions for democratic competition while most of the population remained powerless to intervene, and the Argentine army at the other, departing under a cloud after economic mismanagement and defeat in the Falklands, but most transitions are only possible because a variety of groups take a variety of initiatives at different stages. We now move on from exploring the groups to exploring the actual interactions between them that may produce varied democratic outcomes.

8

The dynamics of transition 3: the resolution of conflicts

The process by which conflicts between the defenders of authoritarianism and proponents of democracy are resolved is not an easy one to observe or analyse. Other types of political conflict are more clearly structured, and have more clearly delineated beginnings and ends: a war is declared and the spoils go to the victors; revolutionaries take to the streets and eventually execute the king; soldiers storm the presidential palace and stage a coup, or the monarch dissolves parliament and an election is won by a leader who can command the support of the newly elected majority. But in a conflict between authoritarians and democrats it is more difficult to know who is on which side; or when, where or how the key contests are being fought, by what means, or over what. Even the original existence of authoritarianism or the outcome may be in dispute. Was India an authoritarian state when Indira Gandhi declared a state of emergency? Did Pakistan become a democracy when General Zia's successors permitted a contested election, and did it remain so after Benazir Bhutto was defeated by an army-supported opposition? Did Nicaragua become a democracy when the Sandinistas took power, or only after they were defeated in a contested election?

The latter type of question may require subjective judgements that are beyond the scope of mere political scientists, though I have attempted to set out different conceptions of democracy earlier in this study. It is the former questions of who, when, where, how and what that are of more immediate interest. What are the ingredients of the various political conflicts that may result in a transition to democracy, how are they resolved, and what bearing does the nature of the process of resolution have on the nature of the democracy which emerges?

In Table 8.1 I suggest five different ways of viewing the process of transition and five possible outcomes which will have a bearing on the way in which the democratic process operates. Without going back to our

Table 8.1 A classification of democratic transitions, and hypotheses on their impact on democratic outcomes

Criteria for classification	Likely democratic or undemocratic outcomes				
	Consensus	*Stability*	*Equality, popular participation*	*Elite veto*	*Military or external veto*
1 Groups dominating transition process (Huntington)					
(a) Government	Indeterminate	Indeterminate	Low	High	High
(b) Opposition	Indeterminate	Indeterminate	Indeterminate	Low	Indeterminate
(c) Balance between government and opposition	High at elite level	High	Indeterminate	Low	Low
(d) External	Low	Low	Low	High	High
2 Processes of transition (Karl)					
(a) Pact	High at elite level	High	Low	High	Possible
(b) Imposition	Indeterminate	Indeterminate	Indeterminate	High	High
(c) Reform and revolution	Low	Low	High	Low	High
3 Compatibility of objectives of different actors (Share)					
(a) Consensus	High	High	Low	Possible	Possible
(b) Conflict	Low	Low	Possible	Possible	Possible
4 Extent and pace of changes (Karl, Share)					
(a) Moderate	High at elite level	Indeterminate	Low	High	Possible
(b) Radical	Low	Low	High	Low	High
(c) Gradual	High at elite level	High	Low	High	Possible
(d) Rapid	Possible	Possible	Possible	Possible	Possible
5 Sequences of changes (Cardoso, Diamond, Ethier). Precedence given to:					
(a) Civil liberties	Indeterminate	High	Low	High	Indeterminate
(b) Participation	Indeterminate	Low	High	Low	Indeterminate
(c) Contestation	Indeterminate	Indeterminate	——Seldom given precedence——→	Indeterminate	
(d) Social reform	High	High	High		High

earlier conceptions of democracy in detail, let us assume that, at a minimum, it requires free contested elections and a degree of freedom of expression and association under the rule of law. Beyond these minimal if vague qualifications, a democratic system may enjoy varying degrees of consensus, stability, equality and popular participation, and may be constrained by the presence or threats of veto by indigenous elites, the military or foreign powers. These variables are set out in the column headings in Table 8.1. In the rows are set out five different criteria which have been used by different authors, explicitly or implicitly, for classifying democratic transitions. These revolve around the questions of:

1 Who dominates the transition? This may turn out to be the government, the opposition(s), a balance between government and opposition, or external powers.
2 What is the process by which conflicting pressures are resolved? Is there negotiation between two or more parties, the imposition of a solution by one party (possibly a foreign power) or a revolutionary overthrow of the existing order? Put symbolically, is the most visible symbol the negotiating table, the white flag or the red flag?
3 To what extent are the objectives of the different actors compatible with one another? Is there room for consensus, or is democracy achieved through a conflict within which there are clear 'winners' and 'losers'?
4 What are the extent and pace of the changes from authoritarianism to democracy? These can be plotted on 'moderate–radical' or 'gradual–rapid' axes.
5 Finally, what is the sequence in which the changes, which mark steps along the road to democracy, occur? If democracy implies the existence of political contestation, participation, civil liberties and, perhaps, an element of social equality to bolster political rights, why may these democratic requirements be conceded to different degrees, and in different sequences, at different times and places, and with what results?

In the body of Table 8.1 certain hypotheses about the likely impact of the row variables on the outcomes in the column headings are advanced. Some of these may be little more than tautologies. It seems obvious, for example, that if a democratic transition is dominated by an external power, that power is likely to be strong enough to exercise substantial veto powers over subsequent events. Similarly, it seems extremely likely, unless some major unforeseen event occurs after democratization, that transitions built around consensus will be more likely to usher in consensual democracies than those built around conflict, or that political systems undergoing radical transformations, or those in which increased popular participation is one of the earliest reforms to be effected in the transitional period, will be more conducive to popular participation in the new order than those systems in which the degree of change is more moderate or the priority in reform is more in the direction of permitting political competition between elites. At the other extreme, the connections between some of the variables and outcomes is so tenuous that I describe them as 'indeterminate'. There is, for example, little clear relationship between the extent of consensus or stability in a democratic system and the extent to which the transition to democracy was initiated by government or opposition. It is the cases between these extremes that are the interesting ones. Here we can note the different emphases of different authors, and consider what light the different perspectives throw on the ways in which the democratic process evolves.

The groups dominating the transition: government, opposition and transplacement

The classification of transitions according to the nature of the group dominating the process is brought out especially clearly by Huntington, who suggests processes of 'transformation' (initiated by governments or elites), 'transplacement' (involving joint action by government and opposition), 'replacement' (initiated by the opposition) and 'intervention' (initiated by a foreign power) (Huntington 1991–2: 582). Of the countries we would normally regard as belonging to the Third World, the only example Huntington offers of democracy through foreign intervention is the dubious one of Grenada, and only Argentina and the Philippines achieved democracy mainly through opposition initiative. The remaining cases are divided evenly between those of government initiative and joint government–opposition initiative.

The qualifications we need to make to such a classification should be clear from previous chapters. Governments and oppositions are not monolithic groups with clearly defined boundaries, and there is room for argument about how far these different modes of transition are independent variables that shape subsequent democracies, or whether they are merely reflections of the reality of power in the countries concerned. Thus, to attribute the relative stability of, but limited participation in, Brazilian democracy, and the high potential for elite or military veto in the democratic process, to a government-controlled transition would be to ignore Brazil's long tradition of a strong state that casts its shadow over both transition and subsequent democracy. The variety of opposition-dominated transitions also requires comment. Unless a regime suffers military defeat (Greece and Argentina), internal collapse (the Philippines) or the loss of a powerful foreign backer (possibly the Philippines), it is difficult for the opposition to exercise much leverage against an intransigent government unless it does it by proxy through the military, as in Ghana in 1966, or through a full-blown revolution. Revolutions are also a rarity in the Third World, for reasons beyond the scope of this study, though the absence of a large urban proletariat is clearly one factor. And when revolutions do occur they seldom facilitate the consensus necessary for democracy.

It would require an extremely deterministic approach to attribute government control, or lack of it, over transitions simply to immovable traditions or power structures. The countries in which, according to Huntington, governments have initiated transitions include relatively integrated ones such as Brazil, and relatively fragmented ones such as Guatemala and Nigeria, relatively professional armies in government such as that in Pakistan, and factionalized ones such as the Nigerian. Similarly, the countries experiencing joint government–opposition initiative vary from the relatively stable Uruguay to the unstable El Salvador, and from the wealth of South Korea to the poverty of Honduras. This might suggest that the source of initiative depends at least partly on the choices made by political actors, and not just on pre-ordained conditions. But what difference does the source of initiative make to subsequent democracies? In Table 8.1 I hypothesize that the variables of stability, non-democratic veto and inequality might be influenced by the extent to which the transition was government-dominated or sponsored jointly by government and opposition. One would expect joint government–opposition action to usher in greater stability if the democratic settlement takes into account the interests of a wider variety of groups, whereas a government-initiated transition may be more the result of unpopular rulers running for cover (Nigeria and Pakistan) or seeking the least harmful means of preserving their interests (Brazil and Chile).

The problem, as in much of this analysis, is to isolate specific variables such as 'degree of government control of transition' from a host of others. 'Other things' seldom remain equal, and there were obvious social and political reasons why government-dominated transitions in Chile or Turkey were followed by greater stability than the more balanced transition of Bolivia, yet the absence of opposition participation does seem to increase the risk of subsequent instability. In some cases it is the problem, noted in the previous chapter, of outgoing military governments prescribing constitutions that are incongruent with political reality and therefore break because they cannot be bent – hence the precariousness of civilian governments in Nigeria and Turkey – and partly a question of freezing out groups which are considered politically unacceptable but cannot be wished away, such as Marxist guerillas in Guatemala. Where opposition groups have played a larger part, as in Uruguay, South Korea or perhaps in the future El Salvador, a more even balance between rival groups may contribute to a more stable and lasting democracy.

The prospect of a veto on the democratic process appears to be greater in democracies built on government-dominated transitions. Such vetoes can be found in even the most 'advanced' democracies, where elites will try to prevent public debate of the privileges they enjoy, but they are much more immediately apparent in the Third World, where elected governments challenge big business, landlords, the army or foreign investors at their peril. The veto is a matter of degree, but a government, and especially a military government, which has kept the process of transition largely under its control is more likely to be able to build in mechanisms for veto, whether constitutionally or informally. The privileges preserved by the

Brazilian and Pakistani military, for example, have at best made a large defence budget sacrosanct in countries where the poor might have different priorities with regard to public expenditure, and at worst left the military as the final arbiter of what is politically acceptable. Even where opposition groups have played a large role in the transition, as in Uruguay and the extreme case of Argentina, armies have secured amnesties for the misdeeds they perpetrated when in power, but that is a more 'defensive' form of veto and has less bearing on day-to-day politics. A recognizable elite, of which the military is only a part, may none the less cast its shadow over most of the fledgling democracies we are considering. This point will emerge again when we look at 'moderate' and (less numerous) 'radical' transitions, but it seems clear that where the government is either the dominant force or a significant force in the transition, we are not going to find participatory or socialist democracies at the end of the road. Governments concede to democratic demands in the expectation that competition for power will not threaten the unequal social and economic structure of which they are the beneficiaries.

The process of transition: negotiating table, white flag and red flag

The tables and the flags are partly metaphorical. Authoritarians and would-be democrats do sometimes sit round a table to secure agreement, as in Uruguay in 1973, but in other cases the dialogue will be more dispersed, or even unspoken. The release of political prisoners, the suspension of violence by the government's opponents and the establishment of a constituent assembly may all be part of a process in which the interaction of government and opposition is clearing the ground for democracy. Similarly, the white flag is an extreme example of the victor imposing democracy on the vanquished, as in the case of the Axis Powers in 1945, but Karl cites cases such as Brazil in 1974 and Ecuador in 1976, in which 'the military used its dominant position to establish unilaterally the rules for civilian governance' (Karl 1990: 9). Red flags come in varied shades, but are borne mainly by non-elite groups that envisage social as well as political change. The 'processes of transition' given in Table 8.1 are a simplified version of Karl's classification, which is based on the dimensions of 'compromise–force' and 'elite strength–mass strength' (Karl 1990: 9–10). The elite–mass dimension overlaps to some extent with the government–opposition dimension of the previous section, but the compromise–force aspect takes us to the heart of our concern with *how* the interaction between authoritarians and their adversaries takes place.

The 'pact' between these groups may, like the negotiating table, be metaphorical – a series of unwritten understandings rather than a sealed document – but it will reflect a relatively stable settlement, irrespective of whether the terms were initiated mainly by the government or opposition, or half and half. Huntington sketches out a typical sequence in which the government begins to lose its authority after allowing some liberalization, and then finds that the opposition exploits this, expands its support and intensifies its actions. The government reacts to contain the opposition, and government and opposition then begin to explore negotiation (Huntington 1991–2: 608–9). Karl elaborates on the 'foundational pacts' which then follow. These make pluralist democracy conditional on the contending forces not harming each other.

> These pacts serve to ensure survivability because, although they are inclusionary, they are simultaneously aimed at restricting the scope of representation in order to reassure traditional dominant classes that their vital interests will be respected. In essence, they are anti-democratic mechanisms, bargained by elites, which seek to create a deliberate socioeconomic and political contract that demobilises emerging mass actors while delineating the extent to which all actors can participate or wield power in the future.
>
> (Karl 1990: 11–12)

Considering the outcomes in Table 8.1, transition by pact scores highly in terms of consensus, at least at elite level, and stability, but poorly in terms of the prospects for equality and mass participation, and leaves a built-in elite veto in place. This does not mean that the new democracy is different only in name from the authoritarianism that went before. Apart from the likely ending of arbitrary arrests, tortures and executions, trade unions may enjoy recognition and voters will at least be able to remove the most unpopular politicians, but capitalists are likely to enjoy guarantees against expropriation, and little is likely to be done to relieve the plight of the poor. Such a description would fit much of post-authoritarian Latin America and Pakistan.

Democracy by 'imposition', in Karl's terminology, occupies the 'force' end of the compromise–force continuum and the 'elite' end of the elite–mass continuum. It may coincide with Huntington's 'democracy by transformation' in which the government takes the lead, but the imposition could come from other sources, such as a foreign invader, the victor in a civil war or an older elite that fills the vacuum left by a discredited military government, as in Greece after the failed invasion of Cyprus. The varied forms of these imposed transitions make it difficult to generalize about the nature of the democracy that will emanate from them, except to predict that the elite which facilitated their creation is likely to wield a powerful veto in the absence of countervailing forces.

Reforming and revolutionary transitions differ from the previous two types in that they are shaped more by the masses and less by elites. Karl distinguishes between the two by associating reforming transitions more with compromise and revolutionary ones with force, but for our purposes we can take the two types together. In Karl's definition, though with some qualifications, Argentina from 1946 to 1951, Guatemala from 1946 to 1954 and Chile from 1970 to 1973 were democracies established through reform, while Bolivia after 1952 and Nicaragua after 1979 (or possibly 1990) were democracies established through revolution. To seek social and economic reform while preserving or extending pluralist democracy and civil liberties may be a laudable objective, but it is likely to leave the door open to deposed elites wanting to return, so that consensus and stability will be under strain and the democratic experiment may have only a brief life, as Karl's chronology shows. While the former civilian elite may have been politically disabled as a redistribution of resources weakened it, the army may still impose the ultimate veto, as may foreign powers which feel that the 'revolution' has gone too far in threatening their economic or strategic interests, as with the American-supported invasion of Guatemala in 1954. For a brief spell, the radical democracy might evoke the praise of idealists for its pursuit of popular participation, equality and social justice but, like a desert flower, its vivid colours may last only briefly until its bloom fades as inclement conditions return.

The compatibility of objectives: consensus and conflict

Share, like Karl, offers a two-dimensional classification which enables him to produce four 'boxes'. In this case the dimensions are consensus–non-consensus and rapid–gradual change (Share 1987: 530). The tempting inference from the former continuum would be that consensual transitions are a 'good thing' because, like transitions based on pacts, they will lay down the rules and conventions for a lasting pluralist democracy, in contrast to the non-consensual transition in Nicaragua, where the incoming regime was intolerant of, and reluctant to concede democratic rights to, its predecessors. A similar point is made by Weiner, who speaks of the need to win over a sufficient section of a military government by showing the moderate or right-wing credentials of its potential successors (Weiner 1987: 863), but doubts creep in at two points.

First, we need to know something about the breadth of the consensus. Hooper (1990) refers to the acceptance of the need for national unity by members of the departing Franco regime in Spain, as an influence on their willingness to secure agreement with the opposition. This priority given to national unity would seem to imply a willingness to accommodate a variety of adversaries, even if they subscribe to radically different ideologies and represent radically different interests. This in turn might provide a basis for an inclusive democracy that is both broad, because it is reluctant to freeze out any significant group, and deep, because it is seen as necessary to maintaining a long-established nation. In contrast, transitions from military government in some African states may also appear to be consensual, in the sense that few people are actively opposing the restoration of pluralist democracy through a given settlement. But this consensus is often a reflection of the convenience of soldiers who have found politics too tiresome, and civilian elites who are thirsty for power. There may not be any deeper concern with the beneficial effects of maintaining the new democracy, or with the threats to other objectives, including national unity, in not maintaining it. As a result, the subsequent democracy may be unstable and short-lived.

Second, on the question of depth of the consensus, there is the danger of focusing on consensus between elites and ignoring the dissent of the masses, whose opinions on the democratic settlement may not have been sought. Gillespie (1990: 53–4) raises the question of the legitimate social order, as well as the political order, in South America. What are the positions of business, the educational system, professional elites or the patriarchal family within the settlement? Even these questions are concerned with counter-elites as much as non-elites, and the latter receive surprisingly little attention in the literature on transitions, beyond observation that they may disrupt the consensus by making unacceptable demands or harbouring unrealistic expectations.

It may be true in the Third World, as it was true in the West in the formative years of pluralist democracy, that the transition is smoother if it is not overloaded with mass demands for increased participation or a wider distribution of wealth, but that is different from believing that it is possible to ignore such demands. Supporters of the 'transition through elite consensus' hypothesis might point out that many countries have achieved relatively stable democracy through this route in recent years, and that the masses have apparently been willing to accept poverty with political liberty as preferable to poverty without such liberty. Whether they will continue to do so, or whether political liberty will merely be regarded as a first instalment of emancipation, is another matter. And if mass pressures do increase, how well equipped will the political system and society be to respond to them? In much of Europe it was possible to channel mass challenges through trade unions and political parties, and thus to retain relative stability while extending equality and participation, but we have seen that in the Third World the era of the mass party, and in many cases the powerful trade union, has been largely bypassed – these may be regarded as post-industrial societies that have not experienced full industrialization. If this is true, then mass pressures may be exerted more through the 'social movements' to which we have already referred, and it is not clear whether, or how, these could be integrated into a stable political system. While few people would prescribe conflict as a desirable means to achieving stable democracy, we must avoid the assumption that recent or current transitions will establish such stability because they are built on 'consensus', if the consensus turns out to lack breadth or depth.

The extent and pace of change: moderation–radicalism and gradualism–rapidity

The moderate–radical axis might appear to be similar to the consensus–conflict one. Moderation will frequently go with consensus and radicalism with conflict, but not invariably. In Spain after the death of Franco there was a broad consensus in favour of what many would regard as radical changes in the political system, while the attempts to restore democracy in Nigeria have generally been characterized by an absence of desire for radical change, in the sense that there has been broad agreement on the desirability of checks and balances, and a continuation of the mixed economy and the role of the chieftaincy, but there has been intense conflict between different ethnic groups over constitutional provisions that would affect their relative strength.

Much of the literature praises moderation, just as it praises consensus, emphasizing both its existence in the minds of the key political actors and its desirability as a goal. Bermeo argues that it is important to keep the political stakes low. Authoritarian rulers may not surrender power if a left-wing party wins an election, and anyway experience of authoritarian rule makes voters moderate. They do not want to vote for parties raising the political stakes (Bermeo 1990: 362–71). We are concentrating, of course, on transitions from non-left-wing forms of authoritarianism to democracy, which constitute the vast majority of transitions in the Third World. Levine, focusing on Latin America and Southern Europe, also argues that transition is helped by the moderate demands of the civilian population, which ensure the election of right-of-centre parties without any need for the outgoing rulers to rig the ballot (Levine 1988: 381–2), but we need to ask at least two questions. First, is 'moderation' an attitude of mind, or something for which people vote in the knowledge that a radical vote would not be acceptable. Second, are the initial elections at the end of authoritarian rule as 'free' as they appear at first sight?

Several key politicians were disqualified from contesting elections in Turkey and Uruguay, the military's manipulation of the electoral system in South Korea ensured a narrow victory for their candidate on a minority vote, and the Pakistan military helped to prevent Benazir Bhutto from winning an overall majority by preventing people without identity cards (generally the poorest citizens) from voting. In Central America, even when elections are not rigged blatantly, the main contenders have been expected to declare their opposition to nationalization, reconciliation with the guerillas or punishment of soldiers for violating human rights. Voters have come to understand that, if they elect a left-wing party, it will not be allowed to take office, and that it is therefore more prudent to restrict their choice to parties acceptable to the outgoing authoritarians. The pattern may be less one of authoritarians and voters (and the parties representing them) subscribing to the same right-of-centre consensus, than of each calculating how far they can go without antagonizing the other to such an extent that the whole transition venture is shelved. The Pakistan military thus allowed an election to be held in 1988 on the tacit understanding that the Pakistan People's Party would tone down the policies it had favoured in the 1970s, and Argentinian parties were careful not to jeopardize the prospects of a free election by promising over-rigorous prosecutions of soldiers who served under General Galtieri.

What are the implications of this willingness to vote for 'moderation' for the future of democracy? Optimists might point out that in Argentina, Brazil, Chile, Uruguay and Turkey voters at least elected parties not favoured by the outgoing authoritarians, even if these parties were not considered to be so radical by the latter as to be banned or harassed. And in Greece and Spain cautious votes for 'acceptable' parties were followed in subsequent elections by votes for parties further to the left. On the face of it, moderation made the transition to stable democracy easier, and opened the door at least a crack to further instalments of democracy, which might reduce the scope for elite or military vetoes and widen the range of ideological choices, but perhaps moderation is a necessary rather than a sufficient condition.

The extent to which perceived radical politicians were handicapped or outlawed in El Salvador, Guatemala and Pakistan may have made for unstable forms of democracy circumscribed by a strong military veto, when a sweeping radical coup against the authoritarians, whether within the military or through a civilian revolt, might have ushered in a less constrained democracy. The obvious example here is Nicaragua, and we have noted the fierce dispute over the democratic credentials of that country. Among the minority who see the prospects for democracy enhanced by a more radical transition, Cammack suggests that democracy may work better in Nicaragua than elsewhere because reforms there have gone beyond mere institutional measures and have empowered the poor (Cammack 1991: 544). If radical changes reflect a broad consensus within society, as appears to have been the case with the transitions from authoritarianism in Eastern Europe and Spain (and an acceptance of liberal democracy in place of fascism does seem to be a radical political change, even if the economic changes were less dramatic), then perhaps a new democratic equilibrium can be achieved. But if, to return to the continuum of the previous section, the changes are the outcome of a fiercer conflict in which older elites reject the new order, the survival of the new order may be more precarious, with a prospect of armed rebellion, together with external subversion if an international as well as a domestic consensus has been broken.

On the gradual–rapid continuum, the immediate problem is whether to make comparisons between different places or different times. If we took the 1688 revolution as the approximate beginning of the British transition and the 1884 Reform Act as the end, we have a transition of nearly two centuries, with stable, relatively consensual government emerging, subject to elite, but not military or external, veto. The German transition which culminated in the Weimar Republic could be measured in decades rather than centuries, and ushered in a much less stable system, but that was still a gradual transition compared with Brazil, where barely twelve years elapsed between the first concessions to democracy by the military government and the free elections that marked the end of military rule. Yet Brazil is regarded as a case of gradual transition by modern standards: as Baloyra (1987: 88) points out, less than seven years elapsed between the deterioration of authoritarianism and the installation of democracy in Latin American countries outside Brazil. As with so many aspects of modern society, what was once regarded as indecent haste is now considered slow and, as in the other aspects of society, this has much to do with modern technology. Mass media and the ability of political leaders, and sometimes followers, to visit countries where pluralist democracy has already arrived make people living under authoritarian governments more aware of the alternatives available, and more impatient to liberalize their own countries.

Gradual change, by modern standards, normally implies the existence of an authoritarian government with enough self-confidence to make some democratic concessions, yet strong enough to control the pace of events. Personal rulers are unlikely to have the humility or flexibility to make step-by-step concessions, and leaders of party governments are likely to face resistance from party functionaries who do not want to lose the spoils of office, but who will quickly desert the sinking ship when popular resistance grows, thus making for a belated but rapid transition. This leaves us with military governments as a possible starting point for gradual transition, and the necessary self-confidence is most likely with a strong, mature army, united by a sense of professionalism. Brazil is an obvious case in point, with the military government largely controlling the pace and direction of change, and ensuring the preservation of a military veto in the ensuing pluralist regime. In most other Third World countries, and indeed in Eastern and Southern Europe, the pace of change has been much more rapid once the vulnerability of the authoritarian regime has become clear. Conservatives might see this as a recipe for instability, with threats to democracy from ousted elites and the military, but, as Share (1987) points out, much will depend on whether the rapid change is based on a broad consensus, as in Spain, or on the old regime being removed against its will by a popular uprising (Nicaragua), an invasion (Germany in 1945), a coup (Portugal) or an implosion as a result of its own incompetence (Argentina and Greece). In Spain most of the old elite was carried along, however reluctantly, in the rapid whirlwind of democratic change. In the other countries mentioned it was not, and much then depended on its willingness or ability to resist the new order.

One danger with the rapid–gradual axis is that it may imply that democratization is a relatively smooth process, whatever its duration. But what of the countries where gradualness involves not slow, steady progress but a form of trench warfare between authoritarians and democrats in which a few miles of democratic territory may be gained in one battle, only to be lost in the next? This has been the case in much of Central America. Or there are cases, as in West Africa, where the war is actually won in the sense of free elections being achieved, only for democracy to be attacked and defeated again a few years later. One could argue that the occurrence of such battles is significant more for what they tell us about the underlying society than for predicting the nature of any democracy which ultimately emerges, but it seems useful to distinguish between a gradualness which allows a steady consolidation of democratic gains, whether in Britain in the nineteenth century or Brazil in the 1970s, and what is merely a long time interval between the initial challenges to authoritarianism and the final democratic outcome, brought about by the ability of authoritarians to retreat and then re-group.

The sequence of changes: civil liberties, participation, contestation and social reform

The virtue of 'gradual' change is not so much the fact that taking a long time to complete a process is necessarily superior to taking a shorter time, as in the production of whisky, but that the longer time can be used (even if it was not so used in Central America) to consolidate one democratic reform before going on to the next. This was one of the arguments of Binder *et al.* (1971), though they dwelt largely on countries which enjoyed the luxury of a longer time-scale than that enjoyed by most Third World countries today. To describe all the changes that are necessary for an authoritarian system to be transformed into a democratic one would be a lengthy and controversial process. Ethier offers a long list of 'principles and categories of social transformation', though the transformation implicit in the list seems to be more political than social. The list begins with basic freedoms, and continues through pluralist competition to the acceptance of the political institutions through which the democratic process works, and participation within these institutions (Ethier 1990: 3–21). For the sake of simplicity, I shall concentrate on changes in the extent of civil liberties, participation, contestation and social reform. Supporters of moderate and gradual change are generally also supporters of consolidating one demo-cratic advance at a time. 'There are no short cuts to political salvation. If the world is to be saved and stable democratic institutions created, it will be done through *incremental* political reform undertaken by moderate, realistic men and women in a spirit of one-soul-at-a-time' (Huntington 1988: 9).

The general preference appears to be the sequence of extended civil liberties first, then increased participation, possibly in electing advisory bodies such as constituent assemblies or relatively weak legislatures, followed by contested elections for the important political offices, with social reform occurring last, if at all (see especially Cardoso 1986–7: 32; Diamond 1989: 155; Munck 1989: 160). The preference of academic observers has co-incided with the actual sequences in many countries. Diamond speaks of authoritarianism being moderated through 'democratic accountability', the rule of law, and an independent judiciary and police (Diamond 1989: 145) before citizens are given the opportunity to make democratic choices. If stability is a high priority, as it always has been with Huntington, then this sequence may be the most appropriate, with a high possibility of elites vetoing changes that challenge their interests, both before and after democracy is established.

The alternative of placing social reform earlier in the sequence, or attempting it simultaneously with the other changes, may seem more attractive to purists who see democracy as incomplete while elites wield heavily disproportionate influence and the poor cannot use their votes to alleviate their poverty, but it is difficult to point to many durable democracies that have been established through this route, apart from the controversial case of Nicaragua. Such reforms are likely to meet with resistance from older elites, and it is easier to combat such resistance through the undemocratic means of the bayonet rather than the democratic means of the ballot box, as the contrasting experiences of Cuba and Nicaragua show. The recent wave of democratizations has been especially difficult for social reformers, occurring as it has in a period of economic retrenchment, and some observers have questioned whether voters have much expectation of radical social changes in the circumstances (see especially Munck 1989: 160; Karl 1990: 16–17).

Economic circumstances aside, the relative failure of 'authoritarianism with social reform' to transform itself into pluralist democracy, in contrast to the relative success of 'authoritarianism with expanded civil liberties', might point to a more general problem. Social reforming authoritarians, using the term in the broad sense of rulers who use the power of the state to alleviate the suffering of the poor, appear to have been better able to put the brakes on the process of democratization when they have wanted to. Ghana under Rawlings, Mexico and Tunisia all serve as examples. This might be because the poor are more easily 'bought off' by material benefits than by intangible civil liberties, but it may also be because 'social reform' implies that the state occupies the driving seat more effectively, to pursue the analogy, and can therefore curtail more easily what has previously been granted. This is especially likely if the authoritarian rulers want to remain in power but fear that the population would vote them out in a free election. Authoritarian rulers who proceed via expanding civil liberties, and thus allow a greater role for autonomous groups in society, may find that the brakes are more difficult to apply as the groups build up their own political momentum.

The expansion of participation before civil liberties also appears to reduce the prospects of democratic transition, and for similar reasons. Governments in Ghana and Uganda set up new structures to encourage mass participation, especially at a local level, while leaving executive and legislative power immune to democratic control and, especially in the case of Ghana, retaining arbitrary powers of imprisonment and restrictions on freedom of association. While the participation might, in theory, be used as a step towards pluralist democracy, in practice it can be restricted or curtailed by the state if it is seen as too much of a threat. Again the constraints on autonomous groups make it difficult for democracy to gather momentum.

Conclusion

We have reiterated that the five perspectives extracted from the literature are subject to considerable overlap, yet each one offers insights that the others do not. Words such as cooperation, pact, consensus, moderation and gradualness may appear to be describing the same phenomena, and transitions that involve one of these variables frequently involve the others. Similarly, opposition initiative, reform, conflict and radical and rapid change might conjure up a picture of a different type of transition, but again the juxtaposition of such variables is a matter of probability rather than inevitability. The danger in relying on the broadly accepted views of writers such as Diamond and Huntington is not so much that they are 'wrong' but that they may leave the unwary reader with too black and white an impression. If we were asked about the relative plausibility of stable, long-term democracy emerging from government–opposition cooperation, pacts, consensus, moderation and gradual change, as against its emergence from opposition, conflict and radical and rapid change, it would be difficult not to accord greater plausibility to the former features. The experience of Pakistan, South Korea and much of tropical Africa and Latin America certainly points in that direction. But that is rather like saying that an empty house is made habitable more easily if it requires only spring cleaning and interior decoration rather than structural alterations. It may be good news for the occupant of the structurally sound house, but it does not necessarily imply that the occupant of the structurally unsound house next door should either make do with a broom and a pot of paint or give up altogether.

Where there are underlying conditions that favour cooperation, consensus and gradual, moderate change, and where political actors exist who are willing to give a high priority to democratic objectives and have the skills to know how to pursue them, it would be foolish to dismiss these assets, but if many of these underlying conditions are absent, it would be dangerous to pretend otherwise. Thus, freezing counter-elites or the masses out of any democratic settlement on the grounds that their heterodox views will threaten consensus, or prescribing gradual change when more rapid change might remove an obstructive elite which could otherwise undermine the democratic process, or failing to remove blatant social injustices in the interests of 'moderation', when these injustices might infect the body politic for years to come, would be to build on unsound foundations while pretending that the structure was basically sound. In the nature of things, one would normally expect the earliest democratic transitions to occur in the countries where conditions were most conducive, even after allowing for differences in degrees of political skill and commitment. Uruguay had fewer obstacles to overcome than Guatemala or Nicaragua, and Zambia has had fewer than Zaire. With communism in retreat in Eastern Europe, transitions based on radical change have been ideologically less fashionable and more difficult to underwrite from outside. But are the recent transitions necessarily a good guide to future ones, which, in many cases, may be attempted in more polarized societies and in international political and economic conditions that no one can predict?

9

The viability of democracy

If a country can negotiate the hazards of transition to democracy, what are the prospects of this democracy surviving? And might it even evolve from a crude system which is distinguished from authoritarianism mainly by the existence of competitive elections, into one in which civil liberties, toleration, citizen participation, stability based on respect for democratic values and social justice all flourish? Latin America had its false dawns in the 1930s, and Africa and Asia in the early post-independence years of the 1950s and 1960s, only for these to be followed by one-party rule, military government or personal dictatorship, or sometimes national disintegration and anarchy. Why should we expect the current wave of democratizations to be any longer lasting? Our task would be easier if we could parade a collection of case studies of viable democracies that have followed recent transitions, or even studies of recently established democracies that reverted to authoritarianism, but it is still early days, and so far we have few cases of anything as dramatic as either the evolution of model democracies or democratic collapse. Countries as diverse as Pakistan, Thailand, Zambia, Guatemala, Uruguay and Chile have all maintained their newly established political competition and kept would-be authoritarians at bay (though with difficulty in the case of Thailand), but is this a cause for congratulation, in the expectation that further instalments of democratic development are on the way, or a cause for indifference or hostility in view of the precarious economic condition of many of these countries and the inability or unwillingness of their rulers to redress the imbalance between rich and poor, and weak and strong?

In the absence of detailed case studies of the recently established democracies, or of a sufficiently long time-scale by which to judge events, this chapter will be largely speculative, though I shall attempt to build on some of the earlier ideas about the conditions conducive to democracy, and to utilize such glimpses as are available of the new democracies in action.

In Chapter 2 I reviewed some of the conditions emphasized in comparative literature as being conducive to democracy, and suggested that economic development, political attitudes, social structures and the development of political institutions were especially relevant to the Third World, even though none of them was a guarantee of democratic success. The relevance of economic development to the recent democratizations can be dismissed without discussion, since most of them, apart from that in South Korea, have occurred against a background of worsening economic conditions, but I shall look again at political attitudes, social structures and political institutions to see if they provide more promising ground for sustaining democracy, and then go on to look at the impact of the mode of transition. Finally, I shall consider the extent to which the actual performance of the new governments may help to strengthen democracy.

Political attitudes and social structure

We have seen in previous chapters that one asset enjoyed by the new democracies is a greater public willingness to sustain them, even when governments are not particularly efficient in managing the economy or sensitive to the needs of the masses, largely because of the exceptional harshness of the previous authoritarian regimes, which had tortured, imprisoned and executed their subjects on an unprecedented scale, especially in Latin America, without being notably more competent in administration than the ailing democratic regimes they had displaced (see especially Cammack 1985; Cardoso 1986–7: 40). It is thus more difficult today to imagine a weak democratic regime, such as that of President Allende in Chile in 1973, being toppled with the support of civilians who felt that the destruction of democracy itself was a price worth paying for the destruction of an unwanted government. If President Allende had been displaced by the traditional military 'man on horseback' who made a few adjustments to the political process and then permitted competitive (if rigged) elections a few years later, few people might have suffered outside the former ruling party and the recipients of its patronage, but the fact that Allende was displaced by a brutal personal ruler who survived for 17 years might serve as a warning to anyone thinking of challenging the democratic process, or supporting such a challenge.

The above argument might suggest an unrealistic degree of 'rationality' in human behaviour. Do rioters protesting against food shortages, speculators who undermine the government's economic policy or soldiers who use armed force to protect their privileges give much thought to the implications of their actions for democracy? Changes in short-term attitudes and behaviour may need to be reinforced or stimulated by longer-term changes in society. Few clear concepts have been developed to spell out clearly the sort of changes that are said to be taking place, but there is broad agreement that the Third World societies over which a growing number of democratic regimes rule are undergoing changes that make them increasingly different from the societies which had been ruled by authoritarians, and by largely unstable democratic regimes before that.

In South Korea the difference may be the familiar one, to Western eyes, of a more industrialized society with all the implications for a larger, more articulate middle class intolerant of the stifling effects of dictatorship, and a growing urban working class better able to assert its demands. The pluralist system that has emerged has often involved violent conflict, but any would-be authoritarian would have difficulty in putting the lid back on the democratic process and demanding the obedience of an increasingly assertive and diverse society. I suggested the somewhat clumsy concept of post-industrial society without full industrialization. In South America Cardoso captures some of the flavour of this with his reference to 'segmented societies', which emphasize professional categories rather than class, neighbourhood rather than state, and parish rather than party (Cardoso 1986–7: 36). 'Social movements' now attract at least as much attention in the literature as political parties. We shall return to some of the implications of this when we look at political institutions, but it could be argued that democracy is more secure if society comprises diverse groups, none of which is strong enough to dominate the polity on its own, rather than a few monolithic groups competing in a zero-sum game in which the stakes become so high that the conflict runs beyond democratic channels. The conflict between the Peronists and their opponents in Argentina might thus be seen as a strain on democracy, with which it could not ultimately cope, and so could the continued, often violent polarization of social groups in Central America. A greater diversity of groups may make compromise a more accepted part of the political process, and curb the pursuit of the more 'extreme' ideologies and demands.

Cardoso noted the decline of left-wing parties as belief in a powerful state waned, even before the collapse of communism in Eastern Europe (Cardoso 1986–7: 40). It would require a long digression to explain the loss of faith in old-fashioned state socialism, but it has been influenced by the inability of socialist governments to deliver the promised benefits, even in the West, and by a realization, especially in the Third World, that a strong state could as easily be used as an instrument for corruption or tyranny as for social welfare, and that a more decentralized form of government might therefore be preferable. With the decline of the more monolithic social groups and the mass parties they had sustained, the wherewithal for establishing a socialist state was also lacking, quite apart from the will to do so. The collapse of the communist bloc merely reinforced trends already at work, though it did help to deprive politicians of the right of a pretext for suspending democracy on the grounds of a 'communist threat'.

Are we in danger of confusing democratic development with mere 'stability'? Are a state with limited planning and redistributive functions, a range of political choices that excludes the 'extreme left' and a society in which non-elite groups are increasingly fragmented really conducive to democracy, or only to a continuation of elite domination in the absence of any effective challenge? The answer may be that no other form of democracy is feasible in the foreseeable future. Social change, economic and administrative constraints, and the absence of a helping Soviet hand all make the establishment of a socialist democracy unlikely. Those who deplore inequality, social injustice or even the dissipation of natural resources have little alternative but to work for change within the existing limited pluralist system.

The social changes in tropical Africa have generally been less far-reaching than those in South America, but they point in a similar direction. Chazan and Sklar have both drawn attention to the myriad of voluntary groups which have provided independent centres of power, at least for modest purposes, where people had previously looked (though often in vain) to an all-providing state or a nominal mass party (Sklar 1987; Chazan 1988: 132). Empty factories, rusting bulldozers, potholed roads and buses abandoned for want of spare parts all provide monuments to attempts at state-initiated development that failed, while the parties have left rather fewer traces. As in Latin America, there has been a realization that authoritarian rule offers few benefits in terms of material progress, stability, national unity or moral rectitude to compensate for the loss of freedom, but whether the social changes that have occurred since the early post-independence years are sufficient to give the new or incipient democracies advantages, which their predecessors in the 1960s did not enjoy, is another matter. The fact that peasants can market their own crops independently of a state marketing board, or can organize their own welfare schemes independently of an increasingly ineffective state, may be an admirable development, but it seems over-optimistic to see such modest developments as bastions against authoritarianism.

Similarly, urban revolts against the hardships attributed to authoritarian governments may suggest signs of less passive populations, but the revolts may be reactions more against hardship than against authoritarianism. Whereas the 'social movements' in Latin America have often contained a 'political' element in the sense that they were making demands which were difficult to reconcile with authoritarianism, the mutual self-help activities of African groups have been more concerned with responding to day-to-day reality, irrespective of who wields power at the centre. Intellectuals continue to provide voices against authoritarianism, just as many of them did in more dangerous times, but it is still difficult to see how any developments in society can make democracy more secure without the development of stronger democratic institutions to match the anti-authoritarian aspirations.

Political institutions

In Chapter 2 we noted the argument that democracy required the development of institutions, such as political parties, interest groups and legislatures, that can filter public demands and facilitate compromises, even if these institutions did not evolve initially for democratic purposes. Have such institutions reached a stage where they are more conducive to democracy than they were before the last authoritarian takeover? Such a question would be easier to answer if there was greater agreement on what sort of institutional arrangements are most conducive to democracy. Huntington's emphasis on 'order', and on containing potentially disorderly popular participation, has been increasingly challenged by writers who see democracy as dependent on a more autonomous society, which can check the power of the state (see especially Gillespie 1989: 95–106). But even then it is not clear whether the ideal is a resurrection of corporatist pacts, albeit on a more democratic basis, between political parties and interest groups, as advocated by Gillespie, or a society in which people participate more directly as individuals instead of having their interests interpreted by leaders of groups, as implied by Dix (1992).

Dix speaks of a greater institutionalization of parties in Latin America compared with the last wave of democratization in the 1960s, with the parties more adaptable, autonomous, coherent and catch-all, and less frequently built around particular individuals (Dix 1992: 505). Such parties might appear more attractive than the early personal supporters' clubs built around a Peron or Stroessner, or parties tied to powerful vested interests, but critics with a sneaking admiration for Huntington's emphasis on order might ask what happens to democracies built around catch-all parties in difficult times. Lacking any depth of commitment, a party's fickle supporters may desert in large numbers if it fails to deliver material benefits. In the West such desertion may involve nothing more serious than defection to another catch-all party, but in the Third World there is a greater danger of people, with a shorter history of commitment to the democratic process, turning against the whole political system and not just the ruling party. Gillespie's alternative of corporate pacts between parties and interest groups seems to imply a more solid anchor for parties than the catch-all model, but he admits that little progress has been made in that direction, with peak associations weak and trade unions more concerned with the effects of inflation than with forging links with parties. In view of what has been said about changes in Latin American society in the previous section, attempts to revive corporate processes would be going against the grain of more fragmented, heterogeneous societies. As in the West, the social pressures favour the catch-all party appealing to voters as diverse individuals, rather than as members of monolithic blocs on the basis of social solidarity but, unlike in the West, catch-all parties are competing for power at the beginning of a pluralist era. In the West the more common pattern was for competition in the early years of democracy to be between parties representing more specific interests, such as organized labour, a religious denomination or a linguistic or ethnic group, so that voters voted as much for a distinctive group as for a set of policies. This preserved a measure of consistency and continuity in parliamentary representation and, ultimately, in the political process as a whole. It has only been at a relatively mature stage of democratic development that catch-all parties have emerged or evolved. Some have occasionally been seen as a threat to democracy, especially those parties exploiting racial prejudices, but, except in cases where massive social and economic dislocation gave rise to fascist governments, the threats have been at the margin. But can less mature democracies start from scratch on the basis of catch-all parties, and survive the massive turnovers of support that ruling parties are likely to suffer?

One mitigating factor might be the presidential systems common to Latin America. Waning support for the majority party will have less political importance if there is a strong executive president elected for a fixed term, but the existence of such a phenomenon pulls the debate back from concern with the stability of the democratic system to concern with the extent to which it is democratic. The checks and balances found in the United States presidential system have seldom been replicated in Latin America where, as in most of the Third World, the difference between being on the winning rather than the losing side is so great that opposition is difficult to sustain. The spectre of elective dictatorship begins to loom, with parties and interest groups becoming weaker as the president grows stronger. Just as catch-all parties may pose a minimal threat to stability if they emerge long after the establishment of democracy, so an executive presidency may pose little threat to democracy if it has been introduced, as it was in the United States, as an institution with limited constitutional power which had to build up its strength through consent and consensus. The presence of a strong president at the democratic dawn may be a more serious problem for democracy.

If we move from Latin America to tropical Africa, the institutional problem is often presented not in terms of political parties, pressure groups or presidents but in terms of the state itself. Parties have shown remarkable resilience in surviving at all, often underground or in exile in the face of persecution, and have re-emerged, usually with different names and sometimes with different power bases, to 'structure the vote' when free elections have been permitted. The significance of this should not be underestimated, especially when it is contrasted with the difficulties in establishing autonomous parties in North Africa and the Middle East and the consequent failure to build democracy there. It did matter, for example, that the voters of Ghana were able to choose between competing parties in 1969 and 1979, even though the policy differences between the parties appeared minimal and the military lurked in the background ready to pounce on any party it found unacceptable. It mattered in the sense that party competition facilitated a circulation of elites and their clients, so that few major groups did not enjoy some of the fruits of office, and in the sense that voting in elections provided at least a safety valve for participants in the political system, the alternatives to which might have been attempts at coercion by an increasingly divided army, or megalomaniac personal rule.

The use of competitive elections at infrequent intervals to elect governments which only survive for two or three years, before being ousted by
the military, does, however, suggest a topsy-turvy world in which authoritarianism is the norm, with political parties only brought in when
there is no other means of resolving crises of authority. In contrast, in a
country like France party politics has been the norm and soldiers have only
intervened occasionally in times of crisis. Can African parties move from
their apparently marginal role of determining political outcomes at times
when colonial or military rule are no longer feasible, to a more central role
in which they aggregate public demands, and provide either a legitimate
basis for government or a means of displacing governments constitutionally?

Optimists might point again to the greater will to make democracy work
after experience of the alternatives, but the countries which have suffered
the most brutal authoritarian regimes, such as the Central African Republic, Uganda and Zaire, have generally made less progress towards pluralism
than countries experiencing the milder constraints of one-party rule, such
as Senegal and Zambia. Indeed, I have argued in earlier chapters that transition from one-party rule to pluralism in Africa is a simpler step than
transition from military or personal rule, because some of the rules of
political conflict are already in place and new parties can learn from the
structures and experience of the formerly dominant one. Transitions from
military rule, in contrast, often involve the military devising rules of conflict that are incongruent with political reality, as in the creation of a two-
party system in Nigeria, so that the succeeding regimes may lack flexibility
or durability.

The 'artificiality' of parties in relation to African society is a thread that
runs implicitly through much of their development since independence.
The attempt in the early years to build 'mass parties' on a nominally Leninist
model never coincided with reality. More recently there has been the
notion that a pluralist system can operate despite the prohibition of some
parties, whether on account of the past misdeeds of their leaders, the heresy
of their ideologies or simply the fact that their presence would exceed the
prescribed number of permitted parties. While such rules are made or
unmade at the centre, what prospects are there of leaders building effective
bases in society? And if society is built more around distinctive ethnic
groups, in contrast to the cross-cutting and overlapping social groups in
Latin America, is there not the possibility of parties building on ethnic
bases and fanning the flames of ethnic conflict (see especially Welch 1987:
196)? Such arguments can be caricatured as explaining African politics in
terms of 'tribalism', and the success of countries such as Botswana, the
Gambia, Senegal and Zambia in holding competitive elections should help
to emphasize that there is nothing in the nature of African society that
precludes party competition. But it faces substantial obstacles in the form
of limited experience in operating such a system over a long period, and
the apparent failure to discover a sustainable party, or party system, that

conforms to generally accepted democratic norms yet is congruent with indigenous society and can build secure bases within society.

Beyond the problem of institutionalizing parties is the question of the state itself. Choosing between competing parties is hardly a worthwhile exercise unless the successful parties can then use the machinery of state to repay their debts to their constituents, whether in material terms or in a modest reshaping of society to reflect current values and priorities. The capacity of the state in Africa was never strong compared with the West, given the extent of national poverty, limited administrative expertise, the limited legitimacy accorded to governments and the laws they passed, and the dependence on uncontrollable external forces, in the form of the Cold War or fluctuations in the price of primary products. But the collapse of many recent authoritarian governments often reflected a new low-water mark in state capacity, as public services and the forces of law and order broke down. It is not clear how far their removal reflected a public preference for democracy over authoritarianism, as was the case in countries such as Chile and Uruguay, or merely a loss of confidence in regimes that could no longer feed, clothe or protect them. A democratically elected government moving into the presidential palace following the departure of the authoritarians might feel like Napoleon entering Moscow. A famous victory has been won, but where are the spoils of office? And once people have discovered that little has changed, or can be changed, as a result of their votes, why should they be anxious to defend democracy if an ambitious young major decides to bring the edifice down again? That is, perhaps, taking the most extreme cases of poverty and state incapacity. Any incoming democratic government in Liberia or Sierra Leone would face immense problems in merely holding the country together, let alone implementing a party programme, but in countries such as Ghana, Nigeria and Kenya, a stronger infrastructure exists and distinctive political choices could be made on matters such as the respective roles of the state, private and voluntary sectors, the extent of the devolution of power and the determination with which corruption was rooted out. The desired statues exist somewhere within the slabs of marble, but the tools available for shaping them in terms of the political institutions available remain crude, and their effective use will require considerable skill, patience and luck.

The modes of transition

I have so far emphasized the importance of the underlying society, political culture, political institutions and, if only indirectly, economy in shaping the prospects for democracy, and all of these factors will play a part in influencing the nature of the demise of the authoritarian government, and thus the nature of the transition to democracy, but we need to allow for specific pressures, political choices and responses to events, which will

Table 9.1 Bases of authoritarian weakness and the possible consequences for democratic successors

Basis of authoritarian weakness	Likely mode of transition	Possible consequences for successor democratic regime
1 Strains within army	Orderly retreat	Continued military veto, continued civilian elite veto
2 Specific unpopular or ineffective decisions	Hasty retreat	Continued military veto, after purge of top ranks; continued civilian elite veto
3 Generally ineffective regime performance	Retreat under pressure	Successor regime may inherit intractable problems, and thus remain weak; continued civilian elite and military veto
4 Disintegration of political and administrative process	Hasty retreat	Little military or elite veto, but democratic regime has very limited capacity
5 Economic disintegration	Hasty retreat	Little military or elite veto, but democratic regime has very limited capacity
6 Uncontrolled social change	Variable	Little military or elite veto; capacity of democratic regime varies with the nature of social and economic conditions

also influence the mode of transition. The mode, in turn, will have consequences for the emerging democracy in terms of the range of choices available to political actors, and the stability and longevity of the democratic system. Six different bases of weakness in the authoritarian system which may lead to a democratic transition are set out in Table 9.1, and I shall consider each of these in turn.

Strains within the army

In the case of a military government it is common for signs of strain to develop as the task of ruling the country becomes increasingly difficult to reconcile with maintaining a disciplined professional army. An army that returns to barracks soon after the symptoms begin to show will, other things being equal, be a more coherent force and one better able to exert influence over the incoming democracy, as in Pakistan, Turkey or Ghana after 1969, than one that has been strained to the point of disintegration, as in Uganda. Critics may point to contrary examples such as Brazil and Chile, where military governments were longer-lived yet armies retained substantial veto powers over their successors, but in the former case the military eased the strain by sharing power with civilians from an early stage, and in the latter the government was more a personal dictatorship than one involving a substantial section of the army.

Specific unpopular or ineffective decisions

Here we allow for an element of free will rather than impersonal forces. It was not inevitable that General Galtieri should invade the Falklands or that the Greek junta should invade Cyprus, but the failure of these decisions to achieve the desired results led to the hasty departure of the rulers. Their going might have been a signal for greater public celebration than the more gradual retreat of authoritarians in other countries, and the army may have suffered at least temporary disgrace, but such a departure implies no radical changes in society. The army, if not its discredited leaders, may still exert substantial veto power, and there is no reason why older civilian elites should not also exert considerable influence on the political agenda.

Generally ineffective regime performance

If an authoritarian regime not merely makes one costly error but generally fails to live up to its own or its supporters' expectations, this might reflect on the calibre of the ruling junta, but it is at least as likely to suggest the existence of intractable problems, as in the case of the Central American military regimes, which have been unable to reconcile the interests of powerful civilian elites with rising mass demands, often backed by violence. Such rulers may find it prudent to cut their losses and withdraw from government but, if they can keep their military power base intact, there is no reason why they and their allies in the civilian elite should not continue to exert a substantial veto power. Any democratic successor regime will be hamstrung by the extent of the veto power and by its inheritance of the same intractable problems.

Disintegration of the political and administrative process

This model is closer to tropical Africa or Bangladesh than to most of Latin America. Benin would be a good example. It is not just that the government performs ineffectively, but that the processes by which the machinery of state functions, in terms of collecting revenue, maintaining order, allocating contracts or maintaining health standards, begins to break down, and authoritarian rulers are left largely defenceless in the face of any revolt against them. There is therefore no question of any veto power being exercised by the former rulers, and in that sense the incoming democrats have a broader canvas on which to paint. They can remould the political structure, to change the metaphor, to their own liking, for example by replacing a Marxist-Leninist approach with a free-market liberal democratic one, but the political disintegration that brought down the previous regime is unlikely to be repaired easily, so the freedom available to the new rulers may resemble the freedom of the beggar to dine at the Ritz Hotel.

Economic disintegration

This will often be closely intertwined with political disintegration. Thus the downfall of the Nkrumah regime in Ghana in 1966 was related to a malfunctioning political structure in which the ruling party lost any control it had had over policy-making and implementation, and administrators were left to oversee unworkable policies, while careless public spending and worsening terms of trade left the economy in chaos and the government with few material rewards to dispense in exchange for public support. The extent to which the main cause of disintegration is political or economic will vary between different countries, but the consequences for the succeeding government are likely to be similar to those in the preceding section. The previous rulers will pose little threat, but the reality of political and economic disintegration will impose its own constraints on the choices available to, and likely longevity of, any incoming democracy.

Uncontrolled social change

Many authoritarian regimes have been swept away by social changes they were ultimately unable to control. Eastern Europe provides dramatic examples, and industrialization in South Korea had similar effects. General Franco's successors also found it impossible to preserve authoritarianism in a Spanish society which was beginning to resemble the rest of Western Europe. Such a fate is less likely to befall 'pure' military regimes, because most of them have too short a lifespan to be able to preside over significant social change, than one-party regimes that are more difficult to dislodge. In the Third World, a search for such regimes takes us mainly to Africa (though Mexico also offers an interesting case of the dilemma of a one-party regime in a hostile environment). A search for parallels between the demise of one-party regimes in tropical Africa and their demise in Spain and Eastern Europe might seem fanciful, but in all these cases there is the common problem of the role of new, enlarged or transformed groups within a system which was not designed to incorporate them, whether it be the East German youth wanting to adopt the lifestyle of his Western counterpart or the Kenyan intellectual despising the pretentiousness of the ruling party and the personality cult of the leader. In such situations the ruling party normally tries to retain support by making some concessions to pluralist demands, only to find that the currents of the changed society sweep it faster and further than it had planned to go, until it becomes completely wrecked. As in political, administrative and economic breakdown, there is thus little prospect of the new rulers being haunted by the ghosts of the old, yet the machinery of state, and in some cases even the economy, may be in a better shape to allow the new democracy to determine its own destiny. Freedom for manoeuvre in such cases is obviously relative. Any future democratic regime in Mexico would enjoy considerable administrative and economic advantages over the new rulers of the impoverished Zambia, but the latter are still in an enviable position compared with the current rulers of Benin or any future democratic regime in Zaire, where political and economic order is minimal.

Performance

Once the new democratic system is in place, how far can it control its own destiny, independently of the forces that brought it into being? And what sort of governmental performances, and public responses to them, are most likely to enable the democratic system to survive or to acquire greater strength? The newness of many of the democracies forces us to rely as much on journalistic reports as on deep academic analysis, but the perception gained from both sources is one of democracies seldom straying far from economic orthodoxy and elite preservation, generally preserving basic civil and democratic liberties, but operating with widely varying degrees of competence within the context of their objectives and ideologies.

Latin American observers are almost unanimous in emphasizing the 'moderation' of the new democratic governments. These are not populist rulers risking economic crises in the pursuit of equality and social welfare, but cautious pragmatists who are at least as competent as authoritarians in dealing with economic growth, inflation, debt and unemployment (Sloan 1989; Remmer 1990: 324–5). Sloan allows for variations in performance being dependent on 'the availability of skilful policy makers' as well as the type of regime (Sloan 1989: 123), and notes the greater flexibility of democratic regimes in shifting priorities to achieve moderate development, in contrast to the more volatile performances of authoritarians, but much of the emphasis is on continued elite constraints. According to Remmer (1990: 335), 'The rise and fall of democracy in Latin America has corresponded less to the whims of the voting majority than to the concerted opposition of business and military elites.'

Cammack (1985) speaks of 'bourgeois hegemonies' which have rejected radical reform and discouraged participation, and Petras (1989) argues that the restoration of democracy has made little difference because the repressive machinery of state, exemplified by the army, police and judiciary, continues to represent a class interest. Reid (1991) describes a post-authoritarian Guatemala with tight constraints on democracy, the left excluded, an alienated population and no public debate on the continuation of unequal land tenure. Rocha describes a Brazil in which democracy is threatened by impoverishment, corruption and military dissatisfaction with low pay, an IMF-imposed austerity programme to repay foreign debts, an unemployment level of twelve million, a breakdown of public services and even the re-emergence of slavery (Rocha 1992: 13).

There is perhaps a danger of selectivity in such reports, and one could argue that the political and economic circumstances in which the democratic transitions took place make it unremarkable that economic miracles and challenges to elite power are few. Did the democracies in the West fare any better in their early years? What is not mentioned in these accounts may be as remarkable as what is. Putting aside the passing reference to slavery, there are no reports of arbitrary arrests or imprisonments, threats to suspend elections or to restore military rule. Brown's account of Pakistan offers a similar contrast between governmental ineffectiveness and the retention of democratic structures. The government, he reported, was failing to cope with economic stagnation, poverty and illiteracy; patronage, corruption, violence and ethnic rivalries were rife, and the army insisted on a high defence budget, yet there was a freer press, rowdy parliamentary debates and an army which continued to support democracy (Brown 1989: 23). One could argue about the relative utility of better health, nourishment and housing in comparison with rowdy parliamentary debates and periodic competitive elections (though there is no guarantee that the suspension of the latter would lead to more of the former), but democracy was never offered as a short-term solution to society's ills in the way that authoritarianism frequently is. If it can survive even in the hostile environment we have described, who is to say that the potential opportunities it provides for articulating mass demands will not eventually be realized?

We should anyway balance the starker descriptions with reports of modest success. Chile has enjoyed relative economic buoyancy since the departure of the military, and there is the prospect of justice for some of General Pinochet's victims, in a country where the rundown of the economy and mass persecution had previously gone hand in hand (Reid 1991). In Argentina the hyper-inflation of the Alfonsin presidency has been succeeded by more effective, if tough and inegalitarian, economic policies under Menem. Many senior army officers have been pardoned for the crimes committed when in government, but the military budget has been cut without any threat of a further military takeover (O'Shaughnessy 1992).

The answer to the question posed at the beginning of this section remains elusive. Have democratic regimes acted in such a way as to help or hinder democratic development? The cases we have examined suggest that they have done more to satisfy civil and military elites and foreign financiers than the masses, but if alienating the former groups would provoke re-intervention by the military, such priorities might be necessary if pluralism is to survive at all. If failure to satisfy mass demands poses more of a threat to democracy in the future, for example through insurrection or a general disregard for legal and democratic processes, governments will obviously have to pay more attention to such demands unless they bring in the armed forces again, and we have noted the sense of revulsion against such a prospect in view of recent experiences of authoritarianism. This still leaves the obvious question of why populations should tolerate existing democratic regimes at all when they are doing so little to alleviate poverty

Table 9.2 Influences on pluralist democracy and social democracy

Variable	Contribution to pluralist democracy	Contribution to egalitarian, participatory democracy
1 Failed Third World authoritarianism	Positive	Neutral
2 Economic recession	Neutral	Negative
3 Governmental problems in meeting popular demands ('overload')	Neutral	Negative
4 Rise of the New Right	Neutral	Negative
5 Collapse of the Soviet Bloc	Possible	Negative
6 Human rights demands in the West	Positive	Neutral

or reduce inequality. One would have to carry out extensive social surveys to seek a satisfactory answer, but an outsider might speculate that the masses have few alternatives to which to turn. There are certainly no benefits in provoking an authoritarian backlash, and a successful popular revolution seems more of a pipe dream than ever with the disintegration of the communist bloc, from whom external aid might once have been sought. This leaves the possibility of using the democratic process to elect politicians who will right current injustices but, quite apart from elite powers which constrain radical politicians in any pluralist system, there are few radical politicians available with plausible solutions to the problems of Third World poverty and inequality.

Conclusion: the re-emergence of democracy in a hostile climate

We have not reserved a special place for 'external influences' in discussing the prospects for democratic development, on the grounds that external actions cannot create democracy, though they can destroy it, subvert it or even help to sustain it once it has been established. But for the most part external pressures percolate through the internal political system, and most influences on the nature and viability of democracy are a mixture of internal or external factors. My purpose in this concluding section is not therefore to add on a set of new influences but to consider democratic prospects in a broader context.

In Table 9.2 I suggest six factors that have affected either the development of pluralist democracy in the narrow sense or the development of a more egalitarian, participatory democracy. (Let us call the latter 'social democracy'. It is distinguished from 'socialist democracy', which is an even more remote possibility, in that social democracy still allows a substantial role for the private sector provided that that sector operates within the context of the regime's objectives.)

What Table 9.2 should bring out is the peculiar circumstances in which the current wave of democratizations is taking place. Had it occurred at a time of relative Third World prosperity, as in the mid-1950s, at a time when social democratic notions of economic planning and social welfare were more fashionable, or when the Soviet bloc was still a dominant force and was seen, though not uncritically, as a source of ideological inspiration and moral and material support, we might be witnessing very different types of democratic development. As it is, we are looking at democracies that owe something to social, cultural and institutional developments, but that owe their existence more than anything else to the brutality of the previous authoritarian regimes, which generally exceeded anything that had gone before, and their failure to meet economic expectations or even to maintain national unity or effective administration. Citizens who pressed for democratization were helped by external powers which became less tolerant of the authoritarians, partly because of these failures, partly because the thawing of the Cold War left them with less strategic need for dubious allies and, though this is more difficult to quantify, partly because Western governments were under greater pressure from 'human rights lobbies', which may have been a reflection of the rise of post-material values or a greater awareness of repression as a result of mass communications. But if these factors favoured pluralist outcomes, there was no obvious reason why they should create pressure for the egalitarianism, participation and social justice that some would regard as essential adjuncts of democracy. Indeed, the collapse of the Soviet bloc might, however unfairly, have discredited such ideas by equating 'social justice' with 'communism', which was now deemed to be impracticable.

At the same time the economic recession, which had helped to undermine the authoritarian regimes, limited the scope for welfare-oriented policies, and put pressure on those governments, whether in the West or the Third World, which attempted to maintain welfare policies and make concessions to mass demands. If Western governments faced a problem of 'overload' in maintaining public expenditure at a level that would satisfy public opinion, more fragile Third World governments with social democratic pretensions faced an even greater burden. This left the door open to the ideology of the New Right, which favoured minimal state involvement in managing the economy or providing social welfare, though not in coercing those who resisted it. This ideology not only was hostile to social welfare and indifferent to social equality, beyond a belief that all citizens had an equal right to use their material resources in whatever way they chose, it also saw 'participation' as an economic activity involving 'one dollar one vote' rather than a political activity involving 'one citizen one vote'. As with most political ideologies, it is difficult to assess how far

New Right ideas took root as a result of the missionary zeal of their proponents, and how far as a result of economic and administrative circumstances that left very limited scope for an interventionist state, or even
because of the perceptiveness of elites who discovered a new way of legit-
imizing their domination, but the result has been the emergence of democracies which have attempted to 'depoliticize' large areas of decision-making
by entrusting them to market forces, and thus to disclaim responsibility for
a range of social problems.

Taking the six influences in Table 9.2 together, two, or possibly three,
have contributed to the development of pluralist democracy and none has
harmed it directly, but none has contributed to social democracy and four
have harmed it directly. Whether these influences, taken together, augur
well for democracy as a whole remains a matter of debate. Those who
hoped that democratic re-emergence would be accompanied by the emergence of a more just society may be disappointed, and may see little reason
to believe that elites will let go of the advantages which the peculiar circumstances of recent democratic transitions have given them – continued
wealth and privileges, yet with a more respectable, and apparently more
durable, legitimate base internally and externally. Opposed to this is the
view that since there are almost insuperable obstacles in the way of social
democracy or socialism, and that politicians who attempt to follow such
paths in the immediate future could easily bring the whole democratic
edifice crashing down on top of them, the sensible response to events is to
celebrate the pluralist achievements which have been accomplished so far.
One might then hope that democracy would consolidate itself the longer
it remained intact, as it has done in the continuous democracies such as
India, Botswana and Jamaica. Equality, participation and social justice
(assuming that these are desired objectives) could then be seen as future
instalments in the evolutionary process. But when these instalments will
become available, and what circumstances might hasten their arrival,
remains a mystery that has yet to be unravelled.

Conclusion

A study of 'Democracy in the Third World' might be taken to assume the existence not only of a 'Third World', but also of distinctive types of democracy shaped by distinctive forces. Even if we treat the 'Third World' countries as no more than a residual category, not belonging to the relatively developed 'West' or to the former communist bloc, a case can be made for such distinctiveness. Most attempts to explain the emergence or survival of democracy in any part of the world have been built on such pillars as economics, political culture, institutions and political behaviour, even though the role and significance given to each of these elements varies between different authors. But almost all authors would agree that the forces which have established and maintained democracy in the West are different from those which have done so in the Third World. (The former communist bloc is outside the scope of this study, but is clearly different again, with extensive political participation and complex industrialization preceding open political competition.)

Empirical observation suggests an immediate contrast between the relative ease with which democracy has displaced authoritarianism in the Third World and the very much more protracted process in the West. While European despots were frequently displaced by other despots, or made only gradual concessions in the direction of extended political rights, until well into the nineteenth century, Third World democracies have emerged with a rapidity that has surprised the former non-democratic rulers and their successors alike. Few people would have predicted at the end of the Second World War that within twenty years most of the existing colonies in Africa and Asia would be ruled by governments elected by universal suffrage. And when most of Latin America was ruled by military dictators in the 1970s, few would have predicted a similar transformation over an even shorter period. Yet there is also a contrast between the greater durability of the Western democracies, unless destroyed by enemy invasion or severe economic crises, and the fragility of most of the Third World democracies, where rulers have often suspended competitive elections or armies have abrogated nominally democratic constitutions. It would be tempting to explain the differences in terms of political rights which have been obtained too easily not being valued, or of nations gaining independence before they are 'ready' for democracy, but even if there is some truth in such assertions, they only take us to the margins of a web of complex processes. They do not explain the varied circumstances in which independence from colonial masters was obtained, the dynamics of the politics of the individual countries after independence, or their interaction with the outside world.

The most obvious area of common ground between the Third World countries, apart from their poverty relative to the West, is in the fact that all those that have strived for, or achieved, some form of democracy have done so in a world where pluralism is a known quantity. Working models exist, in Western Europe, North America and the Antipodes, that did not exist when countries on these continents took their first, and often unintended, steps towards democracy. The presence of this known quantity can be a source of both strength and weakness. It is a strength in that there is experience on which to build and, for the most part, a positive commitment to democracy as an ultimate objective in view of its apparent success elsewhere, but it is also a potential weakness because the desire to achieve the end may overlook the inadequacy of the means.

The argument is not that certain countries or societies are inherently incapable of achieving democracy, but that a desire to do so is not by itself sufficient. What is required in addition to a desire for democracy is more difficult to establish. I have suggested that explanations of the emergence and survival of democracy, insofar as any exist, are to be found somewhere within and between the variables of economic change, political culture, political behaviour and the functioning of political institutions, but it is impossible to prescribe any particular evolution of these variables, or interaction between them, as offering the best prospects. Western countries themselves arrived at pluralist democracy by diverse routes, but common to most of them was a period of sustained social and economic development in which stable institutions evolved that enjoyed widespread legitimacy and could be adapted to a world of universal suffrage and mass participation.

This has not been the pattern in most Third World countries, but many of these countries have differed from one another as much as they have from the West in the circumstances in which democracy has emerged or re-emerged. Economic development may sometimes be a spur, as in the case of South Korea, but in other cases economic stagnation, or even economic collapse, has undermined the foundations of authoritarian governments and paved the way for democracy. In still other cases, economic development may actually strengthen the hands of anti-democratic elites, which can use material resources to reward friends and punish foes. Political institutions have likewise been a mixed blessing. Weak institutions make interaction between government and governed difficult, but over-powerful institutions, in societies where there are often few autonomous centres of power, can leave those who control the machinery of state in an unchallengeable position. The scope for individual political actors, such as Nehru in India or Seretse Khama in Botswana, to mould and preserve a democratic system appears to be greater than in Western countries where political evolution was generally more gradual, yet the constraints on individual actors can be formidable when one considers the paucity of economic resources, the cultural heterogeneity of societies living within frontiers drawn up arbitrarily by colonial powers, and the wide gap between the political perceptions of elites and largely illiterate rural masses.

Even if one could prescribe an appropriate level and pattern of economic development, a set of political processes which could sustain democracy without smothering it, or a desirable set of political attitudes or wise political decisions arising from them, there is still the question of the varied starting points, which provide democracy with varied opportunities and obstacles. The impending dissolution of the British Empire after the achievement of Indian independence was one such opportunity, as was the discrediting of the one-party state when the limitations of the Eastern European regimes were laid bare in the late 1980s, while foreign support for indigenous dictators or internal conflicts bordering on civil war might impose limitations. I have devoted much attention to the concept of 'transitions' to democracy, since the establishment of any democratic system involves a range of processes and interactions. Changes in social or economic conditions, or in prevailing ideologies, may upset the previous political equilibrium; non-democratic rulers and their aspiring democratic successors may interact with each other and with other groups in society, in a variety of ways, and transitions will vary greatly in their pace, extent, processes and degrees of consensus. From this diversity of influences, it is hardly surprising that the democracies which have emerged have varied so greatly in effectiveness, durability, ideological bases and immunity from veto by previous authoritarian rulers or foreign powers. A democracy emerging from an orderly, government-dominated transition in Brazil is thus likely to be very different from one emerging out of government collapse and economic disorder in Benin, and a transition from imperial rule following a steady development of indigenous institutions in India is likely to produce different results from a sudden colonial withdrawal in Zaire.

From out of this diversity we can trace certain common threads. At least three factors have helped to increase the pressure for a restoration of democracy where it has been suspended, or for its continuation where it has not. First, there is the experience of recent authoritarian rule, whether directly or vicariously, which generally failed to deliver the promised material benefits yet was frequently more repressive, especially in Latin America, than anything experienced in the recent past. Since the authoritarians' main claim to legitimacy was their ability to deliver material benefits rather than any claim based on tradition or on popular mandate, this left an ideological vacuum, which leads us on to the second factor. There is, as Diamond has observed, no longer any long-term claim to legitimacy, in most parts of the world, other than pluralist democracy. Outside the Middle East, we no longer have societies that can sustain ruling monarchies or theocracies, and there are no longer communist or fascist regimes in Europe to offer a vision of popular mobilization under the banner of a single party. In the absence of any plausible alternatives, the debate is no longer about whether pluralist democracy is desirable, but about how quickly it should be attained and in what form. Third, there has been a change in the attitudes of the First and Second World powers towards Third World authoritarians and democrats. With the ending of the Cold War, there are fewer pretexts for supporting authoritarians as bulwarks against communism, and there is no longer Eastern European support for the guerilla movements that provided a pretext for authoritarian 'internal security' policies. Western aid is increasingly tied to a commitment to pluralism. Previously there had been a belief that extensive state control was necessary to achieve economic development and social justice. This not only helped to maintain a polarization between traditional 'left' and 'right', which was often too intense to be contained within a democratic framework, but it often left countries with a perverted version of 'socialism' in which state power was frequently associated with authoritarianism, patronage or incompetence rather than development and social justice. The disillusionment of democrats with the strong state, reinforced by the experiences revealed in Eastern Europe, has led to a greater acceptance of both political and economic liberalization – the objectives of competition between parties in place of single-party hegemony, and competition in the market in place of state planning.

The impact of these influences has, of course, varied between different countries. India accepted the virtues of a mixed economy and political pluralism from the start, and steered clear of Cold War entanglements, while the rulers of Kenya and Guatemala have been much more reluctant to concede party competition or a relaxation of 'anti-communist' policies. But few countries can escape entirely from a world in which two pressures, at once complementary and contradictory, are being exerted. On the one hand, there is pressure, both internal and external, to permit open competition for power and the civil liberties which such competition necessitates. On the other there is pressure for 'economic liberalization', which may be seen as an extension of political pluralism, but which also limits democracy in the sense that large areas of decision-making are taken away from the elected majority and left to market forces – a world of 'one dollar, one vote' in place of 'one citizen, one vote'. Few people, even on the 'left', have mourned the passing of the all-powerful state, or of failed attempts to establish it, and there is a long tradition of academic literature that sees a free-market economy as an essential adjunct of democracy by providing autonomous centres of power. There has also been a more recent expression of hope that the process of liberalization will give more freedom not only to company directors, but also to workers and peasants controlling their own destiny through cooperatives, social movements and self-help organizations, where once they were dependent on state patronage, or on monolithic mass parties or trade unions.

This apparent trade-off between economic and political freedom is not unfamiliar in the West, where the citizen often has an ever-widening choice of goods on the supermarket shelves, yet a diminishing choice of policy alternatives as politicians of all the main parties offer only limited variations on the status quo. But in the Third World, the metaphorical supermarket shelves are barer, and the money with which to buy the goods is scarcer. If economic liberalization provides counterweights that limit the power of the state, the counterweights are not necessarily in the hands of the ordinary citizen, and some of them will be in the hands of multinational corporations, which can take decisions that have far-reaching effects on the indigenous population. Again this is not peculiar to the Third World, but the dependence of poorer countries on international market forces is generally greater.

The circumstances in which the recent democratizations have occurred in the Third World thus raise questions about the nature and viability of the new regimes. Democratization in the West was not, for the most part, accompanied by 'economic liberalization' but by policies of social welfare and income redistribution which gave the newly enfranchised groups something tangible in return for their votes. In the Third World today, such policies are rejected as economically and administratively impracticable, and ideologically unsound. For the present, there is little sign of any mass challenge to such assumptions, and recent democratic transitions have been praised for the 'moderation' and 'consensus' on which they were based. Perhaps there has been, as Karl has argued, a lowering of public expectations as democratization has been achieved in a period of economic recession, so that elites remain secure with their wealth, and the masses accept the discipline of the market. One might go on to infer that the recent democratizations mark the 'end of history' in the Third World, just as the evolution of the more mature democracies in the West is alleged to mark such an end. But political entrepreneurship does not remain static any more than economic entrepreneurship. Those who risked their lives and liberty to challenge authoritarianism may accept that a society free from torture, executions without trial, arbitrary arrests and governments unconstrained by the rule of law is infinitely preferable to what they had previously experienced, but they will not necessarily accept that the new order requires no further modification. The economic privileges of elites may then be challenged, just as the monopolization of political power was challenged when the transition to democracy began. This would then raise questions of both the willingness of elites and masses to tackle what Binder et al. (1971) called 'the crisis of distribution' within the framework of a democratic system, and the ability of would-be reformers to produce policy alternatives which are economically feasible and democratically acceptable. The longest-lived pluralist systems in the Third World have generally been those in which opposition challenges have been 'moderate', and elite privileges have not suffered undue challenge. Sporadic radical challenges have been brushed aside, but we still do not know how, or whether, democracy would cope with more sustained challenges. The end of history in the Third World is still a long way off.

Bibliography

Alam, M. B. (1986) Democracy in the Third World: some problems and dilemmas, *Indian Journal of Politics*, xx (1 and 2): 53–68.

Allen, C. (1992) Restructuring an authoritarian state: democratic renewal in Benin, *Review of African Political Economy*, 54: 42–58.

Almond, G. A. and Verba, S. (eds) (1963) *The Civic Culture*, Princeton, NJ, Princeton University Press.

Alubo, S. O. (1989) Crisis, repression and the prospects for democracy in Nigeria, *Scandinavian Journal of Development Alternatives*, 8 (4): 107–22.

Amin, S. (1987) Democracy and national strategy in the periphery, *Third World Quarterly*, 9 (4): 1129–56.

Apter, D. (1961) *The Political Kingdom in Uganda*, Princeton, NJ, Princeton University Press.

Austin, D. (1964) *Politics in Ghana 1946–60*, Oxford, Oxford University Press.

Baloyra, E. A. (ed.) (1987) *Comparing New Democracies: Transitions and Consolidation in Mediterranean Europe and the Southern Cone*, Boulder, CO, Westview Press.

Belloc, H. (1970) *Complete Verse*, London, Duckworth.

Bequele, A. (1983) Stagnation and inequality in Ghana, in D. Ghai and S. Redwan (eds) *Agrarian Politics and Rural Poverty in Africa*, Geneva, International Labor Organization: 219–47.

Berg-Schlosser, D. (1985) Elements of consociational democracy in Kenya, *European Journal of Political Research*, 13: 95–109.

Bermeo, N. (1990) Rethinking regime change, *Comparative Politics*, 22 (3): 359–77.

Binder, L. *et al.* (eds) (1971) *Crises and Sequences in Political Development*, Princeton, NJ, Princeton University Press.

Black, G. *et al.* (1984) *Garrison Guatemala*, New York, Monthly Review Press.

Booth, M. and Seligson, M. A. (eds) (1989) *Elections and Democracy in Central America*, Chapel Hill, University of North Carolina Press.

Brett, T. (1992) A nation transformed after dark years of despair, *The Guardian*, 23 April: 10.

Bretton, H. (1973) *Power and Politics in Africa*, Chicago, Aldine Atherton.

Brown, D. (1989) When the sun sets, *The Guardian*, 2 May: 23.

Cammack, P. (1985) The political economy of contemporary regimes in Latin America: from bureaucratic authoritarianism to restructuring, in P. O'Brien and

P. Cammack (eds) *Generals in Retreat: the Crisis of Military Rule in Africa*, Manchester, Manchester University Press: 1–36.

Cammack, P. (1991) Democracy and development in Latin America, *Journal of International Development*, 3 (5): 537–50.

Cammack, P., Pool, D. and Tordoff, W. (1988) *Third World Politics*, Basingstoke, Macmillan.

Cardoso, F. H. (1986–7) Democracy in Latin America, *Politics and Society*, 15 (1): 23–41.

Carter, G. and O'Meara, P. (eds) (1985) *African Independence: the First Twenty-five Years*, London, Heinemann.

Chalmers, D. A. (1977) The politicized state in Latin America, in J. Malloy (ed.) *Authoritarianism and Corporatism in Latin America*, Pittsburgh, PA, University of Pittsburgh Press: 38–60.

Chazan, N. (1988) Ghana: problems of governance and the emergence of civil society, in L. Diamond *et al.* (eds) *Democracy in Developing Countries, Vol. II, Africa*, London, Adamantine Press: 93–139.

Chazan, N. (1989) Planning democracy in Africa: a comparative perspective on Nigeria and Ghana, *Policy Sciences*, 22: 325–57.

Chazan, N. *et al.* (1988) *Politics and Society in Contemporary Africa*, Boulder, CO, Lynne Rienner.

Clapham, C. and Philip, G. (eds) (1985) *The Political Dilemmas of Military Regimes*, London, Croom Helm.

Close, D. (1988) *Nicaragua*, London, Pinter.

Cockcroft, J. D. (1990) In Latin America: the new politics challenge, *New Politics*, 3 (1): 16–31.

Cohen, Y. (1987) Democracy from above: the political origins of military dictatorship in Brazil, *World Politics*, 40 (1): 30–54.

Collier, D. (ed.) (1990) *The New Authoritarianism in Latin America*, Princeton, NJ, Princeton University Press.

Crowder, M. (1988) Botswana and the survival of liberal democracy in Africa, in P. Gifford and W. R. Lewis (eds) *Decolonization and African Independence*, New Haven, CT, Yale University Press: 461–76.

Cummings, B. (1989) The abortive abertura: South Korea in the light of Latin American experience, *New Left Review*, no. 173: 5–32.

Dahl, R. A. (1971) *Polyarchy*, New Haven, CT, Yale University Press.

Davidson, B. (1988) Conclusion, in P. Gifford and W. R. Lewis (eds) *Decolonization and African Independence*, New Haven, CT, Yale University Press: 505–14.

Diamond, L. (1988) Introduction: roots of failure, seeds of hope, in L. Diamond *et al.* (eds) *Democracy in Developing Countries, Vol. II, Africa*, London, Adamantine Press: 1–32.

Diamond, L. (1989) Beyond authoritarianism and totalitarianism: strategies for democratization, *The Washington Quarterly*, 12 (1): 141–63.

Diamond, L., Linz, J. and Lipset, S. M. (eds) (1988) *Democracy in Developing Countries, Vol. II, Africa*, London, Adamantine Press.

Diamond, L., Linz, J. and Lipset, S. M. (eds) (1989) *Democracy in Developing Countries, Vol. III, Asia*, London, Adamantine Press.

Dix, R. H. (1992) Democratization and the institutionalization of Latin American political parties, *Comparative Political Studies*, 24 (4): 488–511.

Dodd, C. H. (1979) *Democracy and Development in Turkey*, Beverley, Eothen Press.

Dunn, J. and Robertson, A. F. (1973) *Dependence and Opportunity: Political Change in Ahafo*, Cambridge, Cambridge University Press.

Duodo, C. (1991) Britain's gift of shame that betrays Ghana, *The Observer*, 29 December: 14.

Edie, C. J. (1991) *Democracy by Default: Dependency and Clientelism in Jamaica*, London, Lynne Rienner.

Ethier, D. (1990) *Democratic Transition and Consolidation in Southern Europe, Latin America and Asia*, Basingstoke, Macmillan.

Fieldhouse, D. (1988) Arrested development in Anglophone black Africa, in P. Gifford and W. R. Lewis (eds) *Decolonization and African Independence*, New Haven, CT, Yale University Press: 135–58.

Flint, J. (1983) Planned decolonization and its failures in Africa, *African Affairs*, pp. 389–411.

Frank, A. G. (1984) *Critique and Anti-critique: Essays on Dependency and Reformism*, Eastbourne, Praeger.

Frank, A. G. (1991) No escape from the laws of world economics, *Review of African Political Economy*, 50: 21–32.

Ghai, D. and Redwan, S. (eds) (1983) *Agrarian Politics and Rural Poverty in Africa*, Geneva, International Labor Organization.

Gifford, P. and Louis, W. R. (eds) (1988) *Decolonization and African Independence*, New Haven, CT, Yale University Press.

Gillespie, C. G. (1989) Democratic consolidation in the Southern Cone and Brazil: beyond political disarticulation?, *Third World Quarterly*, 1 (2): 92–112.

Gillespie, C. G. (1990) Models of democratic transition in South America, in D. Ethier (ed.) *Democratic Transition and Consolidation in Southern Europe, Latin America and Asia*, Basingstoke, Macmillan: 45–72.

Glickman, H. (1988) Frontiers of liberal and non-liberal democracy in tropical Africa, *Journal of Asian and African Studies*, 23 (3–4): 234–54.

Grugel, J. (1991) Transitions from authoritarian rule: lessons for Latin America, *Political Studies*, 39 (2): 363–8.

Hargreaves, J. D. (1979) *The End of Colonial Rule in West Africa*, London, Macmillan.

Heavey, J. F. (1991) Land policy and the economics of colonial exploitation, in R. Noyes (ed.) *Now the Synthesis*, London, Shepheard-Walwyn.

Heper, M. (1991) Transitions to democracy reconsidered, in D. A. Rustow and K. P. Erikson (eds) *Comparative Political Dynamics*, London, HarperCollins: 192–210.

Hewitt, V. (1990) The Congress, the opposition and the transfer of power in India, unpublished paper, Political Studies Association Conference, Durham.

Hooper, J. (1990) The Spanish connection, *The Guardian*, 22 March: 21.

Huntington, S. P. (1968) *Political Order in Changing Societies*, New Haven, CT, Yale University Press.

Huntington, S. P. (1984) Will more countries become democratic?, *Political Science Quarterly*, 99 (2): 193–218.

Huntington, S. P. (1988) One soul at a time: political science and political reform, *American Political Science Review*, 82 (1): 3–10.

Huntington, S. P. (1991–2) How countries democratise, *Political Science Quarterly*, 106 (4): 579–616.

Huntington, S. P. and Nelson J. M. (1976) *No Easy Choice: Political Participation in Developing Countries*, Cambridge, MA, Harvard University Press.

Im, H. B. (1987) The rise of bureaucratic authoritarianism in South Korea, *World Politics*, 39 (2): 231–57.

Jonas, S. (1989) Elections and transitions: the Guatemalan and Nicaraguan cases, in M. Booth and M. A. Seligson (eds) *Elections and Democracy in Central America*, Chapel Hill, University of North Carolina Press.

Jonas, S. (1990) Contradictions of Guatemala's political opening, in S. Jonas and N. Stein (eds) *Democracy in Latin America*, London, Bergin and Garvey: 65–83.

Jonas, S. and Stein, N. (eds) (1990) *Democracy in Latin America*, London, Bergin and Garvey.

Karl, T. (1990) Dilemmas of democratization in Latin America, *Comparative Politics*, 23 (1): 1–21.

Kraus, J. (1985) Ghana's radical populist regime, *Current History*, 84 (501).

Lehmann, D. (1990) *Democracy and Development in Latin America*, Cambridge, Polity Press.

Levine, D. H. (1988) Paradigm lost: dependence to democracy, *World Politics*, 40 (3): 377–94.

Lewis, P. G. and Potter, D. C. (eds) (1973) *The Practice of Comparative Politics*, Harlow, Longman.

Liebenow, J. G. (1985) The military factor in African politics, in G. Carter and P. O'Meara (eds) *African Independence: the First Twenty-five Years*, London, Heinemann: 126–59.

Linz, J. J. and Stepan, A. (eds) (1978) *The Breakdown of Democratic Regimes*, Baltimore, MD, Johns Hopkins University Press.

Lipset, S. M. (1959) Some social requisites for democracy: economic development and political legitimacy, *American Political Science Review*, 53 (1): 69–105.

Loveman, B. (1988) Government and regime succession in Chile, *Third World Quarterly*, 10 (1): 260–81.

Low, A. (1988) The end of the British Empire in Africa, in P. Gifford and W. R. Lewis (eds) *Decolonization and African Independence*, New Haven, CT, Yale University Press: 33–72.

MacDonald, S. B. (1986) *Trinidad and Tobago: Democracy and Development in the Caribbean*, London, Praeger.

Mainwaring, S. (1988) Political parties and democratization in Brazil and the Southern Cone, *Comparative Politics*, October: 91–120.

Malloy, J. (ed.) (1977) *Authoritarianism and Corporatism in Latin America*, Pittsburgh, PA, University of Pittsburgh Press.

Manor, J. (1990) How and why liberal and representative politics emerged in India, *Political Studies*, 38 (1): 20–38.

Miliband, R. (1973) *The State in a Capitalist Society*, London, Quartet Books.

Mitra, S. K. (1992) Democracy and political change in India, *Journal of Commonwealth and Comparative Politics*, 30 (1): 9–38.

Moore, B. (1967) *The Social Origins of Dictatorship and Democracy*, London, Allen Lane.

Muller, E. N. (1985) Dependent economic development, aid dependence on the United States and democratic breakdown in the Third World, *International Studies Quarterly*, 29: 445–69.

Munck, R. (1989) *Latin America: the Transition to Democracy*, London, Zed Books.

Munslow, B. (1983) Why has the Westminster model failed in Africa?, *Parliamentary Affairs*, 38 (2): 218–28.

Noyes, R. (ed.) (1991) *Now the Synthesis*, London, Shepheard-Walwyn.

O'Brien, P. and Cammack, P. (eds) (1985) *Generals in Retreat: the Crisis of Military Rule in Africa*, Manchester, Manchester University Press.

O'Donnell, G. (1979) Tensions in the bureaucratic authoritarian state and the question of democracy, in D. Collier (ed.) *The New Authoritarianism in Latin America*, Princeton, NJ, Princeton University Press: 285–318.

O'Donnell, G. (1986) Introduction to the Latin American cases, in G. O'Donnell *et al.* (eds) *Transitions fron Authoritarian Rule in Latin America*, Baltimore, MD, Johns Hopkins University Press: part II, 3–18.

O'Donnell, G., Schmitter, P. and Whitehead, L. (eds) (1986) *Transitions from Authoritarian Rule in Latin America*, Baltimore, MD, Johns Hopkins University Press.

O'Shaughnessy, H. (1992) Argentines rediscover a sense of their own worth, *The Observer*, 8 March: 16.

Painter, J. (1986) Guatemala in civilian garb, *Third World Quarterly*, 8 (3): 818–44.

Painter, J. (1987) *Guatemala: False Hopes, False Freedom*, London, Latin American Bureau.

Payne, T. (1988) Multi-party politics in Jamaica, in V. Randall (ed.) *Political Parties in the Third World*, London, Sage: 135–54.

Pearce, R. (1984) The Colonial Office and planned decolonisation in Africa, *African Affairs*, pp. 77–93.

Petras, J. (1989) State, regime and the democratisation muddle, *Journal of Contemporary Asia*, 19 (1): 26–32.

Petras, J. (1990) The redemocratisation process, in S. Jonas and N. Stein (eds) *Democracy in Latin America*, London, Bergin and Garvey: 85–100.

Philip, G. (1990) The political economy of development, *Political Studies*, 38: 485–501.

Pinkney, R. (1988) Ghana: an alternating military/party system, in V. Randall (ed.) *Political Parties in the Third World*, London, Sage: 32–56.

Pinkney, R. (1990) *Right-wing Military Government*, London, Pinter.

Pool, D. (1991) Democratisation and its limits in the Middle East, unpublished paper, Political Studies Association Conference, Lancaster.

Price, R. M. (1975) *Society and Bureaucracy in Contemporary Ghana*, Berkeley, University of California Press.

Pridham, G. (1991) Democratic transition and the international environment: a research agenda, Centre for Mediterranean Studies, University of Bristol, Occasional Paper no. 1.

Randall, V. (ed.) (1988) *Political Parties in the Third World*, London, Sage.

Reid, M. (1991) Evangelical wins in low turnout in Guatemala, *The Guardian*, 8 January: 9.

Remmer, K. (1990) Democracy and economic crisis: the Latin American experience, *World Politics*, 42 (3): 315–35.

Rizvi, G. (1985) Riding the tiger: institutionalizing military regimes in Pakistan and Bangladesh, in C. Clapham and G. Philip (eds) *The Political Dilemmas of Military Regimes*, London, Croom Helm.

Rocha, J. (1992) Brazil's democracy at risk as unrest spreads to army, *The Guardian*, 7 April: 13.

Rothchild, D. and Chazan, N. (eds) (1988) *The Precarious Balance: State and Society in Africa*, Boulder, CO, Westview Press.

Rustow, D. A. (1973) How does a democracy come into existence?, in P. G. Lewis and D. C. Potter (eds) *The Practice of Comparative Politics*, Harlow, Longman: 117–32.

Rustow, D. A. (1990) Democracy: a global view, *Foreign Affairs*, 69 (4): 75–91.

Rustow, D. A. and Erikson, K. P. (1991) *Comparative Political Dynamics*, London, HarperCollins.

Sandbrook, R. (1988) Liberal democracy in Africa. a socialist-revisionist perspective, *Canadian Journal of African Studies*, 22 (2): 240–67.

Schatz, S. P. (1987) Laissez faireism for Africa?, *Journal of Modern African Studies*, 25 (1): 129–38.

Schmitter, P. C. (1986) An introduction to the Southern European transitions from authoritarian rule, in G. O'Donnell *et al.* (eds) *Transitions fron Authoritarian Rule in Latin America*, Baltimore, MD, Johns Hopkins University Press: 3–16.

Share, D. (1987) Transition to democracy and transition through transaction, *Comparative Political Studies*, 19 (4): 525–48.

Sincere, R. E. (1991–2) Africa's revolutionary tendency – democracy, *Terra Nova*, 1 (2): 79–90.

Sivard, R. L. (1983) *World Military and Social Expenditures*, Washington, DC, World Priorities.

Sklar, R. L. (1983) Democracy in Africa, *African Studies Review*, 26 (3/4): 11–24.

Sklar, R. L. (1987) Developmental democracy, *Comparative Studies in Society and History*, 29 (4): 686–714.

Sloan, J. W. (1989) The policy capabilities of democratic regimes in Latin America, *Latin American Research Review*, 24 (2): 113–26.

Stephens, E. H. (1989) Capitalist development and democracy in South America, *Politics and Society*, 17 (3): 281–352.

Stoneman, C. (1991) A rough ride on road to market, *The Guardian*, 25 April: 11.

Sunar, I. and Sayari, S. (1986) Democracy in Turkey: problems and prospects, in G. O'Donnell *et al.* (eds) *Transitions from Authoritarian Rule in Latin America*, Baltimore, MD, Johns Hopkins University Press: 165–86.

Sundhausen, U. (1984) Military withdrawal from government responsibility, *Armed Forces and Society*, 10 (4): 543–62.

Tindigarukayo, J. K. (1989) The viability of federalism and consociationalism in cultural plural societies of post-colonial states: a theoretical exploration, *Plural Societies*, 19 (1): 41–54.

Uwazurike, P. C. (1990) Confronting potential breakdown: the Nigerian redemocratization process in critical perspective, *Journal of Modern African Studies*, 28 (1): 55–77.

Valenzuela, A. (1978) Chile: the Chilean military, the 1973 election and institutional breakdown, in J. J. Linz and A. Stepan (eds) *The Breakdown of Democratic Regimes*, Baltimore, MD, Johns Hopkins University Press: 81–110.

Wallerstein, I. (1974) Dependence in an interdependent world, *African Studies Review*, 17 (1).

Weiner, M. (1971) Political participation: crisis of the political process, in L. Binder *et al.* (eds) *Crises and Sequences in Political Development*, Princeton, NJ, Princeton University Press: 159–204.

Weiner, M. (1987) Empirical democratic theory and the transition from authoritarianism to democracy, *PS*, 20 (4): 861–6.

Welch, C. E. (1987) *No farewell to Arms*, Boulder, CO, Westview Press.

Wiseman, J. (1990) *Democracy in Black Africa*, New York, Paragon House.

Young, C. (1988) The African colonial state and its legacy, in D. Rothchild and N. Chazan (eds) *The Precarious Balance: State and Society in Africa,* Boulder, CO, Westview Press: 25–66.

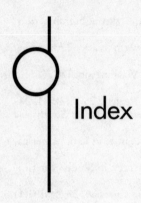

Index